**WITHDRAWN
UTSA LIBRARIES**

STUDIES OF THE AMERICAS

series editor

Maxine Molyneux
Institute for the Study of the Americas
University of London
School of Advanced Study

Titles in this series are multidisciplinary studies of aspects of the societies of the hemisphere, particularly in the areas of politics, economics, history, anthropology, sociology, and the environment. The series covers a comparative perspective across the Americas, including Canada and the Caribbean as well as the United States and Latin America.

Titles in this series published by Palgrave Macmillan:

Cuba's Military 1990–2005: Revolutionary Soldiers during Counter-Revolutionary Times
By Hal Klepak

The Judicialization of Politics in Latin America
Edited by Rachel Sieder, Line Schjolden, and Alan Angell

Latin America: A New Interpretation
By Laurence Whitehead

Appropriation as Practice: Art and Identity in Argentina
By Arnd Schneider

America and Enlightenment Constitutionalism
Edited by Gary L. McDowell and Johnathan O'Neill

Vargas and Brazil: New Perspectives
Edited by Jens R. Hentschke

When Was Latin America Modern?
Edited by Nicola Miller and Stephen Hart

Debating Cuban Exceptionalism
Edited by Bert Hoffman and Laurence Whitehead

Caribbean Land and Development Revisited
Edited by Jean Besson and Janet Momsen

Cultures of the Lusophone Black Atlantic
Edited by Nancy Priscilla Naro, Roger Sansi-Roca, and David H. Treece

Democratization, Development, and Legality: Chile, 1831–1973
By Julio Faundez

The Hispanic World and American Intellectual Life, 1820–1880
By Iván Jaksić

The Role of Mexico's Plural *in Latin American Literary and Political Culture: From Tlatelolco to the "Philanthropic Ogre"*
By John King

Faith and Impiety in Revolutionary Mexico
Edited by Matthew Butler

Reinventing Modernity in Latin America: Intellectuals Imagine the Future, 1900–1930
By Nicola Miller

The Republican Party and Immigration Politics: From Proposition 187 to George W. Bush
By Andrew Wroe

The Political Economy of Hemispheric Integration: Responding to Globalization in the Americas
Edited by Diego Sánchez-Ancochea and Kenneth C. Shadlen

Ronald Reagan and the 1980s: Perceptions, Policies, Legacies
Edited by Cheryl Hudson and Gareth Davies

Wellbeing and Development in Peru: Local and Universal Views Confronted
Edited by James Copestake

The Federal Nation: Perspectives on American Federalism
Edited by Iwan W. Morgan and Philip J. Davies

Base Colonies in the Western Hemisphere, 1940–1967
By Steven High

Beyond Neoliberalism in Latin America? Societies and Politics at the Crossroads
Edited by John Burdick, Philip Oxhorn, and Kenneth M. Roberts

Visual Synergies in Fiction and Documentary Film from Latin America
Edited by Miriam Haddu and Joanna Page

Cuban Medical Internationalism: Origins, Evolution, and Goals
By John M. Kirk and H. Michael Erisman

Governance after Neoliberalism in Latin America
Edited by Jean Grugel and Pía Riggirozzi

Modern Poetics and Hemispheric American Cultural Studies
By Justin Read

Youth Violence in Latin America: Gangs and Juvenile Justice in Perspective
Edited by Gareth A. Jones and Dennis Rodgers

The Origins of Mercosur
By Gian Luca Gardini

Belize's Independence & Decolonization in Latin America: Guatemala, Britain, and the UN
By Assad Shoman

Post-Colonial Trinidad: An Ethnographic Journal
By Colin Clarke and Gillian Clarke

The Nitrate King: A Biography of "Colonel" John Thomas North
By William Edmundson

Negotiating the Free Trade Area of the Americas
By Zuleika Arashiro

History and Language in the Andes
Edited by Paul Heggarty and Adrian J. Pearce

Cross-Border Migration among Latin Americans: European Perspectives and Beyond
Edited by Cathy McIlwaine

Native American Adoption, Captivity, and Slavery in Changing Contexts
Edited by Max Carocci and Stephanie Pratt

Struggle for Power in Post-Independence Colombia and Venezuela
By Matthew Brown

Taxation and Society in Twentieth-Century Argentina
By José Antonio Sánchez Román

Mexico's Struggle for Public Security: Organized Crime and State Responses
Edited by George Philip and Susana Berruecos

Raúl Castro and Cuba: A Military Story
By Hal Klepak

New Political Spaces in Latin American Natural Resource Governance
Edited by Håvard Haarstad

New Political Spaces in Latin American Natural Resource Governance

Edited by Håvard Haarstad

NEW POLITICAL SPACES IN LATIN AMERICAN NATURAL RESOURCE GOVERNANCE
Copyright © Håvard Haarstad, 2012.

All rights reserved.

First published in 2012 by
PALGRAVE MACMILLAN®
in the United States—a division of St. Martin's Press LLC,
175 Fifth Avenue, New York, NY 10010.

Where this book is distributed in the UK, Europe and the rest of the world, this is by Palgrave Macmillan, a division of Macmillan Publishers Limited, registered in England, company number 785998, of Houndmills, Basingstoke, Hampshire RG21 6XS.

Palgrave Macmillan is the global academic imprint of the above companies and has companies and representatives throughout the world.

Palgrave® and Macmillan® are registered trademarks in the United States, the United Kingdom, Europe and other countries.

ISBN: 978–0–230–34070–1

Library of Congress Cataloging-in-Publication Data is available from the Library of Congress.

A catalogue record of the book is available from the British Library.

Design by Newgen Imaging Systems (P) Ltd., Chennai, India.

First edition: October 2012

10 9 8 7 6 5 4 3 2 1

Printed in the United States of America.

Contents

List of Illustrations vii

Preface and Acknowledgments ix

Chapter 1
Extracting Justice? Critical Themes and Challenges
in Latin American Natural Resource Governance 1
Håvard Haarstad

Chapter 2
Post-What? Extractive Industries, Narratives of Development,
and Socio-Environmental Disputes across the
(Ostensibly Changing) Andean Region 17
Denise Humphreys Bebbington and Anthony Bebbington

Chapter 3
More than Beads and Feathers: Resource Extraction
and the Indigenous Challenge in Latin America 39
John-Andrew McNeish

Chapter 4
REDD Gold in Latin America: Blessing or Curse? 61
Anthony Hall

Chapter 5
Extraction, Regional Integration, and the Enduring
Problem of Local Political Spaces 83
Håvard Haarstad and Cecilia Campero

Chapter 6
Resource Extraction and Local Justice in Chile: Conflicts
Over the Commodification of Spaces and the Sustainable
Development of Places 107
Jonathan Barton, Álvaro Román, and Arnt Fløysand

Chapter 7
Territorializing Resource Conflicts in "Post-Neoliberal"
Bolivia: Hydrocarbon Development
and Indigenous Land Titling in TCO Itika Guasu   129
Penelope Anthias

Chapter 8
The Governing of Extraction, Oil Enclaves,
and Indigenous Responses in the Ecuadorian Amazon   155
María Antonieta Guzmán-Gallegos

Chapter 9
Oil Spills, Contamination, and Unruly Engagements
with Indigenous Peoples in the Peruvian Amazon   177
Tami Okamoto and Esben Leifsen

Chapter 10
Nonextractive Policies as a Path to Environmental Justice?
The Case of the Yasuní Park in Ecuador   199
Chiara Certomà and Lucie Greyl

Chapter 11
Extraction as a Space of Social Justice? Commodity
Production and Labor Rights in Brazil and Chile   217
Jewellord T. Nem Singh

Chapter 12
Conclusions   239
Håvard Haarstad

Notes on Contributors   249

Index   253

Illustrations

Figures

Map of Latin America		xi
1.1	Natural resource FDI in Latin America and the Caribbean, percentage of total FDI	2
5.1	FDI in South America, Central America, and the Caribbean, 1980–2010	89
5.2	Bolivian hydrocarbon production and demand scenario, 2011–2020	99
7.1	Location of TCO Itika Guasu and Margarita Gas Field in Bolivia	134
8.1	Oil concessions in Amazonian Ecuador	160
11.1	Share of public and private copper production in Chile, 1989–2009	221

Tables

5.1	Review of investment agreements and other economic agreements for Peru and Bolivia	98
11.1	Petrobras' oil production, explorations, and development share ownership	223

Preface and Acknowledgments

The effects of extractive industries on society can be difficult to comprehend. In the academic literature, extractive resources are shown to have strange properties and destructive effects—weakening democracies, fuelling violent conflict, exacerbating underdevelopment, and driving climatic change. At the same time, modern civilization is founded upon the use of these resources. They have generated massive wealth and not insignificant levels of social welfare. My own country, Norway, consistently ranked highest in the world in terms of human development, can thank its massive oil reserves for much of its wealth. Other places would probably have been better off had their reserves been left in the ground. The people of Latin America never had that choice. There, large-scale extraction predates by a wide margin the emergence of sovereign states, and by an even wider margin the emergence of democracies. The strange properties and destructive effects of extractive resources have throughout modern history defined relations between Latin America and the rest of the world, between people and the elites, and between communities and their land.

Today it seems that the people of Latin American are better positioned than ever before to make informed and democratic decisions about how to extract natural resources and what to do with the revenues. At least that is what many scholars thought a decade ago when the influence of popular movements became visible in national politics, and new-left politicians promised new bargains on extraction, revenue distribution, and environmental management.

An important motivation for this book is to take stock of the changing relationships between natural resources, politics, and social justice at a time when extractive investments are on the rise, and neoliberal governance has presumptively been replaced by (so-called) new-left politics foregrounding participation, local livelihoods, and greater environmental concern. Given the widespread optimism surrounding natural resource–based development prospects in Latin America, both in the business press and in many academic circles, we deem it critical to take a closer look at the constraints and continuities that shape these prospects. We do so through two interrelated analytical frames, *political spaces* and *social justice*. The studies in this book and the conclusions that can be drawn from them call into question many assumptions about the actual content of "post-neoliberalism" and about indigenous peoples' and local communities' relations to extraction. They not only nuance the most optimistic prospects, but also illustrate the progressive dynamics of the new resource politics in the region. The empirical analyses are centered on the Andean and Amazonian regions, where the processes in question are most pronounced. Yet the insights are relevant for understanding the critical development issues of the region as a whole. For better or for worse, the governance of natural resources will be a defining issue in Latin America's development in time to come.

I want to thank the contributors for having faith in this initiative, for responding constructively to comments and suggestions, but first and foremost for sharing their work. This book has grown out of two research projects on natural resources and development in Latin America, the last one titled "Negotiating New Political Spaces: claims for redistribution and recognition in Chile and Bolivia." The Research Council of Norway should be recognized for funding both the projects. It was through the extended network developed through those projects that this book came to fruition. I owe particularly great thanks to the project leader on both projects, Professor Arnt Fløysand, for his constant encouragement and intellectual challenge. The project team, which includes Jonathan Barton, Nina Laurie, Álvaro Roman, Stina Oseland, and Cecilia Campero, has provided a stimulating environment to develop this work. Thanks to the colleagues at the Department of Geography, University of Bergen, for making it a good place to think about nature/society relationships. Maxine Molyneux, the series editor, has been very encouraging and helpful throughout the process of making this book, as have Sarah Nathan and Sara Doskow at Palgrave Macmillan. Even Vaular provided excellent help with preparing the manuscript for submission, and Kjell Helge Sjøstrøm did a great job, as usual, on maps and figures. Finally, I am forever grateful to Anne-Kathrine Vabø for inspiring and supporting me in every way.

Map of Latin America

Chapter 1

Extracting Justice? Critical Themes and Challenges in Latin American Natural Resource Governance

Håvard Haarstad

Natural resources have traditionally been considered a curse on Latin American societies, from the plundering of the colonial era to the ills of commodity dependency in later years. At the present juncture there seems to be widespread optimism due to the belief that natural resource extraction can engender social development and improve livelihoods in the region. Many of the governments have been influenced in a variety of ways by popular demands for more equitable models of development and more participatory politics. Some have characterized this as a departure from the widely unpopular neoliberal governance regimes that failed to satisfy people's development aspirations and the emergence of a "post-neoliberal" era in which different types of alternative models are constructed (Rodríguez-Garavito, Barrett & Chavez, 2008; Sader, 2008). This is particularly the case in Andean societies, where indigenous and "new" social movements have over the past two decades successfully mobilized and campaigned for substantive rights, territory, and inclusion, as well as a greater share of extraction revenues.

Financial analysts also see prospects for strong economic development trends as a result of expanded natural resource extraction. The *Economist* has called this decade the "Latin American decade," pointing to prudent management of commodity revenues, increased foreign direct investment (FDI), and the increasing resource demand for Latin American resources in Asia (Reid, 2010). While foreign investments are falling in developed countries, FDI inflows in Latin America rose 40 percent just from 2009 to 2010. In South America, almost half of foreign investments (43 percent) are now in natural resources (see figure 1.1). China, which is investing heavily in Latin America and is now the third largest foreign investor in the region, places almost all of its investments (90 percent) in natural resources (Economic Commission for Latin America and the Caribbean [ECLAC], 2011). Several concomitant trends have spurred hopes that the current natural resource extraction regimes will foster social and economic development in more democratically legitimate and more environmentally sustainable ways than in the past.

Amidst this optimism and these achievements, it is critical to remain attentive to the enduring challenges that are involved when various social actors make claims to revenues, territorial sovereignty, and participation within expanding extractive economies. Latin American societies are still among the most divided in the world, both in socioeconomic terms and in terms of discrimination against minority cultures; an issue that social movements have powerfully called our attention to over the last couple of decades. As historical experience and extensive academic literature has documented and illustrated, societies dominated by extractive economies often generate increasing inequalities, conflict, environmental degradation, and exploitation. Increased FDI in natural resources can deepen commodity dependency, undermine resource sovereignty, and tie the hands of governments. It can be expected that the expansion of extractive

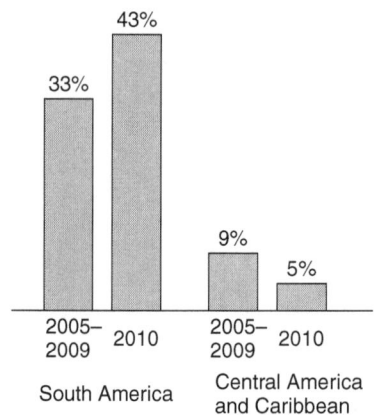

Figure 1.1 Natural resource FDI in Latin America and the Caribbean, percentage of total FDI

Source: Data from ECLAC, 2011.

industries can open up new arenas for political conflict and social friction. Insufficient democratic checks on elites can enable these to undermine distributional mechanisms, while popular sectors that are impatient to see quick and tangible results may support nondemocratic forces if state institutions are seen to be failing to provide the desired results. Both the "resource curse" and a return to populist authoritarianism are lurking in the shadows.

Put simply, there are real grounds for optimism that natural resource extraction can now improve livelihoods in the region, but at the same time there are many pitfalls and lingering problems that can undermine a just distribution of risks and benefits.

This book explores emerging governance processes (models, practices, and conflicts) surrounding natural resource governance in Latin America and the extent to which these contribute to social justice. It seeks to address this critical issue for Latin America's development by bringing together contributions that shed light on this subject from different perspectives and on the basis of different case studies. The overall debate addresses these problematics with reference to Latin America as a whole, while the case studies are primarily focused on the Andean region, where the issues at hand are most pronounced. This admittedly leaves out several important countries where recent developments could provide relevant insights (Argentina, El Salvador, Venezuela, and Mexico come to mind). Still, the Andean countries, with significant and mobilized indigenous populations, recent experiences with post-neoliberal governmental platforms, and long histories of mineral extraction, remain the central cases in shedding light on this problematic.

Our intention is that the book will point to ways forward in several interconnected but typically divided academic debates. In recent years, significant attention has been paid to the political economy of neoliberal reform, the ways in which this has circumscribed citizenship, democracy, and natural resource extraction, and how indigenous movements in particular have mobilized against these reforms. The current juncture has provided us with the opportunity to move beyond the preoccupation with mobilization against neoliberalism in order to analyze the development models that are coming out of this mobilization; how the characteristics of post-neoliberal models (if such things exist) are constructed and negotiated; enduring constraints on equitable policy; the complexities of integration in international markets and territorial-political conflicts between states and local sovereignties.

The discussions in the book are guided by two analytical frames. The first is that of *political spaces*. "Political space" has both metaphorical and geographical elements here, in that it alludes both to the enabling and constraining factors in opportunity structures, and to the sociospatial changes in relations between localities, states, and the various processes associated with globalization. This frame posits that the region is undergoing broad structural changes in terms of political institutions, political discourses, and economic relations, which reshape the opportunity structures of various actors. The new political spaces are rooted in the structural changes pointed to above: consolidation of democracy, strengthened discourses of rights, emergent economic possibilities, and more. These changes bring about new possibilities for civil society actors, in particular, to press claims toward governance models and practices and negotiate for different distributions of risks and benefits. As an overall project, the book aims to answer the question: *How can we understand the political spaces for civil society actors to press claims toward the ways in which natural resources are governed?*

The other analytical frame that this book posits is that of *social justice*. This is in recognition that models of natural resource governance cannot only be evaluated on the basis of how they generate economic growth or possibilities for the types of actors that are typically well positioned to gain access to them. Extraction has profound effects, both positive and negative, on local communities, environmental conditions, socioeconomic structures, and poverty. As opposed to the dominant resource curse literature, which mainly addresses macroeconomic factors and the technicalities of "good governance," we hold that a broader range of implications and effects have to be taken into account to properly understand the complex relationships between natural resource extraction and development. Employing Nancy Fraser's three dimensions of justice—redistribution, recognition, and representation—the book aims to answer the question: *How are the emerging models and practices around natural resource governance contributing to improving social justice?*

The remainder of this chapter does the following. First it elaborates on the new political spaces in Latin American natural resource governance, against the backdrop of neoliberalism and its "other." Second it disaggregates the notion of social justice with reference to Fraser, and discusses the different ways justice is understood in relation to natural resource governance. Third, it introduces the chapters and the way they link up to these frames.

Political Spaces from Neoliberalism to Its "Other"

At the time of writing, parties and political leaders representing "leftist", "popular," or "progressive" political agendas govern in Argentina, Bolivia, Brazil, Cuba, Ecuador, Nicaragua, Peru, Paraguay, Uruguay, and Venezuela. This "wave" of leftist electoral victories have been seen as indicative of a new-left or a "post-neoliberal" era in Latin America (Kozloff, 2008; Rodríguez-Garavito et al., 2008), and as an outcome of the broad political reaction to the neoliberal reforms that were implemented across the region from the late 1970s and onwards. At the same time, the current wave of new-left politics in the region must be seen as more than simply a backlash against neoliberalism (Haarstad & Andersson, 2009). It can be argued that while neoliberal reforms aimed for rather narrow forms of democracy and little state involvement in economic arenas, they opened up spaces for social mobilization that ultimately strengthened more substantive forms of democracy and, in some cases, a return to greater state involvement, particularly in extractive sectors. In complex and contradictory ways, these reforms created new political spaces for claims for cultural recognition and territorial sovereignty. Several writers have suggested that political spaces that were opened up by neoliberal citizenship reforms helped to spur on indigenous movements—movements that soon mobilized beyond the political spaces that had been opened by these reforms (Hale, 2002; Postero, 2006).

Neoliberal discourses of citizenship advocated individual autonomy and responsibility as part of a program that was based on granting political and civil (but not necessarily social) rights (Yashar, 1999). In the 1990s, a range of countries (Colombia in 1991, Bolivia in 1993–1997, Ecuador in 1998, and Venezuela in 1999) undertook radical constitutional reforms that established new rights, which in turn resulted in the political incorporation and heightened mobilization of previously excluded groups, and helped ethnically based parties achieve significant electoral success (Van Cott, 2003a, 2003b; Zamosc, 2007). The new constitutions enacted in Ecuador (2008) and Bolivia (2009) have gone a long way in terms of granting rights to participation and indigenous territorial autonomy, while asserting the right of the state to exploit nonrenewable resources. Several countries in the region have ratified the Convention on Indigenous and Tribal Peoples by the International Labour Organization (ILO 169), which stipulates that indigenous peoples must be consulted with regard to extractive projects in their territories. ILO 169 was ratified by Bolivia, Paraguay, Peru, and Colombia already in the early

1990s, with Venezuela, Ecuador, Brazil, Argentina, and eventually Chile following suit more recently. Indigenous and social movements press a complex set of claims, which are not easily categorized simply as demands for cultural recognition. Socioenvironmental conflicts, including those where indigenous movements are involved, comprise a range of deep-seated grievances that span across theoretical notions of recognition, redistribution, and representation.

Given the electoral success of self-proclaimed "post-neoliberal" governments, the strengthened rights discourses across the region, and favorable conditions for extractive economies, it would seem that there are wide political spaces for promoting new forms of extraction that would take various social demands into account. But as several authors, and many of the contributors of this volume point out, contemporary forms of extraction do not appear qualitatively different from those of the past. It is still an open question whether the "post-neoliberal" or new-left political regimes are able to satisfy the aspirations, ambitions, and demands of the social movements that have helped bring them into office. When I put quotation marks around "post-neoliberalism" here, it is to recognize that it remains an ambiguous idea with few distinctive practices that can define it. Lacking a precise identity, it is perhaps best understood simply as neoliberalism's "other." Gudynas (2009) posits that there exists a "progressive neo-extractivism" under leftist governments that displays some differences in relation to past forms of extraction or those under nonleftist governments, including a more active, developmentalist, role for the state, and a legitimation through redistributive agendas. But they continue to rely on productivist appropriation of nature, weak economic diversification, and a dependence on integration in international markets (Gudynas, 2009). It is unclear whether this reorientation actually represents a reshaping of the political spaces for governments or civil society actors to employ the extractive economy in serving social development. A shift to a leftist orientation in government or a rhetorical break from neoliberalism are not sufficient to overcome the structural problems involved in engendering more socially sustainable forms of natural resource extraction and governance.

Therefore, this book does not attempt to isolate a "post-neoliberal" governance model or a "post-neoliberal" form of extraction, or assume that these are qualitatively different from others. It is interested in how such ideological markets play into resource politics and government legitimation, but assumes that to properly understand the structures, processes, and practices of resource governance and politics one needs to look deeper into the conflicts and interest negotiations taking place around extraction and governance. The cases are drawn both from countries that are associated with the "post-neoliberal" trend and countries that are less so, and illustrate the similarities in problematics faced in the region as a whole.

The new political spaces in natural resource governance in Latin America must be seen in connection with more general shifts in governance structures and the spatial reorganization of politics. The counterpart of the renewed focus on "the local" in participatory development and social movement–based alternatives discussed above is the trend toward regional cooperation and the transnationalization of political and economic governance. Several of the chapters highlight these transnational connections, both in terms of policy formation and within activist networks, illustrating how "local" socio-environmental conflicts are typically shaped by processes at higher scales. The governments in the region, including those that are self-proclaimed "post-neoliberal", are seeking international economic integration and FDI. A number of international treaties and agreements, from bilateral treaties, the World Trade Organization (WTO), Reduced Emissions from Deforestation and Forest Degradation (REDD) to the ILO 169, have introduced mechanisms that bind governments to particular courses of action in ways that shapes political spaces for natural resource and environmental governance. Peru recently became a compliant country in the Extractive Industries Transparency Initiative (EITI), which means that it has committed to a process of making information about any revenue from extractive industries and how it is spent publically available. In other words, political spaces in natural resource governance are increasingly shaped by processes above the national scale.

Governments in the region are also creating regional initiatives, partly in an attempt to carve out political spaces for new development paths. *Banco del Sur* (Bank of the South), the *Alianza Bolivariana para los Pueblos de Nuestra América* (Bolivarian Alliance for the Peoples of Our America, ALBA) proposed by Hugo Chávez or the *Conferencia Mundial de los Pueblos sobre el Cambio Climático y los Derechos de la Madre Tierra* (The People's World Conference on Climate Change and the Rights of Mother Earth) in Cochabamba in 2010, are presented as home-grown alternatives to those promoted by the Western-controlled global institutions. MERCOSUR is, at the time of writing, both expanding to include Venezuela and finalizing a trade agreement with the European Union, which will establish that trade block as a global player. Regional initiatives in the area of energy policy are maturing as well, as can be seen in the case of the Initiative for the Integration of Regional Infrastructure in South America (IIRSA), which seeks to integrate the infrastructure in the fields of transport, energy, and communication with a portfolio of more than 524 projects with a total cost of USD96 billion. With UNASUR and *Comunidad Andina*, South American countries are strengthening their regional alliances and coordination in policy areas including energy and natural resource governance.

However, internationalization and transnationalization are not exclusive to public institutions. Some have pointed to the rise of "transnational indigenous rights movements" that span the Andean region and beyond, with strong linkages to activist circles elsewhere (Martin & Wilmer, 2008). Globalization has opened political spaces for transnational networks bringing together indigenous political actors with nongovernmental organizations (NGOs) from the north, which has made indigenous actors more influential in local and transnational political processes and enabled them to engage with neoliberal agendas. Terming this "globalization from below," Radcliffe, Laurie, and Andolina (2002) argue that the transnational networks of indigenous politics actors have taken advantage of opportunities within neoliberal development agendas that stress the importance of ethnicity to press their demands for territory, language rights, and local politicocultural autonomy at the national level.

The upshot for our purposes is that the political spaces for shaping and contesting natural resource governance are the result of pressures at a range of scales. Disentangling these political spaces and how social actors and governments maneuver within them is one of the tasks that this book sets itself. The chapters emphasize different scales to different degrees, but they all acknowledge the interrelations between what is going on locally, nationally, and internationally.

Natural Resources and the Multiple Dimensions of Social Justice

Much of what is currently written about development and natural resources revolve around concepts of the "resource curse" and "good governance." Political scientists and economists working within this perspective argue that the development prospects and growth performance among resource-rich countries is primarily due to how rents are gained and distributed by the state, and the quality of horizontal "checks and balances" on elite groups. The "curse" of low economic growth, increasing instability, and declining quality of governance can be avoided by countries with sufficiently high-quality institutions with distributional mechanisms in place (Collier & Goderis, 2008; Mehlum, Moene & Torvik, 2006a, 2006b). There are significant insights to be gained from this perspective to understand contemporary socio-environmental conflicts and development paths in Latin America. For example, the dependence on extractive revenue may to some extent explain why self-proclaimed "post-neoliberal" governments fail to follow through on their preelection promises to reorient their economies away from expanding extraction. The resource curse theory predicts a limited space for resource-dependent governments in need of revenue to fund social programs, which corresponds well with the findings of several of the chapters in this volume.

Ultimately, however, the resource curse literature is prohibitively narrow in terms of assessing current socio-environmental conflicts and the range of effects that extractive industries have on societies. This is in part because the focus is almost exclusively on macroeconomic variables and the redistributive arrangements within political institutions at the national level (McNeish, 2010). Also, some authors have suggested that countries in Latin America differ from the typical resource curse cases in Africa, in that resource wealth has encouraged, rather than undermined, democratic transitions (Dunning, 2008; Karl, 1987). Yet our main concern here is that we want to capture a more diverse set of experiences, political practices, and claims than merely those aimed at the formal distributive mechanisms and "checks and balances" at the national state level (though those are definitely important as well). The frame of *social justice* is one that is better adjusted to capture this breadth.

Why should social justice even be considered in relation to natural resource extraction? One might say that such extraction is so technologically complex and economically important that it is best left to bureaucratic technocrats and engineers to devise the appropriate strategies to transform resources into state revenue. Against such a view, objection can be made through several points. First, ample experience has shown that it is those who are living in the vicinity of extraction that suffer most of the negative consequences. This suggests that one considers how to govern extraction in ways that mediate negative impacts and consider various forms of compensation. Second, extractive models benefit social groups in different ways, and these groups differ in terms of their power to promote their interests. Political decisions taking justice considerations into account are necessary to balance these power differentials to some degree. Third, resource extraction implicates other social, environmental, political, and economic issues with profound effects on social justice. These include rights to land, state jurisdiction versus local autonomy, employment versus environmental protection, and so on. Resource extraction shapes the societies in which it takes place, and cannot be seen as something to be simply *administered*. So how might social justice be linked to natural resource extraction in theory and practice? Nancy Fraser's conceptual work on social justice, which defines it as a combination of redistribution, recognition, and representation, provides a useful tool to disentangle the abstract and normative notion of justice, and creates a framework through which the case studies here can be reviewed. *Redistribution* refers to claims over the allocation of material resources, while *recognition* refers to the acceptance of cultural difference, and *representation* concerns procedures for participation and inclusion in the political realm (Fraser, 2008). While these three dimensions of justice are intricately interlinked in practice, their conceptual separation creates room for assessing different justice aspects of resource governance models and political claims toward them. An argument that this book explores is that, for natural resource extraction to respond to the broader needs of society, natural resource governance must accommodate these three dimensions of justice reasonably well.

Environmental and natural resource concerns in Latin America are deeply woven into the fabric of popular mobilization for social justice (Van der Ploeg, 2011). As contemporary struggles over natural resources and the governance of their extraction illustrate, the field of competing claims for redistribution, recognition, and representation, and proposals for how these issues should be resolved between local communities, states, and international markets is a complex one. Increasingly, claims from *below*, from communities demanding being taken into account, and pressures from *above*, from transnational social movements and international governance initiatives, challenge the models and institutional arrangements through which public goods are governed by national states (Bulkeley, 2005; Martin & Wilmer, 2008; O'Faircheallaigh & Corbett, 2005; Swyngedouw, 2004). Adding to the complexity, different notions of justice (different understandings of what is just and of what types of justice are most important) are competing. Natural resource governance appears as one of the main arenas where competing notions and claims for justice clash, and different proposals and counterproposals for a "just" governance of natural resources have been put forward by a wide range of actors at different scales.

Often these conflicts involve local claims for recognition of territorial sovereignty, representation in forums where decisions are made, and redistribution of benefits derived from extraction, all mixed in together. The concept of "*buen vivir*" has gained popularity among communities and social movements across the region. It can be roughly translated as "living well" or as collective well-being, as opposed to "*vivir mejor*," the continuous search to maximize individual and material wealth. "*Buen vivir*" is included as a defining principle in the 2008 Ecuadorian Constitution, and it promotes appeals to broader notions of justice than just the economic and distributional alone. It is concerned with the sustainable use of natural resources governed in a way that will encourage democracy and citizenship from below and harmonious coexistence with nature (Welsh, 2010). At the same time, the demands of indigenous groups are also grounded in their economic marginalization throughout history, and are inherently claims for a greater share of the vast revenues that are generated in and around their communities. It is important to avoid essentializing indigenous groups as living "in touch with nature" and unconcerned with the material aspects of well-being. John-Andrew McNeish stresses this point forcefully in his chapter. Finally, socio-environmental conflicts are often grounded in local actors' sense of being excluded from decision-making that affects them. Several of the chapters here illustrate the grievance that surfaces when rights to participation or self-determination are perceived to have been broken. Devising practical governance models that accommodate these different claims for justice has proven difficult, to say the least. Particular proposals for policy reform in the governance of natural resources are typically in the name of some particular notion of justice at a particular scale, but tend to emphasize one aspect of justice and one scale more strongly than others. When Bolivia's Evo Morales points out, to those who campaign for "Amazonia without oil," that without hydrocarbons there would be no cash transfer programs and little for Bolivia to live off of (see chapter 2 by Denise Humphreys Bebbington and Anthony Bebbington), he is right. The policy strategy of expanding extraction to pay for social programs makes sense for redistributive justice at the national scale. But it can be questioned whether this strategy is sustainable if it fails to accommodate other aspects of social justice at least reasonably well.

    There are legal mechanisms in place that attempt to protect rights to recognition and representation within extractive governance. ILO 169 and rulings of the Inter-American Commission (1998) and the Inter-American Court on Human Rights (2007) hold that the state must ensure the right of local peoples to give or to withhold their consent with regard to projects that may affect their territory

(Finer, Jenkins, Pimm, Keane, & Ross, 2008). States have typically been slow to put this into practice in a substantive way, but several countries have legislation that grants the right to indigenous communities to be consulted about extractive projects, including Bolivia, Columbia, Ecuador, Chile, and most recently Peru with its *Ley de Consulta* passed in 2011. Several countries also have mechanisms in place that are intended to distribute revenues from extractive projects to regional governments, municipalities and local communities. Although these legal mechanisms are in place, and local actors seem increasingly competent in using them for their purposes (often with the help of NGOs), it is the state that is the ultimate arbiter of how they are put into practice. The same states are responsible for, and have significant interests in, the expansion of the extractive sectors. The specific practices that are established and implications of these practices for social justice depends on the pressures on and incentives for state actors, in other words, on political spaces.

The Chapters in the Book

As stated at the outset, the discussions in this book are guided by two analytical frames, looking at the political spaces for civil society actors to press claims within natural resource governance, and the ways in which governance models contribute to social justice. The different chapters contribute to the general conclusions by focusing on particular aspects of these frames, either through overarching discussions on sociopolitical aspects of resource extraction, or through case studies focused on sociopolitical dynamics of extraction in particular contexts. The more overarching chapters are placed in the beginning of the book, to give context to the case studies that follow. The last chapter draws together the main insights and discusses the implication of these for the research questions.

Chapter 2 by Denise Humphreys Bebbington and Anthony Bebbington reflects on the conundrum pointed to above, namely that there is a striking convergence between so-called post-neoliberal forms of extraction and the forms promoted by previous regimes or regimes less associated with post-neoliberalism. They assess developments in Peru, Bolivia, Ecuador, and Columbia in particular, and look for the causes behind this convergence and continuity in the ways that extractive industries structure and limit spaces for governmental action.

John-Andrew McNeish, in chapter 3, takes issue with dominant depictions of social conflicts over extraction and particularly those involving indigenous peoples. These dominant depictions are close to essentializing indigenous peoples as "ecological noble savages" in ways that fail to take account of their more complex relations to capital and modernity. He stresses that indigenous responses to extractive activity should not be interpreted as a rejection of such activity or industrial modernization in general, but rather as desires for participation and struggles for autonomy and livelihoods.

Anthony Hall, in chapter 4, asks whether new climate mitigation mechanisms being implemented in Latin America can constitute another type of resource curse for the region. This issue is becoming increasingly relevant, as dozens of REDD and REDD+ projects are in the process of being designed or implemented with the support of countries in the north or multilateral institutions. His chapter raises doubts as to whether the neoliberal framework based on economic incentives will be effective among socially and culturally diverse populations in forested areas such as Amazonia.

Chapter 5 by Håvard Haarstad and Cecilia Campero returns to the question of the continuity between the so-called post-neoliberal and other regimes in terms of extractive strategies, and looks in particular at regional initiatives aimed at increasing sovereignty and policy space in the extractive sector. There is a clear regional "countermovement" against the international governance regime that promoted international arbitration mechanisms such as International Centre for Settlement of Investment Disputes (ICSID), but it can be questioned whether this "countermovement" reconnects the different governance scales and increases local spaces for participation.

Chapter 6 by Jonathan Barton, Álvaro Román, and Arnt Fløysand takes the discussion to relations between resource extraction and local justice in their case study of Chile. By outlining four different socio-environmental conflicts that have unfolded in recent years, they reveal the diversity of claims, alliances, and practices of the central stakeholders. What they see as an underlying dynamic across these conflicts is the tension between the centrally promoted free market, export-oriented model on one hand, and local justice claims on the other, or in other words the tension between the commodification of *spaces* versus the sustainable development of *places*.

The theme of contradictions between different logics within extractive strategies is developed further in chapter 7 by Penelope Anthias. In doing this, she stresses the importance of placing contemporary conflicts over extraction in the context of broader and longer-term struggles for justice. The extractive strategies of the Morales government in Bolivia maps onto preexisting geographies produced through uneven processes of colonization and nation building, and is only one of the many factors that shape the *guaraní* campaign for land and territory. She also stresses the shifting dynamics of resource conflict under Morales, and the strategies used by the *guaraní* to press their claims.

Chapter 8 by María Antonieta Guzmán-Gallegos is the first of two that deal with the establishment of enclaves, or spatial strategies of detachment for oil operations, and different types of indigenous responses. Enclave formation is based on a specific state-company partnership that delegates public service provision, infrastructure construction and control of space to oil companies. In looking at this phenomenon in the Ecuadorian Amazon, she emphasizes how enclave formation shapes flow of resources and goods connected to extractive activity, and creates highly differentiated access to public services across indigenous communities.

In chapter 9, Tami Okamoto and Esben Leifsen explore the diverse strategies of detachment and "unruly engagements" employed by an oil company to manage critique, knowledge, and participation. They make clear how a relative detachment of the oil industry from surrounding areas and negative environmental effects are made possible by the weak governance of the state in Amazonian areas. They use a case study of the aftermath of a June 2010 oil spill into the Marañon river to shed light on how the oil company handled and contained compensation claims from affected indigenous communities, but they also stress how unruly engagements open political spaces for contestation from communities.

In their discussion of the Ecuadorian Yasuní-ITT initiative to leave oil deposits in the ground, Chiara Certomá and Lucie Greyl outline, in chapter 10, the socio-environmental justice implications that it gives rise to. They question the assumption, put forward by many social movement organizations, that a nonextraction policy necessarily advances social justice. Echoing some of McNeish's arguments, they problematize the often romanticized images of indigenous peoples and their claims promoted by the Yasuní-ITT initiative. They also problematize the financial aspects of the initiative, which depend on funding from industrialized countries and the emerging market for environmental services, and its implications for representative and redistributive justice at the local scale.

Finally, in chapter 11, Jewellord T. Nem Singh takes the discussion back to the question of continuities between neoliberal and post-neoliberal forms of extractive governance, in his comparison of institutional developments in Chile and Brazil. He asserts that a post-neoliberal form of extraction would necessarily be able to bring in participation and agency for affected communities, which implies going beyond narrow export growth models. The cases examined illustrate the constraints that exist on leftist parties to promote such a transition, and the legitimation strategies that these parties, once in power, use to assert their leftist credentials. But also, his account stresses the potential role of organized labor as a transformative actor.

The concluding chapter, chapter 12 by Håvard Haarstad, goes back to the overall research questions of the book and synthesizes the findings of the individual chapters.

References

Bulkeley, H. (2005). Reconfiguring environmental governance: Towards a politics of scales and networks. *Political Geography, 24*(8), 875–902.
Collier, P., & Goderis, B. (2008). Commodity prices, growth, and the natural resource curse: Reconciling a conundrum. Oxford: OxCarre Research Paper, 14.
Dunning, T. (2008). *Crude democracy: Natural resource wealth and political regimes*. Cambridge: Cambridge University Press.
Economic Comission for Latin America and the Caribbean (ECLAC). (2011, July). *Foreign direct investment in Latin America and the Caribbean, 2010*. Santiago, Chile: United Nations.
Finer, M., Jenkins, C. N., Pimm, S. L., Keane, B., & Ross, C. (2008). Oil and gas projects in the Western Amazon: Threats to wilderness, biodiversity, and indigenous peoples. *PLoS ONE, 3*(8), e2932. doi:10.1371/journal.pone.0002932
Fraser, N. (2008). *Scales of justice: reimagining political space in a globalizing world*. Cambridge: Polity Press.
Gudynas, E. (2009). Diez Tesis Urgentes Sobre el Nuevo Extractivismo: Contextos y demandas bajo el progresismo sudamericano actual. In J. Schuldt, A. Acosta, A. Barandiarán, A. Bebbington, M. Folchi, CEDLA-Bolivia, ... E. Gudynas, *Extractivismo, Política y Sociedad* (pp. 187–225). Quito, Ecuador: Centro Andino de Acción Popular & Centro Latino Americano de Ecología Social.
Haarstad, H., & Andersson, V. (2009). Backlash reconsidered: Neoliberalism and popular mobilization in Bolivia. *Latin American Politics and Society, 51*(4), 1–28.
Hale, C. R. (2002). Does multiculturalism menace? Governance, cultural rights and the politics of identity in Guatemala. *Journal of Latin American Studies, 34*(3): 485–524.
Karl, T. L. (1987). Petroleum and political pacts: The transition to democracy in Venezuela. *Latin American Research Review, 22*(1), 63–94.

Kozloff, N. (2008). *Revolution!: South America and the rise of the new left.* New York, NY: Palgrave Macmillan.
Martin, P., & Wilmer, F. (2008). Transnational normative struggles and globalization: the case of indigenous peoples in Bolivia and Ecuador. *Globalizations, 5*(4), 583-598.
McNeish, J.-A. (2010, September). *Rethinking resource conflict.* Background Paper. Washington, DC: World Development Report 2011.
Mehlum, H., Moene, K., & Torvik, R. (2006a). Cursed by resources or institutions? *The World Economy, 29*(8), 1117-1131.
Mehlum, H., Moene, K., & Torvik, R. (2006b). Institutions and the resource curse. *The Economic Journal, 116*(508), 1-20.
O'Faircheallaigh, C., & Corbett, T. (2005). Indigenous participation in environmental management of mining projects: The role of negotiated agreement. *Environmental Politics, 14*(5), 629-647.
Postero, N. G. (2006). *Now we are citizens: Indigenous politics in post-multicultural Bolivia.* Stanford, CA: Stanford University Press.
Radcliffe, S., Laurie, N., & Andolina, R. (2002). *Indigenous people and political transnationalism: globalization from below meets globalization from above?* (Transnational Communities Programme, WPTC-02-05). Oxford: University of Oxford. Retrieved from http://www.transcomm.ox.ac.uk/working_papers.htm
Reid, M. (2010, September 11). So near and yet so far: A special report on Latin America. *Economist*, special report, 1-14.
Rodríguez-Garavito, C., Barrett, P., & Chavez, D. (2008). Utopia reborn? Introduction to the study of the new Latin American left. In P. Barrett, D. Chavez, & C. Rodríguez-Garavito (Eds.), *The new Latin American left: Utopia reborn* (pp. 1-41). London, UK: Pluto Press.
Sader, E. (2008, September). *Posneoliberalismo en América Latina.* Colección pensamientos. Buenos Aires, Argentina: Consejo Latinoamericano de Ciencias Sociales.
Swyngedouw, E. (2004). Globalisation or "Glocalisation"? Networks, territories and rescaling. *Cambridge Review of International Affairs, 17*(1), 25-48.
Van Cott, D. L. (2003a). Andean indigenous movements and constitutional transformation: Venezuela in comparative perspective. *Latin American Perspectives, 30*(1), 49-69.
Van Cott, D. L. (2003b). Institutional change and ethnic parties in South America. *Latin American Politics & Society, 45*(2), 1-39.
Van der Ploeg, F. (2011). Natural resources: curse or blessing? *Journal of Economic Literature, 49*(2), 366-420.
Welsh, C. (2010). Development as *Buen Vivir*: Institutional arrangements and (de)colonial entanglements. *Development, 53*(1), 15-21.
Yashar, D. J. (1999). Democracy, indigenous movements, and the postliberal challenge in Latin America. *World Politics, 52*(1), 76-104.
Zamosc, L. (2007, September). The Indian movement and political democracy in Ecuador. *Latin American Politics and Society, 49*(3), 1-34.

Chapter 2

Post-What? Extractive Industries, Narratives of Development, and Socio-Environmental Disputes across the (Ostensibly Changing) Andean Region

Denise Humphreys Bebbington and Anthony Bebbington[1]

Introduction

Lima, 2011: A colleague begins a postgraduate seminar on extractive industries by presenting students, drawn from across Latin America, with a series of quotations on the relationships between extraction, development strategy, and society. The quotations are unlabeled, though the students are told that they come from Latin American presidents and vice presidents, representing political positions ranging from the self-consciously neoliberal to the ostensibly post-neoliberal. The task was to assign the quotations to these politically very different leaders. The success rate was not high. The point, of course, was to suggest that extractive economies can do strange things to politics, reining in the possibilities of innovation even under progressive government.

We ourselves have used a similar strategy elsewhere, exploring executive statements to suggest that the practical governance of extractive industry across neoliberal and post-neoliberal contexts shows far less variation than might be expected (A. Bebbington & Bebbington 2011; A. Bebbington 2009, 2012). To make such an argument, however, is to operate on doubly treacherous ground. First, executive statements cannot be taken to reflect the full diversity of government policy (though they do surely reflect important dimensions of its political conceptualization). Second, to suggest that new-left governments, even those with celebrated links to social movements, might reveal significant similarities to authoritarian neoliberal regimes is to invite criticisms that can range from conservatism to disloyalty and essentialism (see chapter 3 by McNeish, this volume). Yet, regimes that are now populated by an analyst's friends and allies should be no less subject to critique than those regimes from which an analyst feels a self-conscious distance. A change of actor does not necessarily lead to a change of script, and one cannot necessarily take self-declared harbingers at face value. What changes, and what remains the same, is an empirical question, the answer to that lends itself to theoretical interpretation.

Others have noted the same point. Again for the case of extractive industry governance, Gudynas (2010) asks the region's post-neoliberal governments, "If you are so progressive why do you destroy nature?" Dagnino's (2008) more general exploration of the "perverse confluence" is a similar statement of concern regarding the perverse ability of Brazil's Workers' Party government to combine participation in social programs together with sustained neoliberal management of economy and much of society (see chapter 11 by Jewellord T. Nem Singh, this volume). More poignantly still, the resignations of ministers and vice ministers reflect practical critiques of political projects with which they had once identified: one need only think of the resignation of Alberto Acosta, the president of Ecuador's Constituent Assembly (2007 to 2008), José de Echave, Peru's vice minister of environment (2011), and Cecilia Chacón, Bolivia's minister of defense (2011).

In this chapter, we develop further this line of analysis with a particular focus on two phenomena: the continuing presence of socio-environmental conflict across very different political regimes in the Andean region; and the palpable convergences in the ways in which these different regimes approach the question of extractive industry and the trade-offs among extraction, rights, and environment. Whereas we would not claim that the governments of Alan García (Peru), Ollanta Humala (Peru), Evo Morales (Bolivia), Rafael Correa (Ecuador), and Juan Manuel Santos (Colombia) are the same, we do argue that in their management of the extractive economy they reveal some striking "family resemblances" (Peck, 2004, p. 395). Likewise, although we note some of the diverse motivations that appear to underlie disputes over extraction, we draw particular attention to the continuity of those disputes over time and across regime transitions. We reject, *tajantemente*, the notion that this continuity reflects ongoing manipulation by political actors (c.f. Caballero, 2010). Instead we suggest that for some civil society actors this continuity reflects sustained frustration at the ways in which certain rights and approaches to the governance of nature and space are privileged over others, as well as at the ways in which the macroeconomy has failed to generate employment and new livelihood opportunities. Of course, for certain movement leaders additional motivations might also be at play when they organize protest—they may use extractive industry conflicts to broaden their political authority and seek access to rents, or they may deploy strategic essentialisms as a means of pursuing specific material ends. Nonetheless, we would argue that these types of motivation remain insufficient to explain the decisions that broad segments of the population have repeatedly made to dedicate significant resources to protest and to make themselves vulnerable at the moment of open protest. Something else is going on.

Part of our argument is that such continuities across different regime types, over time and across space, reflect the sheer political economic weight of the extractive economy. One part of this weight is a historical heritage, and in this sense there is path dependence to government strategy in the region. This may or may not be a fully blown resource curse, but at the very least such path dependence reflects the fiscal and political constraints within which governments operate and that have structuring effects on their action. Another part of this weight is more contemporary and reflects the actual and potential scales of investment that are at stake. These (actual and imagined) investments create (actual and perceived) incentives and opportunities that are attractive for governments of the moment who have few other (easily imaginable) sources of short- and medium-term fiscal revenue.

We suggest that this combination of constraint and incentive has led governments of different hues to commit to the promotion of extractive industry as the central pillar (or in the language of the current Colombian national development plan, "locomotive") of economic growth. This pillar is then seen as the revenue source for financing programs of social protection and social investment. This model of extractive growth plus redistributive social spending recurs across different regimes. There is some irony here for this model bears resemblances not only to Dagnino's "perverse confluence" but also to the World Bank's 1990 recipe for poverty reduction (World Bank, 1990), a recipe that combined private sector–led growth, public investment in human capital, and social safety nets. Beyond irony, the troubling face of this policy convergence has been the predisposition toward authoritarian imposition of the model combining occasional use of force with efforts to delegitimize those who question extraction. This policy disposition has, in turn, led to social conflicts—some rights-based, some socio-environmental, and some purely redistributive. In particular it has led to difficult relationships with indigenous populations seeking forms of justice that, although evidently having an economic and livelihood component, extend way beyond the mere redistribution of wealth to be derived from extraction or the forms of political representation that are embodied in contemporary postneoliberal governments. Even though some might read such struggles as a fight for broadened and decolonized concepts of nature, culture, and community (Escobar, 2008), here all we wish to assert is that they appear as struggles for rights, citizenship, and the ability to exercise at least some control over political economic processes in their territories.

Next we offer a brief discussion of the context, nature, and scope of the extractive industry economy in the region. We then explore currents in government policy—and in particular executive statements—regarding extraction, development and rights to protest. As part of this discussion, we trace some of the conflicts between government and indigenous populations to which this policy orientation has given rise, and then go on to a slightly broader discussion of the nature of conflicts over extraction. This discussion emphasizes that there are multiple axes of dispute in these conflicts. These axes make clear that what has occurred over the last two decades should not be understood in terms of heroes and villains (though we would also suggest there are some of each in all these conflicts), but rather in terms of contradictions and transformations. We briefly explore some of the possible routes through which such transformations might emerge, with particular focus on how far they might lay the bases of future institutional frameworks in the region. Whether these frameworks will mitigate or aggravate injustice is an open question. What seems clearer is that the way in which this question works itself will not map neatly onto the contemporary differences among political regimes in the region.

A New Extraction

Beginning in the early 1990s, the Andean-Amazonian region has been the terrain of a new and aggressive phase of expanded investment in the mining, oil, and gas sectors. Three broad factors drive this expansion: growing global demand for minerals, oil, and natural gas (especially from China, India, and other emerging economies), coupled with sustained price increases, have offered new investment opportunities and made low grade, poorly accessible, and difficult to extract deposits viable; technological changes have made it possible to extract dispersed ores as well as hard to access hydrocarbons; and a series of policy and institutional changes have provided favorable tax, royalty, and regulatory environments for investors (Bridge, 2004). This has induced expanded investment in new frontiers that have no modern history of large-scale extraction as well as in traditional regions of extraction. Investment has moved to traditional extractive economies (e.g., Chile and Peru for mining; Peru, Ecuador, and Bolivia for hydrocarbons) as well as to countries with little such history (e.g., hard rock metal mining in Ecuador, Argentina, Colombia, and El Salvador; hydrocarbons across Central America). Meanwhile, within the Andean countries, investment has flowed not only to traditional mining regions (e.g., Potosí, Oruro, and Cerro de Pasco) and hydrocarbon frontiers (Loreto, Tarija, and Pastaza) but also to new ones. The past 15 years have seen important mining projects in Piura, Apurimac, and Ayacucho in Peru, as well as new hydrocarbon frontiers opening up in the *altiplano* of Peru, the northern lowlands of Bolivia, and the southeast of Ecuador.

By the end of the 2000s, the NGO Cooperacción estimated that some 55 percent of Peru's highland peasant communities were affected by mining concessions, and that between 2002–2007 the area under concession increased to 77.4 percent (from over 7 million hectares to 13.2 million hectares). Meanwhile, in Peru's Amazon basin, the proportion of land affected by hydrocarbon concessions increased from 14 percent to over 70 percent in under five years (2004–2008), overlapping with protected areas, indigenous territories, and lands reserved for indigenous peoples (Chase-Smith, 2009). Whereas only 10 percent or so of Ecuador is affected by mining concessions, this is still remarkable given that the country has no significant mining history. Meanwhile, some 65 percent of Ecuador's Amazon basin is concessioned or available for hydrocarbon exploration (Finer, Jenkins, Pimm, Keane, & Ross, 2008). According to Bolivia's National Hydrocarbons Agency just under 50 percent of Bolivia's territory is deemed of potential interest for hydrocarbon exploration. In Colombia, between 2002 and 2009, the area covered by mining concessions increased from just over 1 million hectares to 8.44 million hectares (Rudas, 2011). While overlaps with formal indigenous territories are less extensive (Santoyo, 2002), those with environmentally protected areas are considerable: if in 1990 only 74 titles overlapped with protected areas, by 2011 the figure was 785 (Rudas, 2011).

Extraction and Development Policy: A Regional Narrative?

It would be a step too far to suggest that some sort of regional extractive formation had emerged in the Andean region. That said, various authors (Eduardo Gudynas, Maristella Svampa, Alberto Acosta, etc.) have suggested that something of this might be going on. Such a phenomenon might itself be taken to reflect ongoing processes of regional integration. These are brought together most explicitly under the rubric of Initiative for the Initiative for the Integration of Regional Infrastructure in South America (IIRSA). They are also manifest in the increasing regional projection of the Brazilian Development Bank (BNDES), Brazilian companies specializing in extraction (e.g., Vale, Petrobras), and large-scale civil engineering (e.g., Odebrecht). While IIRSA does not focus specifically on extractive industry, many of its scheduled investments in roads, *hidrovías* (waterways), electricity distribution systems, and ports exhibit many synergies with the extractive economy. These regional initiatives also suggest the constellations of power that might support the consolidation of a regionally integrated network of investments in extraction.

In this sense, national political economy and policy dynamics cannot be understood separately from regional dynamics. This articulation between the regional and national might also provides another window on apparent national policy convergence around extraction. The following paragraphs discuss just a few elements of this convergence for regimes as apparently diverse as Peru under García and then Humala, Bolivia under Morales, Ecuador under Correa, and Colombia under Santos. The general claim is that certain themes recur across these regimes' policy and political narratives on extraction and development. These themes are: a commitment to expanding the extractive economy; a coupling of extraction and the financing of social programs; a criticism of protest and mobilization coupled with strategies to undermine protest through discursive delegitimation and/or the use of force; and a prioritization of popular national political projects over subnational or territorial projects. This prioritization is justified through an arithmetical notion of justice in which if more citizens benefit from social investments funded by extraction than lose as a result of the dislocations caused by extraction, then the promotion of extraction is in itself fair, just, and appropriate.

Peru

In December 2007, President Alan García wrote his now infamous manifesto for a modern extractive economy under the banner of

"The Dog-in-the-Manger Syndrome." Carried by the main national daily, *El Comercio*, García's article argued that the main factors preventing Peru from entering into a full-blown Rostovian "take-off" phase of economic growth (Rostow, 1960) were linked to two main problems: a land and resource tenure system that favored collective property regimes (in particular protecting the collective rights of indigenous communities); and the networks of civil society organizations and environmental activists that sought to defend the rights of indigenous peoples and the environment. To García, these organizations represented the dog-in-the-manger—on the one hand, they sought to prevent large-scale capital from deriving value from resources under their control and, on the other hand, they were unable to transform these resources themselves. García (2007) lashed out against those he saw obstructing Peru's development, "there are millions of hectares for timber extraction that lie idle, millions more that communities and associations have not, and will never, cultivate, in addition to hundreds of mineral deposits that cannot be worked." He argued that proposed hydrocarbon investments had been stalled because activists had created the fictive figure of indigenous peoples living in voluntary isolation: "against oil they have created the image of the 'non-contact' jungle native." García also decried efforts to question mineral development, "barely a tenth of these resources are being exploited because here we are still discussing whether mining destroys the environment," an argument that held no sway with García who saw environmentalists as yesteryear's socialists now wrapped in green. García's vision of development for Peru centered on the role of modern technology, private property, large-scale capital, and a combination of both foreign direct and domestic investment as paramount—a development process led by capitalists and in which the rest of the population would participate as beneficiaries. Indeed, Chase-Smith has argued that this was a manifesto for a "clear project of state reform that leads to an ultra-neoliberal model oriented toward the concentration of land and natural resources in private hands" (Chase-Smith, 2009, p. 51).

Shortly following García's statements, his office passed a "torrent" of decrees (Campodonico, 2008) under temporary powers granted to the Executive by the Peruvian Congress to draft and pass legislation for implementation of the Free Trade Agreement signed with the United States in 2006. Over one-hundred decrees were issued within a six-month period. Together these laws were perceived as weakening communal forms of property, of fomenting private investment in areas historically occupied and claimed by peasant and indigenous communities, and of strengthening the hand of the state in terms of pursuing its territorial projects in these areas. This in turn catalyzed an "Amazonian strike" led by indigenous organizations and involving river blockades and the occupation of hydrocarbon installations. That strike ended when the government agreed to revisit some of the laws, but when by 2009 government was still dragging its feet, indigenous organizations mobilized again. That mobilization culminated in a standoff between protestors and the police on a stretch of road outside the town of Bagua. By the end of the day, 33 people had been killed, including 23 policemen, 11 of whom had been held hostage at an oil pumping station and deliberately murdered by their *awajunwampis* captors in retaliation for the shooting of indigenous people.

The events of Bagua rocked political debate and everyday conversation, and absorbed pages in both the national and international press (e.g., Vidal, 2009). In the months following, the government formed commissions to investigate events and convened dialogues with indigenous leaders to forge agreements. However, at the same time, public prosecutors accused some of those indigenous leaders as being the intellectual authors of the deaths in Bagua. Indeed Alberto Pizango, president of the Inter-Ethnic Association of Indigenous Lowland Peoples (AIDESEP) fled Peru for Nicaragua, where he spent more than 11 months in exile. One post-Bagua CNR report (Coordinadora Nacional de Radio, 2008) found that the Executive Office had exceeded and abused its power by decreeing a number of laws that had nothing to do with the Free Trade Agreement. Indigenous organizations, human rights groups, and the Ombudsman office argued that some of these laws should have been subject to a consultative process—under the provisions of Peru's Constitution and the ILO (International Labour Organization) 169—and thus they were unconstitutional (Chase-Smith, 2009; Rénique, 2009).

The remainder of the García administration was characterized by a continuing commitment to extraction coupled with social conflict and periodic use of government force (as evident in the periodic reports on social conflict by the Human Rights Ombudsman's office: Arellano-Yanguas, 2012). Interestingly, however, the first six months following the installation of the center-left government of Ollanta Humala have suggested relatively little change—either in the dynamic around conflict or in practical government policy. Notwithstanding early legislation on free prior and informed consent (legislation not uniformly supported within the government) and less than three months after taking office the Humala administration faced its first serious challenge when multiple protests broke out in October 2011.

One of these conflicts, over Minas Conga, a mine in northern Peru that would be Peru's largest ever single mining investment, culminated in confrontations between protestors (led in considerable measure by the regional government) and government forces. Speaking of the conflict on November 16, 2011, President Humala came out in support of the project, reiterating the argument that such projects were essential for Peru's development: "Minas Conga is an important project for Peru," he said, "because it will allow us to achieve the great transformation and the social inclusion that we are offering to the Peruvian people" (PresidenciaPeru, 2011). Though promising an "improvement" of the project's Environmental Impact Assessment (EIA) in response to protestors' demands, Humala also declared a 60-day state of emergency in four provinces in the Department of Cajamarca and sent in troops to quell protests. Humala's prime minister, Salomon Lerner, subsequently resigned triggering the resignation of the entire cabinet and the replacement of several of the more left-leaning ministers with new ministers who are seen to be more conservative, and in some cases with military backgrounds (including the new prime minister).

At the time of writing, these are still early days for the Humala administration. The initial responses to the Conga conflict, however, already suggest a policy line being traced. Extractive projects will be supported even if regional populations express skepticism, because such projects are envisioned as providing essential financial resources to support social investments programs and social inclusion. Indeed, it would be difficult for the government to walk away from these investments and forgo the income produced through royalty and tax payments. If necessary, it appears, force will be used.

Bolivia

Whether they want it or not this highway is going to be built[2]
(President Evo Morales, June 29, 2011)

On September 25, 2011, a coordinated police raid set upon a group of lowland indigenous marchers just outside the town of Yucumo. The marchers had been slowly making their way from the lowland town of Trinidad to the capital, La Paz, in protest at the government's proposed plan to build a highway through the middle of a recognized indigenous territory and national park (*Territorio Indígena y Parque Nacional Isiboró Securé*—TIPNIS). They were caught completely off guard. Police lobbed tear gas into the makeshift camps to drive out the marchers, then subdued them and forcefully boarded them onto waiting buses and trucks. In the ensuing chaos, families fled into the forest to escape being caught, and mothers and children were separated. March organizers were tracked down, bound, and gagged, and then transferred into waiting vehicles. Images taken of the raid revealed the severe treatment that many marchers received at the hands of the Bolivian police. In its report on the events, the Bolivian Human Rights Ombudsman's Office concluded that police action had violated a series of human rights and was out of all proportion with the behavior of the marchers, that the state had also violated various constitutional rights, and that parts of the government had obstructed the process of the Ombudsman's investigation of the incident (Defensoría del Pueblo, 2011).

At the heart of the conflict is the struggle over the development of a large region in the center of the country. The TIPNIS was first recognized as a national park in 1965 and later recognized as collective indigenous lands (*Tierras Comunitarias de Origen*—TCO). As in the case of Bagua, Peru, the TIPNIS conflict is embedded in longer processes of broad structural change that seeks to open vast, underdeveloped lowland lands for colonization, infrastructural development, and investment. In September 2006, the newly elected Morales government, following the tactics of previous administrations, promulgated Law 3477 declaring the project a "national and departmental priority" and directing public authorities to proceed with the final study to complete the design and construction of a section of highway connecting the lowland towns of Villa Tunari (Cochabamba) with San Ignacio de Moxos (Beni; Crespo, n.d.). As proposed, the 304-kilometer highway would split the indigenous territory and national park in half, despite TIPNIS being formally protected by Bolivian Law.

Notwithstanding its priority status, the road project had initially been put on hold as the Morales government was forced to confront an internal rebellion launched by right-leaning groups (September 2008), then see through the approval of the New Constitution (January 2009), and the election of the new plurinational assembly (March 2009). However, once these challenges were overcome the government turned its attention to the construction of the highway. In May 2010, indigenous Moxeño, Yuracaré, and Chimán authorities of the TIPNIS gathered to discuss the proposed project and emitted a resolution steadfastly rejecting the construction of the highway Villa Tunari-San Ignacio de Moxos (Crespo, n.d.). The indigenous resolution was in response to the government's unilateral decision to build the highway without following established legal and technical procedures, in particular, the environmental impact study and a process of free, prior, and informed consent (FPIC) in violation of Bolivia's new Constitution and international conventions. As the Morales/MAS government sought to move forward with the project, the vice minister of the environment and a subdirector both resigned their positions after refusing to sign off on the environmental license.

While the trigger of the TIPNIS conflict is the proposed construction of the highway and its potential adverse impacts, in particular the concern that colonists would invade the TIPNIS, the road-building project is linked to additional pressures on land and territory. These include potential hydrocarbon exploration and exploitation, logging, and narco-trafficking interests. Indeed in a report prepared by the Fundación Unir Bolivia (2011, p. 18), the authors note that the Morales government has chosen to prioritize the construction of a highway and privilege the agenda of integration (linked to and promoted by the geopolitical interests of its neighbor, Brazil), the expansion of the agricultural frontier, and the exploration and exploitation of hydrocarbons, without due consideration of an alternative development agenda that prioritizes indigenous aspirations for territorial control and self governance or respects existing environmental legislation or broader concerns for environmental conservation.

This reading of government approaches to development appears to be borne out by earlier statements that both the president and vice president have made regarding the centrality of the extractive economy to their political strategy. At different times Morales has asked out loud:

> What, then, is Bolivia going to live off if some NGOs say 'Amazonia without oil'? . . . They are saying, in other words, that the Bolivian people ought not have money, that there should be neither IDH [a direct tax on hydrocarbons used to fund government investments] nor royalties, and also that there should be no *Juancito Pinto*, *Renta Dignidad* nor *Juana Azurduy* [cash transfer and social programs]. (Agencia Boliviana de Información [ABI], 2009).

Once again, extraction is seen as essential for a social investment model in which the rights of the national many trump those of the subnational minority: "necessity obliges us to exploit this natural resource, the gas, the oil, for all Bolivians . . . If there's oil, gas, you know it is for all Bolivians and this money that we collect from oil, from gas, has to go to all Bolivians" (ABI, 2009). Vice Minister

García Linera is yet more to the point: "Is it mandatory to get gas and oil from the Amazonian north of La Paz? Yes. Why? Because . . . combined with the right of a people to the land is the right of the state, of the state led by the indigenous-popular and *campesino* movement, to superimpose the greater collective interest of all the peoples" (Svampa, Stefanoni, & Bajo, 2009).

Some analysts (see McNeish, chapter 11, this volume; Fuentes, 2011) insist that these confrontations in Bolivia cannot be reduced as if this were a simple debate between an ideal form of indigenous communitarianism populated by noble savages and the government's pursuit of untrammelled *desarrollismo*. Quite so, though this is hardly the point. The issue is less one of divergent environmentalisms and instead one of competing notions about rights and democracy. The question that these conflicts pose is whether minorities, localities, or even natures have any special rights within the post-neoliberal model being constructed by the MAS government, or whether the calculi for political economic decisions should be ones that simply tally winners and losers and allow the Executive to determine which rights count more and which counts less. To invoke the noble savage critique seems little more than to repeat and endorse the arguments the Executive Office uses to dismiss criticisms of its policy.

Ecuador

After assuming power in January 2007, Ecuador's president Rafael Correa spoke of his new government as bringing the country out of its "long neoliberal night," one of whose indicators had been the indiscriminate granting of mineral licenses with immensely favorable conditions for license owners. Initially, Correa's government appeared to target the extractive sector as one in which it was going to prove its post-neoliberal credentials and craft new ways of governing the economy and natural resources. Indeed, the first minister of energy and mines, Alberto Acosta, declared a commitment to a different way of managing oil. This proposal hinged around the sensitive field of Yasuní-ITT (*Ishpingo Tambococha Tiputini*), located beneath a protected area of great biodiversity and occupied by the Huaraoni and Ecuador's two remaining indigenous peoples living in voluntary isolation (Rival, 2012). The government committed itself to pursuing an alternative proposal for the governance of ITT, in which the oil would be left underground if the international community guaranteed half the revenue that Ecuador would otherwise have received from the oil. This compensation would be placed in a trust fund that the Ecuadorian government could then use for broad development purposes. The origin of this project is discussed in more detail in chapter 10 in this book (see Certomà and Greyl) as well as by Rival (2012).

Correa and Acosta subsequently parted ways and since late 2008 Ecuador has seen *both* a new legislation that is much more favorable to the large-scale mining sector *and* political initiatives that at a certain point threw the Yasuní experiment into doubt. Indeed, discrepancies over extraction were an important part of the tensions between Correa and Acosta. Although Acosta was presiding over a Constituent Assembly process in 2008 that explored novel ways of regulating and restricting extraction, Correa was publicly delegitimizing such ideas and at certain times intervened directly in Assembly working groups and processes. An Assembly devised "Mining Mandate" that raised many questions about large-scale mining was soon replaced with legislation that would allow such mining (Moore & Velásquez, 2012), and indeed in 2011 the government gave the go-ahead for the country's first large-scale open-cast mine in the southeast of the country.

As Correa was making the case for extraction he was also denigrating those who questioned the wisdom of such opening up new frontiers for large-scale mining. "The ecologists are extortionists. It is not the communities that are protesting, just a small group of terrorists. People from the Amazon support us. It is romantic environmentalists and those infantile leftists who want to destabilize government" (Narváez, 2007). While questioning protest, he sought to protect investors: "I'll say it again, with the law in my hand, we will not allow such abuse, we will not allow uprisings that block roads that attack private property" (Correa, 2008). Once again the rationale was that these subsoil resources are a revenue stream that cannot be ignored for government policy: "It's absurd to be sitting on top of hundreds of thousands of millions of dollars, and to say no to mining because of romanticisms, stories, obsessions, or who knows what" (Correa, 2008).

As the executive's commitment to extraction hardened, the Yasuní-ITT initiative also encountered problems. In January 2010, Correa rejected a long-negotiated deal that had been brokered by his own government with the United Nations Development Programme (UNDP), Germany, Spain, and others that would have secured about half of the money required for the trust fund. Correa argued that donors were attaching too many conditions to the use of these monies. "If that is how it is going to be, keep your money and in June we'll begin to exploit ITT. Here we are not going to trade in our sovereignty" (Correa cited in EFE, 2010). Versions vary as to how far this breakdown was due to intransigence on the part of Correa or of the German minister and over the course of 2011 the government appeared to attempt to once again recover the process. Whatever the case, however, the government is also clear that with or without Yasuní, oil development will continue, and the mining sector will be promoted.

Colombia

The Colombian context differs from that of the other three Andean countries in that it has not undergone any sort of shift to a left of center (far less post-neoliberal) government. Indeed, the authoritarian neoliberalization that deepened under the Uribe government (from 2002 to 2010) has continued under the Santos administration. Though Colombia has a long experience with large-scale extraction of oil and coal, in the metal mining sector the experience has been different. Notwithstanding the country's precolonial and colonial history of metal mining, large-scale extraction of metals is only a recent phenomenon (though there is a longer history of coal mining). The Uribe administration promoted extractive industry as part of this model with a new mining code that weakened regulatory institutions, weakened territorial rights, and led to increasing overlaps among titles to extract and other legal interests in land. The Santos government has intensified this commitment, and its National Development Plan (for 2010 to 2014) identifies five motors for economic growth of which mining is by far the most significant, set to account for 54 percent of all anticipated private investment and 41 percent of that public investment designed to promote growth. These policy changes—the modification of mining codes, the promotion of foreign investment and privatization initiatives, the regulation of consultative processes—have led to problems related to territory, environment, and impacts on agricultural, indigenous, and Afro-Colombian communities (North-South Institute, 2011). This has driven more conflict, with the number of conflicts increasing from 16 between 2003 and 2006 to 29 between 2007 and 2010. In some cases where communities have resisted extractive industry investments (e.g., the Embará in Mandé Norte) physical force has been used.

Although once again the Colombian "model" appears as one that combines the promotion of extraction, social investment, and authoritarian repression it is also characterized by countermovements that are yet more striking than the strength of the Peruvian and Bolivian Ombudsman's offices. Thus the Colombian Constitution of 1991 drew special attention to the ethnically and culturally diverse nature of the country and in turn granted certain rights to the bearers of this diversity. The Constitution laid the basis for recognizing that indigenous peoples had a right to territory, to cultural identity, to self-determination, to self-government and to exercise their own forms of governance and justice, and the North-South Institute has noted that "Colombia boasts one of the most progressive frameworks for ethnic rights protection in the world" even if it is often the case that "rights are not held up in practice" (North-South Institute, 2011). That said, in 2010, the Constitutional Court passed a ruling (T-1045A) that requires FPIC on mining projects in Afro-Colombian territories, as well as plans to protect basic rights. We will return to the significance of this enigma.

A Common Regional Narrative of Extraction and Development?

The general pattern across Peru, Bolivia, Ecuador, and Colombia appears to be that central government—and particularly the Executive Office—is consistently promoting the expansion of extractive industry and regional integration, prioritizing national agendas over the territorial demands or livelihood concerns, and using discursive and/or material force in order to push this policy agenda through. Different tropes are used to justify hostility to those who question or oppose this agenda, and they run from the invocation of sovereignty, through the urgency and necessity and on to the denigration of critics as stupid, selfish, infantile, leftist, terrorist, corrupt, and right wing. Although the willingness to use physical force shows more variation, with Bolivia, until recently, showing more restraint, the determination to push the extractive frontier outwards is clear in all these countries.

The ingenuous question must be "why?" One interpretation is that as García, Humala, Correa, Morales, García Linera, and Santos survey their own macroeconomic prospects, each concludes that resource extraction is where their macroeconomies' main comparative advantage lies. They might also feel that revenue from extractive industry is easier to appropriate and control than are the more dispersed and difficult-to-tax revenues deriving from the smaller-scale, informal economy. Furthermore, such centralized revenues might seem an attractive means of financing the sorts of centrally provided state services that are more effective in generating political capital and votes than would be the case with more decentralized, bottom-up forms of development. Finally, it may be that these presidencies recognize the risks associated with extractive industry but feel that *this time* they can do things differently, and in that way appease movements' concerns about government's ability to ensure adequate regulation of extraction, to protect citizens' rights and to share the benefits of extraction more broadly. This said, whereas fiscal concerns may constitute one set of factors that lead toward expanded extraction, another is undoubtedly interest group and coalition politics.

More perplexing is why such thinking so easily translates into authoritarianism and the use of force. One answer might be that these presidencies and their respective parties just happen to have authoritarian tendencies. Another answer might be that these regimes see extraction as their *only* option. This is worrying because it would speak to just how constrained they see their policy options as being and also because it would imply that they are gambling that their future will be different from their past. It is concern about just such scenarios that underlie a growing interest among civil society thinkers to imagine what "postextractive" economies would look like.

Conclusions

The increasing levels of social conflict that have accompanied these government commitments to the expansion of extractive industry defy singular explanations. Our own research on conflict dynamics across a range of territories in the region suggest that protest has been driven by a range of motivations, anxieties, grievances, and tensions that are oftentimes exacerbated by and intertwined with historical disputes.[3] This combination of motivations suggests that the juxtaposition of "greed and grievance" in explanations of conflicts around extraction is an unhelpful simplification (Caballero, 2010; Collier & Hoeffler, 2004, 2005).

Some protests and conflicts are best understood as responses to uncertainty and perceived risk. These conflicts typically manifest themselves subsequent to the granting of concessions to conduct exploration but prior to exploitation. In many instances these occur before any actual exploitation has occurred (e.g., much of Ecuador; Piura, Islay, Tambogrande, Puno in Peru; and Norte La Paz in Bolivia). A second group of protests seem more motivated by annoyance and frustration at actual dispossession. In these conflicts, grievances include the payment of very low prices for land that later prove to be immensely valuable, the drying up or actual contamination of water courses, the loss of territorial autonomy, or the loss of authority among local elites. A third set of conflicts reflects demands for opportunities. Here conflict is used as a way of forcing extractive industry to recruit their services locally or to provide local benefits of some sort. Fourth are mobilizations facilitated by political authorities, who may see them as a mean of enhancing their electoral prospects or of increasing the revenue that these authorities derive from extraction.

If the factors that underlie protest are so diverse, several things become evident. First, extractive industry conflicts cannot be reduced to Manichean oppositions between good and bad, or between one set of interests and another. Instead, they can be better understood as the manifestations of different types of overlapping contradictions: among different forms of governing space, among different modes of property ownership, among noncompatible environmentalisms, among incompatible notions of the sacred and the culturally significant, and among claims on resources that cannot be satisfied jointly and simultaneously. Second, the conceptions of justice at play in these conflicts are multiple and not necessarily compatible. Hence any viable way forward will have to accommodate multiple conceptions of justice—simply imposing the conceptions favored by the Executive (on the grounds that it is progressively post-neoliberal) will simply not do. Third, simple fixes are not likely to work in the medium term— certain frustrations, aspirations, and grievances will remain unattended by one-dimensional interventions. Fourth, and by implication, institutional innovations that stand any chance of providing medium-term responses to these conflicts and their associated demands for different forms of justice will have to be flexible and most probably complex.

This begs the question—where might such innovations come from, for some actor will have to produce them. From the discussions above, one thing seems evident—the capacity for such nuanced and iterative innovation is not likely to be found in the offices of the presidency. The recurrent tendency of the Executive toward imposition and authoritarianism is not a quality associated with flexible innovation. Social movements are clearly one of these pathways insofar as they exert the pressure that opens the political space that is essential for any viable innovation. Indeed, absent the sustained exercise of pressure, innovation will not occur. However, in the analyses of both our own and of most published work, such movements have rarely been able to turn their demands into actionable institutional changes that will deliver enhanced justice of one or another form. Other actors that have appeared in some of the vignettes reviewed in this chapter have, however, achieved this. In this regard, the Colombian case becomes particularly interesting because even in a context of authoritarian neoliberalism and expanding extraction, significant progress has been made in recognizing diverse rights and in inscribing these recognitions in law. In this process the combined efforts of social movements, legal activists in civil society and an equally activist Constitutional Court have been paramount. Routes in Peru have been somewhat different—in that instance, the Human Rights Ombudsman has been especially important in creating legitimate spaces within which to discuss institutional change, and then to craft the outlines of such change. In Bolivia, there are nascent signs that the Ombudsman's office might come to play a similar role, even if the political space open to it is more limited.

Looking across the (still limited) range of conflicts discussed in the prior section, the sorts of institutional change needed, will have to address a range of issues and claims for "justice." Some of these changes will have to relate to the administration of processes of consultation and consent prior to exploration (thus nipping in the bud the worst of risk-and-uncertainty-induced conflicts), the planning of land use before and after exploration (so that existing forms of territorial governance are not systematically and inevitably displaced by the expansion of extraction) and the criteria on which benefits from extraction will be distributed both socially and spatially. They will also have to involve innovations in capital markets so that new forms of investment emerge in the regional economy that are able to offer forms of employment that do not depend only on extraction (none of the actors mentioned in earlier sections are particularly up to this vital task).

Delivering this package of transformations will be no simple task, and careful social science understanding of how such innovation can occur and with what effects will be invaluable in helping illuminate the process. Social science also has a role to play in exploring and making explicit the diverse conceptions of justice that have affected, and continue to affect, the extractive economy in the Andes and Amazon. For what is palpably clear in these conflicts is that different social actors feel the weight of different injustices that they feel have been meted out to them over the years. What is also quite clear is that extraction only ever has a chance of being "just" if it is governed in ways that recognize, *from the outset*, the coexistence of, and the need to attend to, diverse and equally legitimate conceptions of justice and perceptions of injustice.

Notes

1. Very many people in Latin America, Europe, and North America have helped make this chapter possible—though none are implicated in its argument. In particular we are grateful to Håvard Haarstad for his patience, and to the Ford Foundation and Economic and Social Research Council for financial support at different moments.
2. Original quote: "Quieran o no quieran vamos a construir este camino"
3. See A. Bebbington, 2012; D. H. Bebbington, 2010, and www.sed.manchester.ac.uk/research/andes.

References

Agencia Boliviana de Información (ABI). (2009, July 10). Morales Denuncia Estrategias para Evitar Exploración de Hidrocarburos en Bolivia. *Hidrocarburos Bolivia*. Retrieved February 6, 2012, from http://www.hidrocarburosbolivia.com/bolivia-mainmenu-117/exploracion-explotacion/19445-morales-denuncia-estrategias-para-evitar-exploracion-de-hidrocarburos-en-bolivia.html

Arellano-Yanguas, J. (2012). Mining and conflict in Peru: Sowing the minerals, reaping a hail of stones. In A. Bebbington (Ed.), *Social conflict, economic development and extractive industry: Evidence from South America* (pp. 89–111). London, UK: Routledge.

Bebbington, A. (Ed.). (2012). *Social conflict, economic development and extractive industry: Evidence from South America*. London, UK: Routledge.

Bebbington, A. (2009, September/October). The new extraction: Rewriting the political ecology of the Andes? *NACLA Report on the Americas, 42*(5), 12–20.

Bebbington, A., & Bebbington, D. H. (2011). An Andean avatar: Post-neoliberal and neoliberal strategies for securing the unobtainable. *New Political Economy, 16*(1), 131–145.

Bebbington, D. H. (2010). *The political ecology of natural gas extraction in Southern Bolivia*. (Unpublished doctoral dissertation). University of Manchester, Manchester, UK.

Bridge, G. (2004). Mapping the bonanza: Geographies of mining investment in an era of neoliberal reform. *The Professional Geographer, 56*(3), 406–421.

Caballero, V. (2010). Conflictos Sociales y Socioambientales en el Sector Rural y su Relación con el Desarrollo Rural. In P. Ames & V. Caballero (Eds.), *Perú: el Problema Agrario en Debate* (pp. 439–487). *SEPIA XIII*. Lima, Peru: SEPIA. 2010.

Campodonico, H. (2008, June 30). Huayco Legislativo y Nuevo Régimen Laboral. *La República*. Retrieved February 6, 2012, from http://www.cristaldemira.com/articulos.php?id=1739

Chase-Smith, R. (2009, July 20). Bagua, Peru: La verdadera amenaza. *Poder 360°* (Lima), 5, 48–53.

Collier, P., & Hoeffler, A. (2004). Greed and grievance in civil war. *Oxford Economic Papers, 56*, 563–595.
Collier, P., & Hoeffler A. (2005). Resource rents, governance, and conflict. *Journal of Conflict Resolution, 49*(4), 625–633.
Coordinadora Nacional de Radio (2008, August 27). *Ejecutivo Hizo Uso Incorrecto de Facultades Legislativas Otorgadas por el Congreso*. Retrieved from http://www.cnr.org.pe/noticia.php?id=23385.
Correa, R. (2008). *Cadena Radial*, October 11.
Crespo, C. (n.d.). El Estado contra los Comunes del TIPNIS. *Territorio Indígena y Parque Nacional Isiboro Sécure*. Retrieved September 16, 2011, from www.isiborosecure.com/tipnisdocucrespo.htm
Dagnino, E. (2008). Challenges to participation, citizenship and democracy: Perverse confluence and displacement of meanings. In A. Bebbington, S. Hickey, & D. Mitlin (Eds.), *Can Ngos make a difference. The challenge of development alternatives* (pp. 55–70). London, UK: Zed Books.
Defensoría del Pueblo. (2011, November). *Informe Defensorial: Respecto a la violación de los derechos humanos en la marcha indígena*. La Paz: Defensoría del Pueblo. Retrieved February 6, 2012, from http://www.cejis.org/sites/default/files/ informe%20defensoria%20intervencio%20marcha%20indigena.pdf
EFE (2010, January 9). Correa Considera "Vergonzosas" las Condiciones del Fideicomiso del Proyecto ITT. *EFE* (Quito, Ecuador). Retrieved February 6, 2012, from http://www.elsiglodedurango.com.mx/noticia/247801.html
Escobar, A. (2008). *Territories of difference: Place, movements, life, redes*. Durham, NC: Duke University Press.
Finer, M., Jenkins, C. N., Pimm, S. L., Keane, B., & Ross, C. (2008). Oil and gas projects in the Western Amazon: Threats to wilderness, biodiversity, and indigenous peoples. *PLoS ONE, 3*(8), e2932. doi:10.1371/journal.pone.0002932
Fuentes, F. (2011, September 9). Amazon protests in Bolivia: Development before environment? Message posted on http://boliviarising.blogspot.com/2011/09/bolivia-amazon-protest-development.html. Retrieved September 11, 2011.
Fundación UNIR Bolivia. (2011, October). *Análisis de la Conflictividad del TIPNIS y Potenciales de Paz*. La Paz: Fundación UNIR Bolivia. Retrieved from http://es.scribd.com/Gobernabilidad/d/70101462-Analisis-de-la-conflictividad-del-TIPNIS-y-potenciales-de-paz
García, A. (2007, October 28). El Síndrome del Perro del Hortelano. *El Comercio*. Retrieved February 6, 2012, from http://elcomercio.pe/edicionimpresa/html/2007-10-28/el_sindrome_del_perro_del_hort.html
Gudynas, E. (2010, April). Si eres tan Progresista ¿Por qué destruyes la naturaleza? Neoextractivismo, izquierda y alternativas. *Ecuador Debate, 79*, 61–82.
Moore, J., & Velásquez, T. (2012). Sovereignty negotiated: Anti-mining movements, the state and multinational mining companies under Correa's

'21st century socialism'. In A. Bebbington (Ed.), *Social conflict, economic development and extractive industry: evidence from South America* (pp. 112–133). London, UK: Routledge.
Narváez, X. (2007, December 5). Ecuadorian president says "ecologists are terrorists" (M. Allen, Trans.). Message posted to redamazon.wordpress. com/2007/12/05/ecuadorian-president-call-ecologists-terrorists
North-South Institute. (2011, Spring). *A house undermined: Transforming relations between mining companies and indigenous peoples in the Americas.* Ottawa, Canada: The North-South Institute Policy Brief.
Peck, J. (2004). Geography and Public Policy: Constructions of neoliberalism. *Progress in Human Geography, 28,* 392–405.
PresidenciaPeru (2011, November 16). Conferecia de Prensa Presidente Ollanta Humala y Conflicto Sociales [Press conference] [Video file].Video posted to http://www.youtube.com/watch?feature=player_embedded&v=MDKT6q-dWsk&list=PLC01443B5BFAF9CFF
Rénique, G. (2009). Law of the jungle in Peru: Indigenous Amazonian uprising against neoliberalism. *Socialism and Democracy, 23*(3),117–135.
Rival, L. (2012). Planning development futures in the Ecuadorian Amazon: The expanding oil frontier and the Yasuní-ITT initiative. In A. Bebbington (Ed.) *Social conflict, economic development and extractive industry: Evidence from South America* (pp. 153–171). London, UK: Routledge.
Rostow, W. W. (1960). *The stages of economic growth: A non-communist manifesto.* Cambridge: Cambridge University Press.
Rudas, G. (2011, August 3). Contexto del Sistema Nacional Ambiental y la Minería. Uso del suelo, recursos tributarios y capacidad de regulación [Workshop presentation]. *Taller sobre Minería y Proyectos Extractivos. Sus Impactos en Territorios Étnicos* [*Workshop on the impacts of mining and other extractive projects on ethnic* territories]. Bogotá, August 2–4, 2011.
Santoyo, G. J. (2002, August). *Possibilities and perspectives of indigenous peoples with regard to consultations and agreements within the mining sector in Latin America and the Caribbean: thematic exploration.* Ottawa, Canada: The North-South Institute.
Svampa, M., Stefanoni, P., & Bajo, R. (2009, September 11). Bolivia's vice-president defends MAS government's record (R. Fidler, Trans.). (Original article published in *Le Monde Diplomatique,* Bolivian edition, August 2009). Retrieved September 23, 2009, from www.links.org.au/node/1241
Vidal, J. (2009, June 13). We are fighting for our lives and our dignity. *Guardian.* Retrieved from http://www.guardian.co.uk/environment/2009/jun/13/forests-environment-oil-companies
World Bank. (1990). *World development report, 1990: poverty.* Oxford / New York, NY: Oxford University Press.

Chapter 3

More than Beads and Feathers: Resource Extraction and the Indigenous Challenge in Latin America

John-Andrew McNeish

Introduction

Recent violent clashes have drawn new attention to the persistence of conflicts between indigenous peoples, states, and private interests in Latin America. The media coverage and commentaries that followed events such as those in Bagua, Peru in 2009, and Yucumo, Bolivia, in 2011, made it evident to a wide audience that severe contestation surrounds the plans of Latin American governments to further promote and introduce new projects for natural resource extraction and supporting infrastructure. This chapter is written recognizing these conflicts, but also in critical response to green-washed interpretations of recent clashes between indigenous peoples and states. Although it is correct to highlight the seriousness of confrontations and the failures of current governments in the treatment of these cases, I question whether the images of indigenous resistance and environmentalism created in relation to these events are not dangerously oversimplified. Current depictions of environmental conflicts involving indigenous peoples, states, and the private sector reinforce stereotypes that make it appear as though indigenous peoples are the natural allies of the natural environment—and thus of the environmental movement—and are incapable of anything but confronting and rejecting change. Moreover, they frequently appear in these reports and articles as one-dimensional, anachronistic, and incapable of thinking critically about their own development. In this chapter, I highlight a different depiction of indigenous peoples.

The statements of indigenous peoples themselves, existing ethnography, the growing literature on indigenous development as well as my own research on resource politics (McNeish & Logan, 2012) point to a much larger spectrum of positions and responses to extractive and infrastructure initiatives in Latin America and beyond. Indeed, with prejudices and injustice still abounding, it is important to recognize that the indigenous lobby is far from as downtrodden as popular media or activist organizations often portray. In most Latin American countries there has been a slow, but a steadily growing acceptance of the need to recognize cultural diversity and to respond to indigenous peoples' rights and interests. In this new climate, indigenous movements express a new confidence where veto or rejection of consultation processes are alternatives, but outright rejection of all projects for extraction and the construction of infrastructure is rare. In providing a rough panorama of some of the different indigenous positions and actions in relation to extractive practices, the chapter aims to demonstrate the interests of indigenous communities and their political movements to push for more than recognition and environmental protection. Although the protection of the environment (including monitoring and reporting on damages) remains a central factor of indigenous campaigning, it is included primarily in the context of what is typically the main demands; the protection of autonomy and livelihoods. Crucially we also see that whilst conditions, environments, and histories differ, and severe imbalances of power remain, there are clear signs of a desire for participation and of reaching another result than a simple standoff.

Resource Extraction and Contestation in Latin America

Encouraged by the current high prices for commodities on the international markets, many Latin American governments have implemented a significant expansion of extractive industries as a pillar of their national macroeconomic strategies. Hydrocarbons and mining have recently seen hikes in capital investment largely driven by the demand for raw materials amongst the fleet of emerging economic powers led by China. In direct support of new extractive efforts many Latin American governments have also sought to further develop national infrastructure capabilities, that is, the further expansion of road networks and other forms of communications. The most significant and expansive of these infrastructure programs is the Initiative for Integration of Regional Infrastructure in South America (IIRSA), a pan-South American agreement signed at a presidential summit in Brasilia in 2000. Aiming to construct a bi-oceanic trade corridor from the Atlantic to the Pacific, the initiative will also build a massive network of roads, ports, waterways, hydroelectric plants, pipelines, and other major pieces of infrastructure aimed at the integration of the continent.

The claims made by governments supporting the developments in extraction and infrastructure—such as Brazil, Venezuela, Ecuador, Peru, and Bolivia—are that, given currently high international commodity prices, they represent an opportunity to generate the state coffers necessary for wider economic development, poverty reduction, and social investment.[1] In some cases, such as Brazil, Venezuela, and Bolivia, public highlight is made by governments that increased public funding coming from these sources have been essential in providing the basis for large-scale public programs that have reduced poverty levels and improved a range of human development indicators. The linkage of state financing gained from expanded extractive activities to economic diversification and a range of social programs and cash transfer schemes—of which Brazil's *Bolsa Família* program is the strongest representative—have had significant results in reducing poverty levels and inequality in a number of countries in the region.

Although with possible social and economic gains, the expansion of the extractive and infrastructure frontier in Latin America has also significant costs. In the process of expansion there are pressures and requirements to open up territory that previously was isolated or protected, and which are often biologically fragile environments populated by vulnerable populations who share their land with minerals and energy sources. The statements of government representatives claim that in respect of these sensitive conditions their programs for extraction and infrastructure are being carried out responsibly and with respect to evolving national laws and regulations governing questions of environmental security and human rights. The practical legal implication of these conventions and operating principles has been the rapid increase in number and intensity of prior consultation exercises. Despite these exercises a rising number of clashes between indigenous peoples and national authorities have demonstrated that state and private sector claims of responsible action are questioned by the indigenous communities most directly affected by development. Indeed, travelling from north to south through Latin America it is hard to pass through a country where there are not conflicts of a socio-environmental character, or where indigenous peoples are not pitted against extractive or infrastructure interests in their territory. The Goldcorp mining project in Guatemala, the Camisea gas-pipeline project and Bagua confrontation in Peru, the Belo Monte dam in Brazil, the Chevron case in Ecuador, the la Minga mobilizations in Colombia, and the recent *Territorio Indígena y Parque Nacional*

Isiboró Securé (TIPNIS) march in Bolivia are all *cause célèbre*s in what is really a much longer list of registered, but lesser known, confrontations caused by extractive and infrastructure activities in indigenous territories stretching the length of the continent. As has been noted by a number of authors (A. Bebbington, 2009; Gudynas, 2010; Sawyer & Terence Gomez, 2008), these conflicts are also notable in that they arise in countries whose governments reflect a range of political options ranging from right to left of the political scale. Despite the current Bolivian government's claims to represent a radical plurinational alternative, Anthony Bebbington (2009) has for example argued that "while approaches to the ownership of the extractive industry clearly vary . . . , approaches to the environmental and social implications of extraction may be less different." (p. 15). Bolivian and Ecuadorian governments, both characterized as progressive, seem just as likely as Peru's to tell activists and indigenous groups to get out of the way of national priorities, just as likely to allow extractive industry into fragile and protected ecologies, and just as determined to convince indigenous peoples that extractive industry is good for them too, without fulfilling their rights. Whilst recognizing substantial ideological differences between Andean governments, Gudynas (2010) also argues that Bolivia belongs to a group of "neo-extractivist" countries, which while reemphasizing the role of the state and the redistribution of surplus to the population, repeats the negative environmental and social impacts of old extractivism.

Environmental Avatars and the Noble Savage

Despite governmental claims of appropriate action, socio-environmental conflicts are taking place in a range of different political environments throughout the region. While other authors highlight of the expansion and violence of extractive economies throughout the Americas is undoubtedly important, I see however as much more problematic a tendency in recent academic writing (A. Bebbington & D. H. Bebbington, 2011) and environmental campaigns[2] to characterize these struggles as taking place under "Avatar"-like conditions. Even though it is correct to highlight the seriousness of current confrontations and the failures of current governments, I question here whether the images of indigenous resistance and environmentalism created in relation to these events have been over simplified.

Drawing on Stuart Hall's (1996) influential conception of black cultural politics, de la Cadena and Starn (2007) have proposed that indigenous activism is "without guarantees." Despite earlier anthropological efforts to isolate and contain the singularity of indigenous cultural identity and interests through ethnographic description these authors argue that indigenism has never been a singular ideology, program, or movement, and that its politics resist closure.

Although indigenous activism can be linked to social justice and inspire transformative visions, as a political order it can equally be motivated by different ideological positions, all of them able to effect exclusions and forced inclusions. Indigeneity that is, being indigenous, while being concerned with specific origins is also not necessarily a condition of separateness. Indeed, as de la Cadena and Starn (2007) recognize, it is relational in nature. Indigenous peoples are the product of different colonial experiences including processes of mixing, *mestizaje*, and of enforced separation or racial apartheid. Indeed, their identities have in some cases, such as Mexico and Indonesia—and thinking about economic migration from the highlands to the lowlands in Bolivia—been formed as much as a result of internal colonization as by external processes of colonization and conquest.

Indigeneity today should then be seen as a process and not a fixed state of being (de la Cadena & Starn, 2007). In its most ambitious expressions, and articulated to alter-globalization processes, the new indigenism seeks to undo hegemonic signifiers. However, not being a monolithic entity it is also necessary to recognize that some of indigeneity's fractions are included in the dominant and hegemonic—and still others are straddling both.

Most indigenous groups possess a strong sense of rootedness to the land, that is. of territoriality, and of prior occupation to foreign invaders, characterized by distinctive historically and culturally shaped understandings and connections to an intimately known landscape. Land and water were the basis of indigenous life in the past, and remain so today. However, struggles over territory are seldom neatly cohesive or driven by noble or utopian ideals alone. Money and corporate appetites enter the mix, often creating dissention within native groups or pitting them against one another.

We are then faced with a very different kind of indigenism than the closed, corporate, and static stereotypes produced in early anthropology, and repeated in both government policies and the environmental activist ad campaigns common today. Over the past few decades, environmentalist thinkers have increasingly looked to indigenous peoples for inspiration and guidance. Native American beliefs and myths have, for instance, greatly inspired environmentalists; the founders of Greenpeace saw themselves as the Rainbow Warriors who, according to Cree myth, would come to the Indians' rescue and "teach the white man reverence for the Earth."[3] Environmentalists regularly invoke native traditions and philosophies when they articulate their own visions of the ecologically ideal society, and they frequently seek to enlist indigenous peoples as allies in environmental struggles. However, for every success story and for every productive alliance between environmental advocates and indigenous peoples, there is a matching story; a story of misunderstanding and conflict. Environmentalists and indigenous people have frequently found themselves on opposing sides in particular environmental struggles (Nadasdy, 2005, pp. 291–292).

Criticizing the wanton naivety of environmental analysts and organizations that have employed stereotypes of indigenous peoples living in harmony with the environment, or as the protectors of the forest, some writers have pointed out the similarities that exist between the images used today and earlier colonial stereotypes. Redford (1991) has for example coined the term "ecologically noble savage," highlighting the deep roots that exist between today's imagery with older colonial imagery of ecological nobility. Despite its intentions to create positive connotations, this new "noble savage" perspective also denies the realities of native people's lives, reducing the rich diversity of their beliefs, values, social values, social relations, and practices to a one-dimensional caricature. It also acts to create an unattainable ideal that acts to divide rather than serve indigenous interests. As with older incarnations of the noble savage stereotype, the image of ecological nobility also authorizes Euro-Americans to judge how "authentic" indigenous people are. Thus, when environmentalists unexpectedly find themselves opposed by indigenous people, there is a tendency to dismiss any opposition as a result of cultural loss or "contamination" rather than to take indigenous people's concerns seriously. Those who do not measure up to the stereotypical "beads and feathers" ideal of indigeneity—or the hyper-real indian (Ramos, 1998)—find themselves stigmatized as *mestizos*, as half-breeds, assimilated, or as imposters.

The tendency of environmental organizations, and also of other development policy-makers, to operate such stereotypes of course creates difficult decisions for indigenous peoples themselves. In the search for support and financing of their campaigns and development interests, indigenous peoples are forced to take on masks of identity that are sympathetic to wider audiences. By invoking the *beads and feather* image, environmentalists and indigenous people alike tap into the image's rhetorical power, enabling them in some instances to galvanize broad—even worldwide—support for particular communities and struggles (Conklin & Graham, 1995). By representing themselves as ecologically noble, indigenous peoples in Latin America and further afield gain access to a vast amount of symbolic capital. As is widely known, the political and legal pressure brought to bear by international environmentalist-indigenous alliances on private companies and governments have led to unprecedented gains—not only for environmental compensation and clean up—but direct control over territory. However, in doing so we should also be aware that the result of making this strategic decision has been that a range of wider indigenous interests that do not fit with the static nature of ecological nobility (e.g., autonomy, political representation outside traditional territory, local economic development, and gender rights) may be silenced.

Although the regional campaign for cultural recognition have secured constitutional recognition of rights to identity and autonomy, the essentialized and concessional terms in which these processes have been won, have had the unintended consequences of reducing the spaces available to indigenous organizations to negotiate the further expansion of political and economic rights (Engle, 2010). Moreover, as this chapter means to convey, the reduction of indigenous peoples to stereotypes of ecological nobility threatens to close down the possibility of recognizing and learning from a more nuanced understanding of the way in which they are at once tied to similar historical processes and differentially understand the linkages between development and environment.

Militant Pragmatism

From 2008 to 2011, I carried out several periods of field research on the politics of hydrocarbons in the Department of Tarija in Bolivia, the region where 70 percent of Bolivia's hydrocarbon wealth is found. During my period in Tarija, I conducted interviews with the leaders of two of the indigenous communities within the department, the *guaraní* and the *weenayek*.[4] Both of these communities had histories of confronting plans to expand hydrocarbon production in their traditional territories. These clashes have taken place despite the existence of legislation mandating prior consultation in the case of extractive projects.[5] This legislation was tightened up following nationalization of the hydrocarbons industry, including changes to the Constitution in 2009 that declares the United Nations Declaration of the Rights of Indigenous Peoples (UNDRIP) to be national law and the introduction of a legal norm that regulates the consultation procedure in the hydrocarbon sector (SD 29033).

In the case of the *guaraní*—Bolivia's third largest ethnic group—a long campaign had been carried out by the *Asamblea Pueblo Guaraní* (APG) with the assistance of the Tarijeño Regional Research Centre (CERDET) to pursue Spanish REPSOL for compensation relating to environmental and social damages connected with the exploitation of resources and pipeline construction from Campo Margarita, one of Bolivia' principal oil fields (see figure 7.1). With the transference of the fields to the national oil company (*Yacimientos Petrolíferos Fiscales Bolivianos*—YPFB) new plans were launched to expand pipelines and bore another 23 wells in the region, sparking a new round of confrontations and tensions around the time of my arrival. As well as new conflicts in the *Guaraní* territory of *Itaka Guasu* (Rio Grande) bordering Cochabamba to the north of the department, tensions had also risen in connection with plans to reopen a set of previously abandoned oil wells together with Oriental Oil within the Aguaraqüe National Park close to the southern border with Argentina. Although a protected area, the communities living close to the park borders claimed that the oil wells within the park—established by Standard Oil in the late 1920s—had been leaking into their drinking water supply for well over a decade. Following years of being ignored by consecutive governments, there was little faith in the new government's promises of cleaning up this contamination in the course of reestablishing the wells using new technologies.

In the case of the *weenayek*, a community of 3,500 people in 25 settlements along the left bank of the Pilcomayo river that runs through the city of Villamontes, nationalization had similarly brought with it plans to expand gas production within their territory. The *weenayek* also had to experience confronting companies searching for gas within the bounds of their registered indigenous territory (*Tierras Comunitarias de Origen*—TCO).[6] At the time of my arrival in the department the *weenayek* were once more confronting plans proposed by the YPFB and an international partner, British Gas, to expand gas production and to construct a network for transport and processing of condensates.

Interested in capturing insight into these cases, my interviews with the *guaraní* and *weenayek* were aimed at probing local perspectives on hydrocarbon exploitation in their territories. The responses I received from the local leaders were notably very different to those that I had expected to hear. Rather than an account of a story of clear resistance, the answers I received from the leaders expressed much more willingness to push for accommodation with the oil and gas companies and the government than I had expected. In the case of the *weenayek*, though recognition was made by a Capitan Grande of the damaging effects of seismic testing on the game animals, on which their hunting depends, he pragmatically stated that:

> If they are willing to provide the good money, we are willing to discuss. This time we have a long term development plan, twenty years, resources that are to arrive as projects. We state the amount and what these are for, productive activities, clean water etc. We work with the Ministry of Hydrocarbons to define this in consultation ... We are flexible. (Weenayek Capitan Grande, interview with author, February 2009, Tarija)

In the case of the *guaraní*, militant protests had mounted blockading roads and efforts had been made to mount a legal case against both Repsol and YPFB. However, there was no real interest on the part of local leaders to put a stop to all production in their territory. Rather there was an emphasis on seeking dialogue and to negotiate settlements that would be beneficial to community development. APG talked openly about its experience of working politically around the edges of legal claims to achieve settlements out of court. Though not entirely avoiding setbacks and governmental contradictions, this strategy has secured the APG a series of advances. Although never entirely honored by the company and begrudgingly accepted by the local community because of its low level, in 2001, an out of court settlement resulted in Repsol's funding of the establishment of community environmental monitoring and a local development fund.[7] Also in May 2008, APG together with the *weenayek* signed an agreement with the government covering nine different points, the most concrete among which was the state's commitment to respect legal requirements of consultation, to consider a commitment of 2 percent of all departmental hydrocarbon royalties to local indigenous development funds, to provide the local indigenous community with gas for domestic cooking, payment for environmental damages, funding for socio-environmental monitoring, and incorporation of local leaders in official discussions about the reform of the Hydrocarbons Law.[8] This agreement followed months of consultation, backed up by periodic protest action in which the *guaraní* and *weenayek* separately blocked roads and occupied public buildings to draw attention to their interests.

Despite statements by key official figures such as the director of YPFB to the newspapers about how APG were standing in the way of necessary development, a mixture of militancy, negotiation, and legal action won the APG a series of further agreements with the Morales government. In May 2010, agreements were signed by APG and the government regarding recognition and registration of the autonomy of *guaraní* territories in Tarija, in accordance with the new plurinational constitution. In May 2011, the APG also negotiated an out of court settlement with the government for USD14.8 million in connection with compensation for damages incurred in the Caipipendi block within the Itika Guasu territory[9].

APG's participation in the recent TIPNIS (National Park and Indigenous Territory of Isobore Secure) march and parallel negotiations with the government also delivered results. My own research on the march in 2011 reveals that although the march was initially organized in opposition to a road project and in defense of the autonomy of the indigenous populations living within the park (*mojeños, yuracarés, chimanes*), through their use of experience and sheer numbers, the APG had convinced the march organizers—CIDOB (Indigenous Confederation of the Bolivian Orient) and the subcentral of the TIPNIS—to include their interests among the demands presented by the protest leaders to the government. As is now a matter of record, despite tremendous opposition from the government and some sectors of the rural population including violent police action, the TIPNIS march succeeded in gathering sufficient attention and support that on October 24, 2011, the government bowed to public pressures by reversing its plans for the road. In the negotiations surrounding this decision the APG also managed to receive response to its demands, not to stop planned extraction, but rather to develop a sustainable development plan for the Aguaraqüe National Park that takes account of its contamination, local economic interests, and guarantees respect of the earlier agreements on consultation and territorial autonomy.[10]

Of course, for the indigenous protest marchers from Isobore Secure, the government's stoppage of the road project appeared at first glance to be a major success. However, considering the unexpected nuances of indigenous positioning on issue of resource governance, it is important to note the disappointment voiced by the leaders of the march the day after the decision by the government to declare the TIPNIS territory as "intangible" state property, that is, indefinitely stopping all forms of extractive and infrastructure projects in the park area. Although aiming to stop the road project, indigenous leaders had no desire for all productive activities in the park to be restricted. As Pedro Vare, vicepresident of the TIPNIS subcentral stated to the Bolivian media:

> The theme of conservation is directed at conserving resources, as part of a strategic development plan. You know that to conserve means that one can keep in one moment, a thing, and in the other, later, at another time, make use of it. (Propuesta Indígena tiene 4 ejes, Cambio 04.11.11[11])

The indigenous protesters from the area argued that intangible should only apply to "terceros" (third parties), that is, actors who are not indigenous from the area, such as coca-growing farmers entering the area or other external commercial interests. Early on proposals had been made to the government by community leaders that the road should rather follow the route of the River Secure where most of the local communities are located. It was argued that such a routing would help connect them to necessary services and markets outside of their territory, but at the same time allow greater possibility for the protection of the mass majority of the park—including areas that are sacred and environmentally sensitive. Initially there had been proposals to the government about alternative routes, but with the government's refusal to enter into dialogue on these points, its failure to respect the law regarding impact studies, to carry out genuine widespread consultation and signing of a contract with a Brazilian company to go ahead with the project, the demands of the protest had become increasingly recalcitrant in rejecting the road entirely. As well as noting the role of APG above, the other demands included in the list presented to the government also emphasized that the indigenous protesters were interested not only in the protection of the biodiversity on which they relied. The demands state very clearly local interest in securing territorial boundaries and assistance with development challenges such as schools and education, women's rights, and the development of a carbon fund where their provision of environmental services would be possible.[12] By emphasizing their close relationship to the natural environment the TIPNIS march appeared to fit the "green" mold assigned to them by environmental and rights organizations. However, even though protection of the natural environment was important to the marchers, this was not expressed as a value in its own right, but rather as a point used to reinforce issues they saw as priorities, that is, the defense of territory and autonomy, with biodiversity following after. For example, asked about the cause of the march, a leader of the subcentral of Secure (TIPNIS) responded to me in an interview that:

> The defense of the territorial autonomy of the TIPNIS comes first. This is the spearhead (punto de lanza) of the march. We are defending our rights against what we see is a slow crime. The road threatens our culture, customs and the biodiversity of the territory. (Subcentral leader, interview with author, October 2011, Tarija)

Indigenous Protagonists

Processes of prior consultation and legal action perhaps represent the most common manner in which indigenous concerns and interests are now expressed. The formation of international conventions and parallel legal reforms has channeled a significant proportion of indigenous demand-making off the streets and into courts and meeting rooms. There are now a series of well-known cases of prior consultations and court cases where indigenous claims have gained formal legal analysis and process. Some of these cases, such as the 18-year-long court case by Ecuadorian indigenous groups against Chevron, the US-based oil company, have drawn considerable media and political attention within and beyond the region. Ecuadorean indigenous groups in the province of Sucumbíos have claimed that Texaco, Chevron's forerunner in oil production in the region, dumped more than 18 billion gallons (68 billion liters) of toxic materials into unlined pits and rivers between 1972 and 1992. According to scientists working for the communities and the environmental organizations that have financially supported their case, these contaminants led to a 150 percent increase in the incidences of cancer in the local population. Although final payment is still resisted by the company, the Ecuadorian court concluded the case in 2011 by fining Chevron USD 9.5 billion to cover environmental damages in the Amazonian lowlands and their clean up costs. Bucking the more normative accounts of this case such as given in Berlinger's film *Crude* (2009), detailed research on this case has revealed the manner in which indigenous struggles over land and oil operations in Ecuador were as much about reconfiguring national and transnational inequality—that is, rupturing the silence around racial injustice, exacting spaces of accountability, and rewriting narratives of national belonging—as they were about the material use and extraction of rain forest resources (Sawyer, 2004).

In the high profile prior consultations taking place in Peru between the *aschuar* and the Canadian oil company Talisman, other nuances must also be noted. For over 40 years the *aschuar* have been affected by the contamination entering the Corrientes River Basin from oil exploration carried out by Occidental. Government tests have demonstrated that the *aschuar* in this area have life threatening levels of cadmium and lead in their blood streams. With over 40 years of experience of the effects of oil exploration in this area the *aschuar* now oppose efforts by Talisman Energy to open new oil fields in the Western Pastasa and Morona River Basins. Unfortunately, in the rush to secure financing and support many of the statements by local indigenous leaders have been edited by Nongovernmental Organizations (NGOs) to suggest that environmental protection is the only goal of the campaign.[13].Again a closer look at the case demonstrates that there is more nuance at stake. Although environmental concerns are in place, the statements of local leaders themselves, disregarding NGO voice-overs, suggest that self-determination is also a key point in their campaign. Consciously or not, there are signs here and elsewhere of environmental NGOs tending to background issues, such as the protection of territory, that indigenous peoples attempt to foreground in their open statements and political strategies. It is evident that the principle reason for the *aschuar* to ask Talisman to leave their territory was as much their failure to respect local claims for collective autonomy as it was concern with further environmental contamination. In traveling to the shareholders meeting of Talisman in Calgary, Canada, in April 2011, focus was given by the *aschuar* leaders to the way in which the process of prior consultation carried out by the company ignored traditional leadership structures and had by arriving at agreements with eight communities failed to achieve real consensus support for their activities. Indeed, highlight was made of the way in which the company's efforts to carry out prior consultation had divided their community. The statements of the *aschuar* leaders made it very clear that they were not outright opposed to oil exploration, but that any decision on oil exploration must be determined by the community as a whole.

> We want to live healthy, peacefully amongst ourselves, without discrimination, without internal conflicts. Practicing self-determination. We want to be autonomous in our territory (*Aschuar* Leader, Linton Rengifo Hernandez).[14]

There is an echo of similar emphasis in the statements made during the *u'wa* case in Peru. The *u'wa* case was considered a landmark case by many indigenous and environmental organizations because of the success of the solidarity campaign in expelling the oil company Occidental from their territory in the late 1990s. Although granted financial assistance by a number of international environmental NGOs including Oil Watch and Amazon Watch in their fight to stop Occidental from drilling in their territory, the statements of the *u'wa* themselves expressed more a concern with the way in which leadership structures had been ignored and the lack of consultation granted by the company and state. For example:

> For the u'wa, making decisions implies a long process. We must talk to our . . ., with all our people, and with all our councils. Our shamans, who work to maintain the equilibrium of the world, must in turn communicate with the gods, in order to know the correct road

and thus guide the people. With their guidance, the u'wa make decisions amongst the whole people. Our spokespeople or representatives are then charged with communicating or carrying them out.[15]

Experiences from extraction and infrastructure projects and road-building in other parts of Latin America also suggest that more care needs to be taken when looking for insight into indigenous positioning in relation to these events. Even though in a series of well-known Brazilian cases such as the Belo Monte Dam and the road-building projects BR-163 (Cuibá–Santarém), BR 364 (Cuibá–Porto Velho), and BR 319 (Manaus–Porto Velho) local populations and NGOs are clearly concerned about their environmental consequences, indigenous campaigning is commonly founded on greater concerns with their impact on territorial integrity.

Frustrations with governmental or corporate avoidance of existing laws and regulations governing prior consultation and impact studies, appears in review as one of the principle catalysts explaining why the sentiments of local populations develop a more confrontational character. However, as Rodríguez-Gavarito (2011) and Engle (2010) have observed the official emphasis on legal process either through prior consultation exercises or through the operation of the courts have in their own right led to growing frustrations among indigenous groups. As Rodríguez-Gavarito (2011) writes about consultations processes:

> Beyond the physical and economic coercion, the effect of domination operates by more subtle and indirect means. Mere participation in consultation processes or litigation related to them place the indigenous cause within the logic of procedure, which has costs, as it limits what can be said, demanded and achieved. (p. 38)

In recognizing, like these authors, the limits of legal or militant confrontation, some indigenous groups have chosen instead to wage their campaign for self-determination and economic development by working with rather than against the dominant paradigm of market-led development. Representatives from many of the region's leading indigenous organizations[16] have for example taken part in initiatives sponsored by the World Bank to create round-tables between themselves, Latin American states, and the private sector—including oil and gas companies. These initiatives have specifically sought to circumvent through the creation of common agreements the stipulation in current international agreements the requirement of "consent" instead of a softer term of common engagement, that is, "consultation." According to a policy document from one of these round-tables a common refrain from leaders and representatives of indigenous peoples is that

> indigenous people understand that direct actions such as national or regional strikes, work stoppages, and disruptions of [resource] facilities may lead to undesired and unpredictable outcomes. However, in most cases, whenever the indigenous communities undertake direct actions, they do so to press for dialogue with governments and [resource] companies. They emphasize that they take such actions solely in the absence of alternatives such as a joint policy or project planning.[17]

Here emphasis is placed on dialogue and consultation to avoid confrontation, and on working with extractive businesses to ensure an outcome favorable to indigenous interests. A series of projects for participatory environmental monitoring (e.g., the Yanacocha mine in Peru, Glamis Gold Mine in Sipacapa, Guatemala) have also been the result of further round-tables where indigenous peoples, states, and companies have taken part and discussed common principles.

More surprising still are the efforts by a number of indigenous people to take things further by attempting to establish their own oil companies.[18] In the last few years a number of small indigenous-owned extractive companies have been established.[19] All of these companies have attempted to establish themselves as operators within the Ecuadorian Amazon and with a view to establishing more socially responsible business. In the case of Keyano-Pimee Exploration a joint-venture deal was struck with Amazon Gas, a local indigenous entity, where they were to retain 45 percent ownership and agreements were signed for the transference of technical knowledge and management of the field into indigenous hands within the first five years. Although the project eventually failed as a result of disagreements between company authorities and local leaders, one of the key figures in the projects commented at a conference that

> it is not as difficult as it may seem for indigenous peoples to enter into the formal economy, to participate in businesses of this dimension. We realized that we have to work a lot more in education, training and leadership, under a perspective of entrepreneurship. Until now, the policies have been protectionist, 'poor little Indians, we will have to give them something, we will have to help them survive.' That is why when we started this project we did not have a single indigenous capacitated. (Edwin Puma[20])

Other examples of indigenous business entrepreneurship within and beyond the fields of extraction now start to abound. For example, many indigenous communities including the *surui* of Brazil and the *ashaninka* of Peru have entered into agreements with either international NGOs or with private business to develop projects for carbon sequestration (REDD projects) and payments for environmental services (PES) aimed at the protection of forests and other areas of conservation (see chapter 4 by Hall, this volume). Interestingly the shareholders in many of these projects include banks, extraction, and energy trading companies including Barclays Capital, Bank of America, Merill Lynch, Goldman Sachs, Shell, GE, Allied American Power, and Gazprom. It is also of note that in the recent TIPNIS march mentioned earlier in this paper, one of the key demands presented by the leaders of the protest to the government was for the creation of "green funds" that would operate and allow them to privately profit in a similar way to these other carbon-offsetting projects. Also gaining some significant profile are the efforts by indigenous peoples to develop networks, research, and knowledge geared toward assisting them in more entrepreneurial endeavors. In September 2010, the second Fostering Indigenous Business and Entrepreneurship in the Americas (FIBEA) conference was held in Manaus, Brazil.

Relationships to Capital and Modernity

Rather than matching environmental stereotypes and typical academic assumptions, we see here that indigeneity in Latin America expresses a great deal of complexity and ambiguity. Indigenous peoples express different positions, but in general it is possible to see from this rough panorama more of a desire for participation and protagonism than outright rejection and confrontation of extractive interests. Although perhaps uncomfortable from the position of more green or red progressive interests, we see here that indigenous peoples while challenging states and private companies actively seek possibilities for participation and are often extremely tolerant of failures to respect their legal rights and claims.

It is important to note that in no cases of indigenous contestation or protagonism is there an attempt to claim separation or opposition to state development. Rather, we see in the course of this rough review of protagonism that far from looking for ways to retract from processes of development, indigenous peoples are more often than not interested in using these processes to deliver possibilities for defending their territorial sovereignty and producing opportunities for economic and social development within the state. As such we need to accept that indigenous peoples are equally as involved in processes of thinking through the meaning, possibilities and meaning of modernity, or critical modernity (Peet & Hartwick, 2009), and significance of human relations with nature and resources, as we nonindigenous are. We need to also recognize that indigenous peoples through their protagonism and expressions of alternative approaches to development represent important alternative voices of stateness, and as such have and continue to influence state formation (something that can explain constructs such as the plurinational state).

In producing environmental caricatures, there is indication that current interpretations appear to have forgotten, or ignored a history of debate within anthropology in which indigenous practice and thought is seen to be critically connected to capitalist economies and to processes of state formation, globalization, and development (Gupta & Sharma, 2006; Hansen & Stepputat, 2006; Harris, 1995; Mintz, 1986; Nash, 1993; Taussig, 1980). It is important, I think, to draw from these debates and to give renewed emphasis in the current context of current extractive conflicts to the point that indigenous peoples do not live beyond a relationship to capital and development. The meaning and use of resources, commodities, and the market are similarly transformed and contentious in indigenous thought as they are in other societies. The historical experiences of indigenous peoples in the Andes are clearly different to those in the Amazon and Lowlands, but because of histories—that are both local and global and involve constant movement in-between, we cannot assume that simple separation of rationalities exist. Even accepting that different peoples construct the relationship between society and nature differently, the efforts by phenomenological oriented social scientists and environmentalists to identify entirely distinct cultural categories of thought about the natural environment are out of step with the materiality of historical and political experiences.

In short, in daily practice, tradition and resistance are required by the circumstances of history and global economic pressures to be balanced with an interconnected discussion about modernity and exploitation. Just as we do, indigenous populations in Latin America face untenable decisions between development and identity—where traditional modes of production and subsistence might no longer be feasible options. In discussing "hybrid natures" other authors such as Escobar (1999, p. 13) recognize how as a result of history and globalization indigenous groups are required to incorporate multiple constructions of nature in order to negotiate with translocal forces while maintaining a modicum of autonomy and cultural cohesion. Indigenous groups are also aware that this problem is particularly acute for peoples who have been displaced from their lands or territories. It is for this reason that though economic interests are important, it is above all else territorial autonomy and sovereignty that remain the principle concerns of indigenous peoples facing development and extractive activities. As Alison Brysk (1996) has argued:

> Cultural survival in the sense of the preservation of precontact, low technology indigenous cultures is neither viable nor desired by most groups . . . the important question is who manages the pace and content of development so that indigenous peoples can exercise self-determination. (p. 41)

Conclusions

This chapter has questioned the tendencies of academic, media, and NGO campaigns to characterize the participation of indigenous peoples as natural environmentalists, or Avatars, in recent extractive conflicts. I have argued that recent interpretations of clashes have green-washed the reality of events and positions. Such characterizations are not only overessentialized, but also more importantly they are misleading and dangerous in that they reduce indigenous peoples to one-dimensional stereotypes—the ecological noble savage—that strips them of their humanity and the fullness of their agency. In line with Gow (2008) I argue that there is no single indigenous approach to development and modernity.

Far from comprehensive, the rough panorama of strategies and positions sketched in this chapter suggests that indigenous peoples' relationships to these processes of development, and with them capital and modernity, are far more complex than common presumptions allow. The chapter demonstrates that rather than rejecting all modern development per se, indigenous communities are working critically to consider the pros and cons of proposed projects. As is argued above, indigenous peoples draw on what in many instances is a long and sometimes intimate relationship with global actors, networks, and capital. In the process, resistances and militancy are often expressed, but there are strong signals from campaigns and statements that indigenous peoples are also interested in also using other legal and political mechanisms to respond to both the unavoidable ill effects of extraction and infrastructure, and their economic promises. At times uncomfortable compromises and alliances are created with the extractive business, and in others indigenous peoples are starting to be extractors themselves.

Rather than an outright rejection of all extractive operations or infrastructure building in their territories, we see instead then indigenous peoples utilizing different and often multiple strategies (protest, litigation, prior consultation exercises, round-tables, participatory environmental monitoring, the establishment of indigenous extractive corporations, etc.) not necessarily to stop, but in efforts to tame and guide the outcome of these projects. Where companies are asked to leave a territory and confrontation looked for by an indigenous community, it appears to be more often than not premised on the failure of outside interests—states, companies, and courts—to respect traditional leadership structures and comply with the laws and regulations for consultation and impact study these instances themselves put in place.

Finally, I argue here that recognition of the ambiguity and multiplicity of indigenous positions in relation to extractive and infrastructure projects is important not only to provide a realistic characterization of recent events, but to create opportunity for indigenous peoples' real concerns and challenges to come to the fore. These concerns and challenges are many, but it is also striking that in the place of pure antagonism a host of positions of protagonism are revealed. It is also striking that though environmental concerns and development hopes are important, the abiding issue at the heart of all indigenous struggles in Latin America remains that of self-determination and of territorial integrity. If we are to do justice to indigenous peoples, and allow indigenous peoples to claim their own justice—and this really is the point (see chapter 2 by Humphreys Bebbington & Bebbington, this volume)—it is not externally imposed ideas of environmental conservation or rights, but rather these two seemingly contrasting elements—that may be summed up as agency and sovereignty—that need to be foregrounded in the search for lasting conflict resolution.

Notes

1. See www.ipc-undp.org/pub/IPCWorkingPaper35.pdf
2. See http://amazonwatch.org/news/2010/0827-james-cameron-and-avatar-cast-shine-spotlight-on-real-battles-to-defend-pandoras-on-earth; http://www.fobomade.org.bo/art-749
3. http://archive.greenpeace.org/comms/vrml/rw/text/ztextonly.html
4. Further results from this research can be found in two other publications, that is McNeish (2010) and McNeish (2012).

5. According to Bolivia's MHE between 2007 and 2010, 21 consultations have been concluded. Most of them concerned planned explorations or the construction of gas conduits (see www.hidrocarburos.gob.bo at 26 September 2011).
6. The *Organización de la Capitanía Weenhayek*—ORSAWETA had been formed in the course of negotiations with the US-Bolivian Company Tesoro in the 1990s, and had further success in confronting Transredes and Transierra (D. H. Bebbington, 2010).
7. 180,000 dollars (two years of monitoring), 300,000 (settlement for lost earnings), and 80,000 (community development projects).
8. See http://www.cipca.org.bo/index.php?option=com_content&view =article&id=631:zdpa&catid=81:zdpa&Itemid=121
9. See http://www.derechos.org/nizkor/bolivia/doc/apg21.html
10. See http://www.cipca.org.bo/index.php?option=com_content&view =article&id=2370:css&catid=137:zdpa&Itemid=14
11. See http://www.cambio.bo/noticia.php?fecha=2011-11-04&idn=57778
12. See http://www.somossur.net/documentos/AcuerdosTIPNIS_16%20 puntos.pdf
13. See http://shem.se/index.php?option=com_content&view=article& id=2067:achuar-vs-talisman-energy-the-struggle-continues- &catid=13:environmental-news
14. See http://shem.se/index.php?option=com_content&view=article& id=2067:achuar-vs-talisman-energy-the-struggle-continues- &catid=13:environmental-news
15. See http://saiic.nativeweb.org/actions/urgent8.html
16. That is, the Coordinating Organisation of the Indigenous Organisations of the Amazon (COICA), the Indigenous Federation of the Bolivian Orient (CIDOB), Organisation of the Indigenous Peoples of Surinam (OIS), and Confederation of Amazonian Nationalities (CONAP).
17. Weatherhead Center for International Affairs, "Perspectives on Consultation," Harvard University: Cambridge, Massachusetts, March 2000 at 29. Also see: http://idbdocs.iadb.org/wsdocs/getdocument.aspx?docnum=362175
18. See http://www.landcoalition.org/pdf/08_georgetownuniversity_ conference_indigpeople_latin_america.pdf
19. For example, Arco and Puma Business Solutions of Quito, Ecuador, the Keyano-Pimee Exploration Company Limited of Alberta, Canada
20. See http://www.landcoalition.org/pdf/08_georgetownuniversity_ conference_indigpeople_latin_america.pdf

References

Bebbington, A. (2009, September/October). The new extraction: Rewriting the political ecology of the Andes? *NACLA Report on the Americas, 42*(5), 12–20.

Bebbington, A., & Bebbington, D. H. (2011). An Andean avatar: Post-neoliberal and neoliberal strategies for securing the unobtainable. *New Political Economy, 16*(1), 131–145.
Bebbington, D. H. (2010, July). Anatomy of a regional conflict: Tarija and resource grievances in Morales's Bolivia. *Latin American Perspectives, 37*(4), 140–160.
Brysk, A. (1996). Turning weakness into strength: The internationalisation of Indian rights. *Latin American Perspectives, 23*(2), 38–57.
de la Cadena, M., & Starn, O. (2007). Introduction. In M. de la Cadena & O. Starn (Eds.), *Indigenous experience today* (pp. 1–30). Oxford, UK: Berg.
Conklin, B. A., & Graham, L. R. (1995, December). The shifting middle ground: Amazonian Indians and eco-politics. *American Anthropologist, 97*(4), 695–710.
Engle, K. (2010). *The elusive promise of indigenous development: rights, culture, strategy*. Durham, NC: Duke University Press.
Escobar, A. (1999). After nature: Steps to an anti-essentialist political ecology. *Current Anthropology, 40*(1), 1–30.
Gow, D. D. (2008). *Countering Development: Indigenous modernity and the moral imagination*. Durham, NC: Duke University Press.
Gudynas, E. (2010). The new extractivism of the 21st century: Ten urgent theses about extractivism in relation to current South American progressivism. *Americas Policy Program Report*.
Gupta, A., & Sharma, A. (2006, April). Globalization and postcolonial states. *Current Anthropology, 47*(2), 277–307.
Hall, S. (1996). Introduction: who needs identity? In S. Hall & P. du Gay (Eds.), *Questions of cultural identity* (pp. 1–17). London: Sage.
Hansen, T. B., & Stepputat, F. (2006). Sovereignty revisited. *Annual Review of Anthropology, 35*, 295–315.
Harris, O. (1995). Ethnic identity and market relations: Indians and mestizos in the Andes. In B. Larson, O. Harris & E. Tandeter (Eds.), *Ethnicity, markets and migration in the Andes: At the crossroads of history and anthropology* (pp. 351–390). Durham, NC: Duke University Press.
McNeish, J.-A. (2012). On curses and devils: Resource wealth and sovereignty in an autonomous Tarija. In J-A. McNeish & O. Logan (Eds.), *Flammable societies: Studies on the socio-economics of oil and gas*. London, UK: Pluto Press.
McNeish, J.-A. (2010, April). Sobre Maldiciones y Demonios: Hidrocarburos y soberanía en un Tarija autónoma. *UMBRALES, 20*, 189–221.
McNeish, J.-A., & Logan, O. (2012). *Flammable societies: Studies on the socio-economics of oil and gas*. London and New York: Pluto Press.
Mintz, S. W. (1986). *Sweetness and power: The place of sugar in modern history*. New York, NY: Penguin.
Nadasdy, P. (2005). Transcending the debate over the ecologically noble Indian: Indigenous peoples and environmentalism. *Ethnohistory, 52*(2), 291–331.

Nash, J. C. (1993). *We eat the mines and the mines eat us: Dependency and exploitation in Bolivian tin mines.* New York: Columbia University Press.
Peet, R., & Hartwick, E. (2009). *Theories of development: Contentions, arguments, alternatives* (2nd ed.). New York, NY: The Guildford Press.
Ramos, A. R. (1998). *Indigenism: Ethnic politics in Brazil.* Madison: University of Wisconsin Press.
Redford, K. (1991). The ecologically noble savage. *Orion, 9,* 24–29.
Rodríguez-Garavito, C. (2011). Ethnicity.gov: Global governance, indigenous peoples and the right to prior consultation in social minefields. *Indiana Journal of Global Legal Studies, 18*(1), 263–305.
Sawyer, S. (2004). *Crude chronicles: Indigenous politics, multinational oil, and neoliberalism in Ecuador.* Durham, NC: Duke University Press.
Sawyer, S., & Terence Gomez, E. (2008). Transnational governmentality and resource extraction: Indigenous peoples, multinational companies, multilateral institutions and the state. Geneva: UNRISD.
Taussig, M. T. (1980). *The devil and commodity fetishism in South America.* Chapel Hill, NC: University of North Carolina Press.

Chapter 4

REDD Gold in Latin America: Blessing or Curse?

Anthony Hall

Introduction: Carbon Sequestration as Resource Extraction

The notion of natural resource extraction as a "curse" on development has conventionally been associated with the history of internationally traded commodities such as oil and gas, gold and silver, which yield substantial revenues for governments and private companies. In Latin America, as several of the contributions to this volume make very clear, little of this wealth has trickled down to the wider population. The economic benefits from extractive industries have generally been concentrated in the hands of powerful political and commercial groups, tending to generate national dependence on such exports, reinforcing mass poverty, polarizing income distribution, and causing extensive environmental damage. As the introductory chapter to this collection notes, however, there is now qualified hope that, as the result of political reforms and grassroots pressure, resource extraction on the continent could help foster broad-based social and economic development through more careful management and fairer distribution of commodity revenues.

One of the most promising resource areas in which such a reversal might, in theory, occur involves not minerals or agricultural exports, but a rather more ephemeral and less tangible commodity; namely carbon and its sequestration as a tool for mitigating the effects of global warming. This is particularly critical in Latin America. Forests play a major role in regional and global climate regulation by supplying key environmental services such as carbon sequestration, rainfall regulation, and biodiversity protection (Daily, 1997). In addition, forests support the livelihoods of millions both directly and indirectly. In heavily forested countries such as Brazil, Bolivia, Ecuador, and Peru, deforestation and land-use change typically account for up to 80 percent of national greenhouse gas emissions, compared with just 18 percent globally (IPCC, 2007; World Bank, 2009). Controlling forest loss and enhancing carbon sequestration as a tool of climate change regulation is thus especially critical in Latin America.

Based on the notion that carbon is arguably more easily quantifiable than other environmental services, the idea of rewarding forest users for maintaining standing forest and demonstrating carbon dioxide (CO_2) capture has become a major policy instrument in discussions on action to mitigate climate change (see chapter 10 by Certomà and Greyl, this volume). Whether traded as a commodity in official and voluntary markets or compensated through public funding by international bilateral and multilateral donor organizations, the "extraction" of CO_2 from the atmosphere offers a major opportunity to generate income while addressing climate change and promoting environmentally appropriate forms of development. The idea of providing economic stimuli in the form of payments for ecosystem services (PES) to compensate for maintaining rather than destroying resources has thus become a highly attractive policy option (Wunder, 2005). In the context of forest policy, this instrument has become known as payments for "Reduced Emissions from Deforestation and Forest Degradation" (REDD) and has been lauded by many as something of a "win-win" solution for reducing forest loss.

Yet several key questions will need to be addressed as REDD policies evolve from their present embryonic stage into a more mature framework for action. In the context of developments in Latin America, this chapter will raise doubts over the extent to which a neoliberal framework based on economic incentives can be relied upon to maintain standing forest. It will also examine the related issue of social and cultural diversity of forest populations, particularly relevant in Amazonia, and the need to take due account of multidimensional motivation in conservation behavior. Several major operational challenges that could compromise effective implementation of REDD+ across the continent are also highlighted.

Climate Change, Forests, and REDD Funding

In 1992, the landmark United Nations Conference on Environment and Development (UNCED) or "Earth Summit" was held in Rio de Janeiro and launched international negotiations on climate change.

The UN Framework Convention on Climate Change (UNFCCC) attempted to set common goals and apportion responsibility for tackling climate change. The 1997 Kyoto Protocol, which came into effect in 2005, established binding commitments for 39 industrialized countries and the European Union (known together as Annex I countries) to reduce or "cap" their combined greenhouse gas (GHG) emissions to 5 percent below 1990 levels by 2008–2012, the first commitment period. Industrialized countries are expected to meet their emissions reductions targets through pollution controls and the introduction of greener technologies at home. In addition, new "cap-and-trade" mechanisms were introduced to allow them to offset greenhouse gas emissions over and above their assigned quotas for sale on carbon markets to countries with accumulated unused permitted emissions; for example, through the Clean Development Mechanism (CDM).

Under the principle of "common but differentiated responsibilities," developing (Annex II) countries have no legal emissions reductions obligations during the first commitment period of the Kyoto Protocol from 2008–2012. However, a powerful lobby emerged within the UNFCCC known as the "Coalition for Rainforest Nations," which sought financial support for the maintenance of standing forests as a major contributing factor in the mitigation of global warming. Deforestation and land-use change have conventionally been held responsible for about 18 percent of global CO_2 emissions. Yet under the Kyoto Protocol avoided deforestation projects were excluded from the CDM, which allowed only afforestation and reforestation for carbon offsets.

Following sustained pressure from the Coalition and publication of the "Bali Action Plan" at COP13 in 2007, the concept of providing developing countries with financial compensation for REDD was introduced onto the international policy agenda (now generally referred to as REDD+, which includes enhancement of carbon stocks). Under REDD+ policies, forest users would be given cash incentives to preserve standing forest. The principle of including REDD+ in UNFCCC negotiations was firmly endorsed in 2009 at COP15 in Copenhagen and a year later at Cancún in Mexico. Underpinned by the strong international conservationist lobby, forest protection is one of the few areas in which it has been possible to reach a measure of international consensus around climate change policy. A "REDD+ Partnership" was set up to develop collaborative arrangements among over 70 nations, including most Latin American countries.

At Copenhagen, "Fast Start" funding of USD30 billion for REDD+ was agreed in principle for the period 2010–2012, including USD4.5 billion in "new and additional" resources to support "REDD+ readiness" preparations. There was the further somewhat vague promise of USD100 billion a year by 2020 to be secured from a combination of bilateral, multilateral, and private sources. At Cancún, it was agreed to establish a "Green Climate Fund" with the World Bank as a trustee to manage these longer-term finances.

Literally dozens of REDD and REDD+ projects are in the process of being designed and implemented in Latin America with financial support from a combination of donors such as Norway, the World Bank, and the United Nations. The UN-REDD program and the Forest Carbon Partnership Facility (FCPF) of the World Bank have together pledged large amounts for training and capacity-building to help developing countries prepare national REDD strategies and for sustainable forest management. UN-REDD funds national program planning strategies in nine countries, including in Latin America (Bolivia, Ecuador, Panama, and Paraguay). The World Bank's FCPF has 37 member countries, 15 of which are in Latin America.

Bilateral assistance has come mainly from the Norwegians, whose help has been critical. In addition, the Norwegian government has donated USD120 million to help set up Brazil's innovative Amazon Fund and also granted support for Guyana's REDD+ strategy. In Brazil's case, administered by the National Economic and Social Development Bank (BNDES), with promises of up to USD1 billion by 2015, the Amazon Fund supports a variety of environmental measures including early REDD+ projects (Zadek, Forstater, & Polacow, 2010).

Forestry and other land-use schemes have had to rely on steadily expanding voluntary markets and public funding. REDD credits leapt from 1 percent of the voluntary land-based market in 2008 to 7 percent in 2009. Yet although impressive at first sight, this is but a drop in the REDD sea, so to speak, amounting to a mere 0.22 percent of total regulated carbon market value and 1.1 percent of the total volume of traded carbon (Hamilton, Peters-Stanley, & Marcello, 2010; Waage & Hamilton, 2011). Once REDD+ credits are accepted in a post-Kyoto regulatory regime, the private carbon markets are likely to play a far more critical role in generating new finance, although there is still much uncertainty and speculation over this potential.

Latin American governments have not been universally receptive toward participation in carbon markets for REDD+ funding purposes. Brazil and Bolivia have expressed resistance to the idea on several grounds including; (1) fears that the price of carbon could be driven down if the markets were flooded with forest credits, (2) a reluctance to let industrialized countries "avoid" their environmental commitments by allowing carbon offsets against REDD projects, and (3) in the case of Amazonia, concerns that national sovereignty might somehow be compromised by foreign "interference" in domestic policy. The Brazilian government's nationalistic stance came under strong pressure from a powerful lobby formed by Amazon state governors and civil society organizations, together with the Ministry of the Environment and Ministry of Finance. This campaign proved instrumental in bringing about an official change of heart at Copenhagen in 2009 and has led to a partial acceptance of market instruments in the formulation of a national REDD+ strategy for Brazil.

President Evo Morales remains perhaps the most outspoken critic of carbon markets, declaring at Cancún in 2010 that "we are not here to turn Nature into a commodity."[1] Earlier that year, this antimarket position was firmly endorsed by a world meeting of indigenous groups in Cochabamba, although it is by no means universal among native peoples in Latin America, which are increasingly being attracted by potential revenues arising from carbon markets. Nowadays, it is generally accepted that a combination of donor funding and market-based mechanisms will be necessary to fund future scaled-up REDD+ programs.

There was much initial optimism regarding the potential of REDD to generate substantial extra funding in support of forest policies to mitigate climate change. Expectations, probably unrealistic, were raised that a pot of "REDD gold" would somehow be found from voluntary markets and generous donors to provide the extra financing necessary to address growing deforestation, especially in critical regions such as the Amazon rain forest. An ever-expanding collection of interested parties (or stakeholders) include small farmers, traditional and indigenous forest populations, as well as larger commercial crop producers, not to mention the supporting institutional apparatus behind REDD+ both within government and private sectors as well as civil society.

Stern (2007) estimated that tackling climate change through controlling deforestation would be relatively cheap, requiring an annual expenditure of up to USD10 billion. Globally, it has been estimated that ecosystem service payments of USD30 billion a year channeled into REDD+ projects could alleviate poverty for up to 800 million rural poor (Milder, Scherr, & Bracer, 2010). Another study claimed that reducing deforestation rates in the Amazon by 10 percent could generate up to USD12 billion a year, much of which could be channeled into avoided deforestation initiatives and support for protected areas (Ebeling & Yasué, 2008). It is a moot point whether anything like this amount of funding for REDD+ is likely to be forthcoming.

Preparing for REDD

At this relatively early stage in the evolution of REDD+ in Latin America, therefore, there is what might be called a general qualified optimism regarding its potential to at least make a significant contribution to reducing rates of forest loss and assist in climate change mitigation, and that appropriate financial support will be generated. Latin America leads the world in expanding REDD+ coverage. With the exceptions of Venezuela, Uruguay, Belize, and French Guiana, all Latin American countries are now in the process of developing national REDD+ strategies. As noted above, this is being undertaken with multilateral assistance from UN-REDD and the World Bank's FCPF, as well as from bilateral donors such as Norway and Germany. Costa Rica, Brazil, and Mexico have arguably advanced farthest along the Latin American REDD road.

Costa Rica was the first country in the world to introduce a national system of payments for ecosystem services (PES), predating REDD by over two decades. Landowners are financially compensated for maintaining standing forest (Karousakis, 2007; Pagiola, 2008). Mexico has a long history of community-based forestry held in collective ownership rather than individual private property, which dates back to the Revolution of 1910. A system of PES was introduced in 2004 (now known as *Pro-Árbol*) to promote forest conservation, upon which its REDD+ preparation strategy is based (Corbera, 2010).

During the 1990s, Brazil developed a number of separate projects adopting ecosystem payments, such as the ecological value-added tax and several voluntary carbon sequestration projects (Hall, 2008a). Brazil's first major forest PES initiative dates from 2000 when the *Proambiente* scheme was launched. Aimed at several hundred families in 12 Amazon forest locations, the program was set up by civil society but transferred to the federal government in 2004. However, it met with limited success due to financial shortfalls and lack of institutional support (Hall, 2008b). *Proambiente* was forced to close in 2010 but since 2007 a number of other REDD+ schemes have been initiated in the region by state governments and civil society organizations, including the well-known *Bolsa Floresta* program in Amazonas (Viana, 2010).

Several other REDD+ schemes are at various stages of preparation in Acre, Pará, and Mato Grosso states (Hall, 2011a; May, Millikan, & Gebara, 2011; Moutinho, Cenamo, & Moreira, 2009). In Brazil, Amazon states have taken the initiative to develop their own REDD+ strategies, thus stealing a march on the federal government and lobbying for the development of a national REDD plan, greater involvement in international negotiations, and the adoption of market-based funding mechanisms. Brazil is the only REDD-adopting Latin American country that is not being assisted by the UN-REDD program or the World Bank's FCPF, although it enjoys major support for the Amazon Fund from the Norwegian and German governments.

Beyond these three "leading" countries, the more advanced with their "REDD+ readiness" preparations are Bolivia, Colombia, Ecuador, Guyana, Paraguay, Panama, and Peru. Arguably, Bolivia heads the list, having set up the pioneering if controversial Noel Kempff Mercado Climate Action Project (NK-CAP) in 1996 as the largest deforestation avoidance and carbon sequestration project in the world at the time. Despite its current antimarket rhetoric, Bolivia was a founding member of UN-REDD and in 2010 received a preparation grant of almost USD5 million. At the time of writing in mid-2011, other Latin American countries were still in the very early stages of formulating proposals with UN-REDD and the FCPF; namely, Argentina, Chile, El Salvador, Guatemala, Honduras, Nicaragua, and Suriname, while others trail behind.

In all of these cases (with the exception of Brazil, which does not receive multilateral assistance for this purpose), donor funding has been concentrated on preparing countries to adopt and administer national REDD strategies: for example, in compiling forest inventories and setting baselines; monitoring deforestation; analyzing the major forces driving deforestation; updating conservation laws; preparing the institutional structure involving government, civil society, and private sector organization; training personnel in key areas, including monitoring, reporting, and verification (MRV) of carbon emissions; and setting up consultative bodies with the participation of major stakeholders involved in REDD such as indigenous populations and small farmers as well as larger commercial producers.

REDD Realities: Conceptual and Operational Limitations

Despite its superficial attractiveness as a potential "win-win" solution for conserving trees while providing livelihood-support payments to forest users, REDD+ faces major challenges both in terms of its conceptualization as well as operationally. First, serious questions need to be asked about the neoliberal assumptions that underpin REDD; namely, whether forest dwellers can actually be persuaded to adopt conservationist behavior simply by being paid to preserve, either through the provision of direct economic incentives or other benefits. Second, underestimation of the diversity and complexity of forest populations, their livelihood dynamics and their political importance threatens to undermine the impact of REDD initiatives. Third, a number of technical complications concerning the effectiveness of emissions reduction strategies (relating to leakage, additionality, and permanence) may frustrate REDD policies once beyond the pilot phase.

Economic Incentives

Attributing economic values to nature and ecosystem services has allowed new policy instruments to be developed that go beyond command-and-control approaches, aiming to provide economic incentives and disincentives to assist in the pursuit of environmental goals (Goldman, 1998; Daily, 1997). This is an instinctively appealing proposal in light of the history of tropical forest settlement in areas such as Amazonia, where perverse incentives have traditionally encouraged forest removal as an indicator of "development" (Hall, 2011b). REDD+ has been in the international spotlight as a PES tool to assist in forest conservation. In Latin America, this would typically involve paying farmers to switch from destructive slash-and-burn farming to more ecologically sound activities such as agroforestry, extractivism, and sustainable forest management as well as adopting other more sustainable land management practices. Such (usually) voluntary arrangements allow demand and supply requirements for ecosystem services to be met; providers supply services to purchasers wishing to offset their verified emissions at an appropriate price (Engel, Pagiola, & Wunder, 2008; Wunder, 2005).

Under this logic, previously "free" environmental services have now become "commodified"; that is, they have acquired a scarcity value and may be traded between willing buyers and willing sellers. The intellectual foundation for this rationale lies in Coasean-based economics, centered on the role of market trading in efficiently addressing externalities. Bargaining is seen as an effective tool as long as there are no serious obstacles such as high transaction costs or poorly defined property rights (Coase, 1960; Gómez-Baggethun, de

Groot, Lomas, & Montes, 2010). Under REDD+, the value of carbon captured should exceed the costs of service provision, including the opportunity costs of destructive activities foregone as a result of the scheme. The ultimate aim should be to create a multilevel payments system, a "payments culture" that will reduce emissions and enhance forest carbon stocks (Angelsen, 2009; Wunder, 2009).

More generally, this approach is predicated on the increasingly popular assumption in policy circles that behavioral change can be induced in various walks of life through the provision of appropriate economic stimuli. Thus, "choice architects" of economic, social, and (in this case) environmental strategy are considered to have the power to "nudge" participants in preordained, "desirable" directions to improve their lives (Thaler & Sunstein, 2008).

In many respects, the approach taken to PES and REDD+ mirrors the introduction all over Latin America of conditional cash transfer (CCT) programs as a social policy tool for poverty alleviation. Regular cash payments are targeted at the poorest groups provided that certain conditionalities are met, including regular school attendance and participation in health checkups (Barrientos, Gideon, & Molyneux, 2008; Hall, 2008c). It is perhaps no coincidence that Brazil and Mexico, both REDD+ pioneers, are also home to the world's two largest CCT schemes (*Bolsa Família* and *Oportunidades* respectively). However, as noted below, conditionalities in the case of social policy may prove rather easier to deliver.

There are several problems associated with the neoliberal economic paradigm underlying REDD+. First, analysts have pointed to the dangers of overreliance on cash payments as a driver of behavioral change, especially in the context of traditional and indigenous forest communities. Muradian, Corbera, Pascual, Kosoy, and May (2010, p. 1205), for example, note that "economic incentives are just one of the multiple drivers that may influence behavioural patterns in relation to land use and the provision of environmental services." The social "embeddedness" of economic relations belies expectations of "rationality" in terms of there being an automatic link between cash incentive and producer response (Granovetter, 1985). If inappropriately applied, therefore, economic stimuli may clash with and "crowd out" wider "moral sentiments," such as cultural beliefs in the intrinsic value of forests held by many indigenous groups. Seen as part of a wider "social market," economic transactions may weaken motivation and lessen people's self-esteem by encouraging them to think in selfish, instrumental terms rather than considering what is best for the common good (Ariely, 2008; Vatn, 2010).

Thus, responding to a carbon price cannot be viewed simply as an individualized, neutral monetary transaction along Coasean lines, but must be seen within its social, cultural, and political context. Gowdy (2008, p. 632) observes that "the standard economic approach to climate change policy, with its focus on narrowly rational, self-regarding responses to monetary incentives, is seriously flawed." As Vatn further notes (2010, p. 1250), a "price is not just a price . . . it is not just about opportunity costs but about maintaining relationships." The Coasean model has come under heavy criticism because "it does not pay enough attention to the role of institutions and shared beliefs in shaping PES design and outcomes" (Muradian et al., 2010, p. 1205).

Research in Cambodia points to the complexity and diversity of incentives in community-based forest conservation schemes, and draws attentions to the need to incorporate locally developed rules and norms within PES design in order to avoid failure (Clements et al., 2010). For example, incentives other than direct payments may be as effective as, or even more successful than cash transfers in supporting households' conservationist behavior. Such evidence is beginning to emerge from REDD projects in Latin America. In Brazil's abovementioned *Proambiente* scheme, farmers received less cash compensation than originally promised, which reduced its relative importance as a motivating factor. However, farmers placed a high value on associated rural extension support. Due to the history of farmer mobilization and organization in certain parts of the Amazon, there was also a significant level of commitment to conserving trees irrespective of the scheme (Hall, 2008b; Bartels, Schmink, Borges, Duarte, & dos Santos Arcos, 2010).

Overall in REDD-type initiatives, PES payments have tended to form a small proportion of household income and have done little to lift people out of poverty, raising doubts about their real influence on conservation behavior. However, such payments are relatively more important for poorer families, as noted in the case of Mexico (Corbera, 2010). Some REDD schemes invest in production and community infrastructure alongside household income transfers, in a more integrated and holistic attempt to address basic needs. Brazil's *Bolsa Floresta* program in Amazonas state is a case in point, where in addition to a monthly stipend for families there is an investment program in schools, clinics, and roads as well as income diversification through community-based agroforestry (Viana, 2010). Mexico's long-running national PES program, which will form the basis of its REDD+ strategy, also complements cash incentives with investments in common goods (Corbera, 2010).

Social Complexity

Closely intertwined with the issue of cash incentives as an overriding mechanism for modifying resource user behavior is the sheer social and cultural diversity of forest populations. The more complex are the groups embraced by REDD+, the greater is the need to take due account of the inherent variety of their livelihood dynamics and of the sociocultural and political factors that influence conservation behavior. It would be a fundamental mistake to assume that all forest groups can be influenced by cash inducements irrespective of other considerations. Nowhere is the social diversity of forests more evident than in Amazonia, where a large proportion of Latin American REDD+ projects and stakeholder groups are presently concentrated.

Although the situation has changed in recent years with the political mobilization of indigenous, small farmer, and extractivist groups in many parts of Latin America, and especially in the Amazon region, some research maintains that they still "share a condition of social and economic invisibility" (Brondizio, 2008, p. 184). Ethnographic studies point to the noncapitalist economic relations that pervade many cultures, the local dynamism that goes unperceived by outsiders and the heterogeneity of livelihood activities that allows them to provide flexibility while reducing risk. These may embrace one or more of a number of productive pursuits, including extraction of nontimber forest products, farming, fishing, logging, livestock, and nonagricultural pursuits such as informal gold mining (Harris, 2008; Brondizio, 2008). Conservation decisions by forest populations may well be affected by any reduction in their dependence on natural resources that comes with the diversification of livelihoods, even with compensatory cash payments.

Studies of land-use patterns in the Amazon in Brazil, Ecuador, and Peru reveal the many different production patterns and resource use as determined by the household life cycle in specific contexts, resulting in different mixes of crops, livestock, and forest cover. Rubber tappers in Brazil's extractive reserves have in some instances been forced to break the rules, contrary to planners' expectations, by introducing cattle to compensate for loss of income as subsidies for latex have been removed (Salisbury & Schmink, 2007). Rather than following a linear trajectory in adapting to frontier settlement conditions, decisions about retaining forest cover in relation to other farming and livestock activities are variable and unpredictable, taking many directions (Browder et al., 2008; Browder, Pedlowski, & Summers, 2004). Wider forces may also intervene, such as accelerating rural-urban migration, resulting in growing demand for forest products and higher rural household incomes, as noted in parts of the Brazilian and Peruvian Amazon (Padoch et al., 2008). These developments may have the effect of strengthening market demand near large urban centers and influence conservation priorities irrespective of possible REDD+ incentives.

Other less tangible social factors could influence patterns of forest use and conservation decisions. Futemma (2008), for example, demonstrates how social networks and kinship structures by blood, affinity, adoption, and godparentage exert a direct influence on stratified access to forests, pasture, and farmland in an Amazon community. At the same time, planners' assumptions about the unified "community" and its inherent propensity for collaborative action in favor of maintaining forest cover will not necessarily apply. As noted by many studies, "communities" are as likely to be characterized by internal division, inequality and conflict as by shared goals, equality, and cooperation (Agrawal & Gibson, 1999; Guijt & Shah, 1998; Hall, 1997). The propensity of particular forest groups to maintain standing forest must therefore be considered within this dynamic in order to avoid simplistic assumptions being made in the design of REDD+ interventions.

Another area of complexity that threatens to undermine REDD+ arises from the variable and uncertain conditions of landownership, security of tenure, and user rights. As already noted, Coasean economics underpinning the concept of ecosystem payments such as REDD+ is based on the principle of clearly defined property rights (Muradian et al., 2010). In Latin America, as elsewhere in the developing world, this is very much the exception rather than the rule. Although some countries such as Costa Rica and Mexico have introduced PES systems based on fairly well-established structures of individual and collective land ownership, most other nations in the region have serious lacunae in this department. Land titles are often either absent or fraudulent.

In Brazilian Amazonia, a key REDD+ region, just 4 percent of properties have legal titles verified by the land agency INCRA. A further 23 percent have nonvalidated titles, 9 percent is in the hands of squatters, 21 percent are unprotected public lands, and over 40 percent lie in officially protected areas (Brito & Barreto, 2009). In Latin America overall, governments own around 43 percent of forests, with 32 percent in private hands, and 25 percent administered by communities and indigenous peoples, only 7 percent of which is recognized under statutory tenure law (Hatcher, Bailey, Purdy, & France, 2009).

Up to 70 percent of national forests in would-be REDD+ countries in Latin America is in the hands of community and indigenous groups.[2] A rights-based approach to REDD would take into account the human right to property to ensure broad-based land titling for the wider population (Lawlor & Huberman, 2009).

For indigenous groups more specifically, rather than just formal property ownership, it is important that "bundles of rights" should be recognized relating to legal and customary entitlements such as physical access, resource use, exclusions/inclusion, and alienation. These issues will have a major effect on carbon rights and subsequent income-generating potential under REDD+ arrangements. Thus, REDD+ initiatives involving traditional and indigenous groups "should recognize local diversity and not impose blueprints" (Larson et al., 2010, p. 1). Fundamentally, governments and private companies should apply the principle of "free, prior and informed consent" (FPIC) determined by international law (Colchester, 2010).[3]

An encouraging sign for REDD+ is the fact that forested lands are increasingly being transferred to indigenous groups, arguably their most effective custodians. Furthermore, the legalization of traditional indigenous lands and the involvement of their inhabitants in planning for REDD+ is one of the major prerequisites of current national "Readiness" preparations funded through UN-REDD and the FCPF. It is hoped that these demands will help avoid further rural violence and conflicts over access to natural resources.

However, early REDD+ plans under the FCPF, for example, have already come under criticism for allegedly being developed with "minimal or no consultation with forest peoples" (Griffiths, 2010, p. 19). Another major report accused the FCPF of failing to address key issues such as clarifying and securing land rights as well as dealing with corruption and weak governance (Dooley, Griffiths, Martone, & Ozinga, 2011). It is hoped that this issue will be addressed, if only due to grassroots pressure from increasingly discontented forest populations. In this process, what is certain is that the extremely varied cultural, social, and spatial characteristics of indigenous populations will require well matched, sensitive REDD+ design solutions (CIFOR, 2010).

Operational Challenges

If REDD+ faces major challenges in terms of putting into place appropriate financial and other incentives within situations of complex social and cultural diversity, other complications threaten to undermine its effectiveness as a climate change mitigation option. These more general technical concerns relate to the overall effectiveness of REDD+ as a tool for avoiding deforestation, enhancing carbon stocks, and reducing emissions. Specifically, they concern (1) leakage, (2) additionality, and (3) permanence.

"Leakage" refers to the problem of illegal deforestation simply being displaced directly from one controlled area to another that is unprotected, thus undermining the REDD+ process. Any serious attempt to monitor and control for leakage would require strong command-and-control mechanisms such as surveillance and imposition of sanctions as part of a cross-sector, holistic approach to deforestation. In addition, measures would have to be taken to address the commercial and political drivers of deforestation to reduce pressures conducive to leakage.

A closely related second challenge is how to guarantee "additionality"; that is, how to be sure that deforestation and emissions really have been reduced by the REDD project or program. To achieve this, it is necessary to have in place a reliable system for monitoring, reporting, and verification (MRV) of changes in forest carbon stocks as well as levels of deforestation. Most countries in Latin America, with some notable exceptions such as Brazil, are poorly equipped for these tasks and require considerable investments to bridge the capacity gap. Furthermore, even if such evidence is forthcoming, actually enforcing conditionality is highly problematic most of the time. The majority of REDD+ projects are in effect "PES-like" schemes in which benefits are assumed rather than proven (Wunder, 2005). Wider processes may also compromise additionality. Doubts have been raised, for example, over the effectiveness of Costa Rica's widely acclaimed national PES policy in reducing deforestation. Various studies have suggested that the system was introduced when rates of forest loss were already declining and that it has made almost no difference (Pattanayak, Wunder, & Ferraro, 2010).

REDD+ may compensate developers for not chopping down trees they might otherwise have destroyed (avoided deforestation). However, rewarding traditional forest guardians such as indigenous and community groups must also be factored into calculations of how benefits should be distributed. For example, one-quarter of Brazil's Amazon forest is protected in officially demarcated indigenous areas, whose very existence serves as a deterrent to would-be loggers. In fact, several tribal groups, notably the *surui*, have started to develop REDD+ carbon financing initiatives as a form of compensation for their roles as historical and contemporary forest guardians (Instituto Socioambiental & Forest Trends, 2010).

A third issue concerns the "permanence" or sustainability of any deforestation controls or emissions reductions. These could be undermined in the long term by commercial pressures from logging, mining, and agricultural interests, by new waves of farmer settlement or even by interruptions in the flow of cash compensation. Following the logic discussed in the section above, pure economic factors are less likely to condition the conservationist behavior of smaller farmers, traditional communities, and indigenous groups in REDD+ schemes.

There are other concerns relating to the design and operation of REDD+ policies. The first of these concerns the debate over achieving "efficiency versus equity" gains (Wunder, 2007). In order to maximize "efficiency" in emissions reductions financial incentives should logically be targeted at the main drivers of deforestation: large commercial farmers, livestock producers, and logging interests. Yet to alleviate poverty, strengthen livelihoods, and encourage forest populations in their stewardship role, benefits should be more equitably distributed among community and indigenous groups.

For the moment, emerging national REDD+ strategies in Latin America funded by the UN and World Bank are generally poverty-focused, aimed at forest populations of community and indigenous groups. Yet sooner or later policy-makers will come up against the "efficiency versus equity" dilemma in pursuing emissions reductions through REDD+ and a balance will have to be struck. This issue has received attention in the Brazilian Amazon, for example, where a mix of approaches is emerging (Hall, 2011a; May et al., 2011).

A second practical concern is the risk of corruption. Although this problem has so far been highlighted in connection with REDD projects in Africa and Asia rather than Latin America, Transparency International (2011) has drawn attention to the issue as a potentially global phenomenon. Even Interpol has raised the prospect that "organised crime syndicates are eyeing the nascent forest carbon market . . . [and] . . . Redd schemes are open to wide abuse" (Vidal, 2009). For example, cases have been uncovered in Papua New Guinea of fake carbon credits being issued with official connivance, while communities have been hastily dragooned into schemes without proper consultation as a front for generating carbon revenues. Similar stories of corrupt deals being struck within a burgeoning "carbon capitalism" industry have been documented in Liberia, Cameroon, and Indonesia (Astill, 2010). There is no reason why such practices could not be extended more widely given the financial temptations involved, and the prospect of REDD+ funding becoming more real as climate change negotiations progress.

Yet a third preoccupation that could frustrate REDD+ ambitions has to do with Latin America's limited institutional capacity to implement development initiatives in a timely and efficient manner. REDD+ proponents often claim that promised funding falls far short of what is required to reduce current rates of forest loss. Yet many incipient programs appear to have trouble in spending even the limited monies they have been allocated for the task. At this very early stage in the development of national REDD+ strategies, a "pledge-implementation gap" is emerging in FCPF and UN-REDD programs, as reflected in low disbursement and implementation rates (IDEAcarbon, 2011).

A further operational requirement is that governments should have in place appropriate legislation to facilitate payments for ecosystem services. Nations such as Costa Rica and Mexico have a long track record in this field, while Brazil is currently in the process of approving a national PES legal framework. In Brazil's case, state authorities such as Amazonas, Acre, and Mato Grosso have taken the initiative to institute legal provision to enable payments systems to be introduced and, more importantly, sustained over the longer term.

Conclusions

In answer to the rhetorical question posed in the title to this chapter, REDD+ is probably neither a blessing nor a curse: at best, it could be labeled a "mixed blessing." It will neither save the rain forest, nor will it result in the environmental, economic, and social aberrations characteristic of so many resource exploitation processes in other sectors such as mineral and oil extraction. It has the potential to make a small, possibly significant, contribution to addressing climate change in the Latin American context.

However, oversimplistic assumptions made by planners and policymakers could undermine the effectiveness of REDD+: principally the highly optimistic expectations over the power of cash incentives to modify the behavior of forest populations in support of conservation. Furthermore, there is a marked tendency to underestimate the social complexity of forest user groups and the ease with which they can be easily incorporated into standardized, top-down planning strategies.

Notwithstanding these very real challenges, however, there is another overarching danger that could turn REDD+ into a resource "curse," even if indirectly. Its deservedly high political profile as a new avenue for promoting conservation and sustainable development, capable of attracting substantial new funding for the forest sector, could serve to divert attention from the need to address the more fundamental drivers of deforestation. Most internationally funded REDD+ policy documents include an obligatory emphasis on the need to tackle the root causes of deforestation. However, there is little indication that national governments are on the whole doing much to tackle the core drivers.

In most Latin American countries, small farmers and indigenous groups are not the main culprits in this regard; commercial and political interests allied to government export and regional development policies are, accounting for roughly three-quarters of forest loss on the continent. Without a concerted, parallel effort to deal with these wider forces such as the impact of commodity prices, poorly planned infrastructure, and road expansion, and the perverse financial incentives that support them, it is highly unlikely that REDD+ will have any major impact on reducing rates of forest loss on a significant scale.

Although REDD+ policies are often presented as having the ability to tackle national or regional deforestation rates, they will probably make only a minor, complementary contribution. Only a major financial and political commitment by national governments themselves to addressing the more fundamental causes of deforestation alongside REDD+ would make a difference in this respect. However, if the lessons learned from these early experiences could eventually be incorporated into wider policies in favor of conservation and more environmentally friendly forest use, REDD+ may after all prove to be a blessing in disguise.

Notes

The author would like to thank The British Academy and the LSE for financial support that made this research possible.

1. John Collins Rudolph, In Cancún, a roar of indignation from Bolivia, New York Times, December 10, 2010.
2. In Mexico 70 percent of forests are managed by indigenous and community populations. For the Amazon region the figures are: Ecuador, 65 percent; Colombia, 65 percent; Bolivia, 26 percent; Brazil 22, percent; and Peru, 17 percent.

3. See International Labour Organization Convention ILO 169 (1989) and UN Declaration on the Rights of Indigenous Peoples, DECRIPS (1977).

References

Agrawal, A., & Gibson, C. C. (1999). Enchantment and disenchantment: The role of community in natural resource conservation, *World Development*, 27(4), 629–649.
Angelsen, A. (Ed.). (2009). *Realising REDD+ national strategy and policy options*. Bogor, Indonesia: CIFOR.
Ariely, D. (2008). *Predictably irrational: The hidden forces that shape our decisions*. London, UK: Harper Collins.
Astill, J. (2010, September 25). Seeing the wood: A special report on forests. *Economist*, pp. 1–14.
Barrientos, A., Gideon, J., & Molyneux, M. (2008). New developments in Latin America's social policy. *Development and Change*, 39(5), 759–774.
Bartels, W.-L., Schmink, M., Borges, E. A., Duarte, A. P., & dos Santos Arcos, H. D. S. (2010). Diversifying livelihood systems, strengthening social networks and rewarding environmental stewardship among small-scale producers in the Brazilian Amazon: lessons from Proambiente. In L. Tacconi, S. Mahanty, & H. Suich (Eds.), *Payments for environmental services, forest conservation and climate change: livelihoods in the REDD?* (pp. 82–105). Cheltenham, UK: Edward Elgar Publishing.
Brito, B., & Barreto P. (2009, March). Os riscos e os princípios para a regularização fundiária da Amazônia. *O Estado da Amazônia, 10*, IMAZON. Retrieved February 2, 2012, from http://www.imazon.org.br/publicacoes/o-estado-da-amazonia/os-riscos-e-os-principios-para-a-regularizacao/at_download/file
Brondizio, E. (2008). Agriculture intensification, economic identity, and shared invisibility in amazonian peasantry: caboclos and colonists in comparative perspective. In C. Adams, R. Murrieta, W. Neves, & M. Harris (Eds.), *amazon peasant societies in a changing environment: political ecology, invisibility and modernity in the rainforest* (pp. 181–214). New York, NY: Springer.
Browder, J. O., Pedlowski, M. A., & Summers, P. M. (2004). Land use patterns in the Brazilian Amazon: Comparative farm-level evidence from Rondônia. *Human Ecology, 32*(2), 197–224.
Browder, J., Pedlowski, M. A., Walker, R., Wynne, R. H., Summers, P. M., Abad, A., . . . Mil-Homens, J. (2008). Revisiting theories of frontier expansion in the Brazilian Amazon: A survey of the colonist farming population in Rondônia's post-frontier, 1992–2002. *World Development, 36*(8), 1469–1492.
CIFOR. (2010, August). REDD+ in indigenous territories in Latin America: Opportunity or threat? *Infobrief, 24*. Bogor, Indonesia: CIFOR. Retrieved

February 1, 2012, from http://www.cifor.org/publications/pdf_files/infobrief/024-infobrief.pdf

Clements, T., John, A., Nielsen, K., An, D., Tan, S., & Milner-Gulland, E. J. (2010). Payments for biodiversity conservation in the context of weak institutions: Comparison of three programs from Cambodia. *Ecological Economics, 69*, 1283–1291.

Coase, R. H. (1960, October). The problem of social cost. *Journal of Law and Economics, 3*, 1–44.

Colchester, M. (2010, July). *Free, prior and informed consent. Making FPIC work for forests and people.* The Forests Dialogue, Yale University. Retrieved February 1, 2012, from http://www.forestpeoples.org/sites/fpp/files/publication/ 2010/10/tfdfpicresearchpapercolchesterhi-res2.pdf

Corbera, E. (2010). Mexico's PES-carbon programme: A preliminary assessment and impacts on rural livelihoods. In L. Tacconi, S. Mahanty, & H. Suich (Eds.), *Payments for environmental services, forest conservation and climate change: Livelihoods in the REDD?* (pp. 54–81). Cheltenham, UK: Edward Elgar Publishing.

Daily, G. C. (Ed.). (1997). *Nature's services: Societal dependence on natural ecosystems.* Washington DC: Island Press.

Dooley, K., Griffiths, T., Martone, F., & Ozinga, S. (2011, February). *Smoke and mirrors: A critical assessment of the forest carbon partnership facility.* Moreton in Marsh: FERN & Forest Peoples Programme. Retrieved February 2, 2012, from http://www.forestpeoples.org/sites/fpp/ files/publication/2011/03/smokeandmirrorsinternet_1.pdf

Ebeling, J., & Yasué, M. (2008) Generating carbon finance through avoided deforestation and its potential to create climatic, conservation and human development benefits. *Philosophical Transactions of the Royal Society B, 363*, 1917–1924.

Engel, S., Pagiola, S., & Wunder, S. (2008). Designing payments for environmental services in theory and practice: An overview of the issues. *Ecological Economics, 65*, 663–674.

Futemma, C. (2008). The use of and access to forest resources: The Caboclos of the Lower Amazon And their socio-cultural attributes. In C. Adams, R. Murrieta, W. Neves, & M. Harris (Eds.), *Amazon Peasant Societies in a Changing Environment: Political Ecology, Invisibility and Modernity in the Rainforest* (pp. 215–237). New York, NY: Springer.

Goldman, M. (Ed.). (1998). *Privatizing nature: Political struggles for the global commons.* London, UK: Pluto Press.

Gómez-Baggethun, E., de Groot, R., Lomas, P. L., & Montes, C. (2010). The history of ecosystem services in economic theory and practice: From early notions to markets and payment schemes. *Ecological Economics, 69*, 1209–1218.

Gowdy, J. M. (2008). Behavioral economics and climate change policy. *Journal of Economic Behavior & Organization, 68*, 632–644.

Granovetter, M. (1985). Economic action and social structure: The problem of embeddedness. *American Journal of Sociology, 91*(3), 481–510.

Griffiths, T. (2010). Seeing 'REDD'? Forests, climate change mitigation and the rights of indigenous peoples and local communities. In D. Roe & J. Elliott (Eds.), *The Earthscan Reader in Poverty and Biodiversity Conservation* (pp. 341–357). London, UK: Earthscan.

Guijt, I., & Shah, M. K. (Eds.). (1998). *The myth of community: gender issues in participatory development.* London: Intermediate Technology Publications.

Hall, A. (1997). *Sustaining Amazonia: Grassroots action for productive conservation.* Manchester, UK: Manchester University Press.

Hall, A. (2008a). Paying for environmental services: The case of Brazilian Amazonia. *Journal of International Development, 20*(7), 965–981.

Hall, A. (2008b). Better RED than dead: Paying the people for environmental services in Amazonia. *Philosophical Transactions of The Royal Society B, 363,* 1925–1932.

Hall, A. (2008c). Brazil's Bolsa família: A double-edged sword? *Development and Change, 39*(5), 799–822

Hall, A. (2011a). Getting REDD-y. Conservation and climate change in Latin America. *Latin American Research Review, 46* [Special Issue], 184–210.

Hall, A. (2011b). Turning the tide in Amazonia? From perverse incentives to environmental services [Research Paper]. ESPA Research Project.

Hamilton, K., Peters-Stanley, M., & Marcello, T. (2010). *Building bridges: State of the voluntary carbon markets 2010.* Washington DC / New York, NY: Ecosystem Marketplace / Bloomberg New Energy Finance.

Harris, M. (2008). 'Sempre ajeitando' (Always Adjusting): An Amazonian way of being in time. In C. Adams, R. Murrieta, W. Neves, & M. Harris (Eds.), *Amazon peasant societies in a changing environment: Political ecology, invisibility and modernity in the rainforest* (pp. 69–91). New York, NY: Springer.

Hatcher, J., Bailey, L., Purdy, L., & France, M. (2009, May). *Tropical forest tenure assessment: trends, challenges and opportunities.* Washington DC / Yokohama, Japan: Rights and Resources Initiative / International Tropical Timber Organization. Retrieved February 2, 2012, from http://www.indiaenvironmentportal.org.in/files/doc_1075.pdf

IDEAcarbon (2011, June). Assessing the financial flows for REDD+: The pledge-implementation gap [Research Note]. Retrieved February 2, 2012, from http://www.forestcarbonportal.com/sites/default/files/ IDEAcarbon%20Research%20Note%20June%202011%20-%20 Assessing%20the%20Financial%20Flows%20for%20REDD.pdf

Instituto Socioambientale & Forest Trends (2010, September). *Desmatamento evitado (REDD) e povos indígenas: experiências, desafios e oportunidades no contexto amazônico.* São Paulo: Instituto Socioambiental & Forest Trends. Retrieved February 2, 2012, from http://www.forest-trends.org/documents/ index.php?pubID=2692

IPCC (2007). Summary for policymakers. In S. Solomon, D. Qin, M. Manning, Z. Chen, M. Marquis, K. B. Averyt, . . . H. L. Miller (Eds.), *Climate change 2007: The Physical science basis*. Contribution of working group I to the fourth assessment report of the intergovernmental panel on climate change (pp. 1–18). Cambridge / New York, NY: Cambridge University Press. Retrieved February 2, 2012, from http://www.ipcc.ch/pdf/assessment-report/ar4/wg1/ar4-wg1-spm.pdf

Karousakis, K. (2007, May). *Incentives to reduce GHG emissions from deforestation: Lessons learned from Costa Rica and Mexico*, Paris: OECD/IEA. Retrieved February 2, 2012, from http://www.oecd.org/dataoecd/55/54/38523758.pdf

Larson, A., Corbera, E., Cronkleton, P., van Dam, C., Bray, D., Esrada, M., . . . Pacheco, P. (2010). Rights to forests and carbon under REDD+ initiatives in Latin America. *Infobrief, 33.* Bogor, Indonesia: CIFOR. Retrieved February 2, 2012, from http://www.cifor.org/publications/pdf_files/infobrief/3277-infobrief.pdf

Lawlor, K., & Huberman, D. (2009). Reduced emissions from deforestation and forest degradation (REDD) and human rights. In J. Campese, T. Sunderland, T. Greiber and G. Oviedo (Eds.), *Rights-based approaches: Exploring issues and opportunities for conservation* (pp. 269–285). Bogor, Indonesia: CIFOR & IUCN.

May, P. H., Millikan, B., & Gebara, M. F. (2011) *The context of REDD+ in Brazil: Drivers, agents and institutions* (2nd ed.). Occasional Paper 55. Bogor, Indonesia: CIFOR. Retrieved February 2, 2012, from http://www.cifor.org/nc/online-library/browse/view-publication/publication/3287.html

Milder, J., Scherr, S. J., & Bracer, C. (2010). Trends and future potential of payment for ecosystem services to alleviate rural poverty in developing countries. *Ecology and Society, 15*(2), 4. Retrieved February 2, 2012, from http://www.ecologyandsociety.org/vol15/iss2/art4/

Moutinho, P., Cenamo, M. C., & Moreira, P. F. (2009). Reducing carbon emissions by slowing deforestation: REDD initiatives in Brazil. In C. Palmer & S. Engel (Eds.), *Avoided Deforestation: Prospects for Mitigating Climate Change* (pp. 90–109). London, UK: Routledge.

Muradian, R., Corbera, E., Pascual, U., Kosoy, N., & May, P. H. (2010). Reconciling theory and practice: An alternative conceptual framework for understanding payments for environmental services. *Ecological Economics, 69*, 1202–1208.

Padoch, C., Brondizio, E., Costa, S., Pinedo-Vasquez, M., Sears, R. R., & Siqueira, A. (2008). Urban forest and rural cities: Multi-sited households, consumption patterns, and forest resources in Amazonia. *Ecology and Society, 13*(2), 2. Retrieved February 2, 2012, from http://www.ecologyandsociety.org/vol13/iss2/art2/

Pagiola, S. (2008). Payments for environmental services in Costa Rica. *Ecological Economics, 65*, 712–724.

Pattanayak, S. K., Wunder, S., & Ferraro, P. J. (2010). Show me the money: Do payments supply environmental services in developing countries? *Review of Environmental Economics and Policy, 4*(2), 254–274.

Salisbury, D. S., & Schmink, M. (2007). Cows versus rubber: Changing livelihoods among Amazonian extractivists. *Geoforum, 38*(6), 1233–1249.

Stern, N. (2007). *The economics of climate change: The Stern review.* Cambridge, UK: Cambridge University Press.

Thaler, R. H., & Sunstein, C. R. (2008). *Nudge: Improving decisions about health, wealth and happiness.* New Haven / London: Yale University Press.

Transparency International. (2011). *Global corruption report: Climate change.* London / Washington DC: Earthscan. Retrieved February 2, 2012, from http://www.transparency.org/content/download/60586/970870/Global_Corruption_Report_Climate_Change_English.pdf

Vatn, A. (2010). An institutional analysis of payments for environmental services. *Ecological Economics, 69*(6), 1245–1252.

Viana, V. M. (2010). *Sustainable development in practice: Lessons learned from Amazonas.* London: International Institute for Environment and Development.

Vidal, J. (2009, October 5). UN's forest protection scheme at risk from organised crime, experts warn. *Guardian.* Retrieved February 2, 2012, from http://www.guardian.co.uk/environment/2009/oct/05/un-forest-protection

Waage, S., & Hamilton, K. (2011, January). *Investing in forest carbon: lessons from the first 20 years.* Forest Trends, The Katoomba Group, Ecosystem Marketplace and Bio-Logical Capital. Retrieved February 2, 2012, from http://www.forest-trends.org/documents/index.php?pubID=2677

World Bank. (2009). *World development report 2010: Development and climate change.* Washington DC: World Bank.

Wunder, S. (2005). *Payments for environmental services: Some nuts and bolts.* Occasional Paper 42. Bogor, Indonesia: CIFOR. Retrieved February 2, 2012, from http://www.mtnforum.org/sites/default/files/pub/4613.pdf

Wunder, S. (2007). The efficiency of payments for environmental services in tropical conservation. *Conservation Biology, 21*(1), 48–58.

Wunder, S. (2009). Can payments for environmental services reduce deforestation and forest degradation? In A. Angelsen (Ed.), *Realising REDD+ National strategy and policy options* (pp. 213–223). Bogor, Indonesia: CIFOR.

Zadek, S., Forstater, M., & Polacow, F. (2010). *The Amazon fund: Radical simplicity and bold ambition: Insights for building national institutions for low carbon development.* São Paulo, Brazil: Avina foundation.

Chapter 5

Extraction, Regional Integration, and the Enduring Problem of Local Political Spaces

Håvard Haarstad and Cecilia Campero

Introduction

The marches and strikes against road construction and gas extraction in Bolivia's Isiboro Secure National Park and Indigenous Territory (TIPNIS) nature reserve, widely publicized in the international media in the summer and early fall of 2011, brought out the contradictions of the Morales presidency for the world to see. The champion of indigenous rights and self-proclaimed "instrument of the people" was challenged by a movement of his supporters, the indigenous and labor movements, on a road construction project that pitted indigenous rights, local territorial claims, and environmental protection against modernist industrial development. A police raid to break up a protest march left tens of protesters wounded, leading to public outcry and forced Morales to suspend the project. The event illustrated a set of growing tensions during Evo Morales's tenure.

Morales came to power in 2006 on a platform precisely to empower *el pueblo* (the people) to make their own decisions with regard to the governance of their natural resources and to empower indigenous communities in relation to how the resources in their territories are governed. His campaign was bolstered by popular opposition to *neoliberalismo* and extractive politics that were seen as unresponsive to the needs and demands of popular sectors. In his first year in office he nationalized the gas industry, and in 2007 he passed a law mandating that all extractive projects potentially affecting indigenous territories would have to go through a process of prior consultation. Since then, relations between the government and indigenous movements appear to have soured, as the government has sought to intensify gas exploration, and as local actors and community groups have claimed that they are not properly consulted. Tensions between local territorial claims and national extraction strategies have also run high across the border in Peru. The tragedy of Bagua in 2009, where protests in a small Amazonian town escalated into violence that left 34 people dead (including 23 police personnel) and 202 injured, was widely understood as one particularly violent incident in a trend of increasing governmental aggression against indigenous and rural movements and a sharpening of conflicts over the development model of the country (Aiello, 2010). The mining industry has for decades defined national development priorities. Although there have been examples of civil society action changing the course of project development, the strategic position of the industry, and the government positioning itself to sign free trade agreements with, among others, the United States, have meant that local priorities have received little hearing (Aiello, 2010). Former president Alan García made no secret about his disdain for localist claims to indigenous territorial rights and environmental protection initiatives that may hamper the economic development of the country (García, 2007).

The Bagua event contributed to pushing the campaign to strengthen the right to prior consultation, through the proposed *Ley de Consulta*, further up the agenda. It also boosted the presidential campaign of the left-leaning Ollanta Humala, elected in 2011. The agency Associated Press (Salazar, 2011) reported that, as power was transferred to Humala, García left behind a "ticking time bomb" of disputes stemming from conflicts between indigenous groups and the extractive industry. Humala had campaigned on a promise to impose tighter restrictions and higher taxes on mining companies, and received significant backing in regions like Puno, where tensions have run high (Achtenberg, 2011). But just months after his inauguration, Humala was forced to declare a state of emergency in Cajamarca after failing to resolve violent strikes against a mining project by the US-based Newmont Mining Corporation that he had approved.

As these events serve to illustrate, tensions between local rights and national extractive strategies are not easily erased simply through a shift in power from the right to the left, or by installing an *"Indio"* in the highest office. Local-national conflicts over extractive activity and development models appear to plague "neoliberal" as well as "post-neoliberal" development models. If such tensions endure or even intensify, what does that mean for our understanding of emerging models of extraction and the alleged new-left, "post-neoliberal", or "resource nationalist" trends in the region? What is the actual content of this emerging model, and to what extent does it reshape relations between local territorial claims, citizens, and the extractive strategies of states?

A central argument in this chapter is that possibilities for local and national actors to negotiate extraction politics are highly dependent on interstate extractive relations above the national scale. For both Peru and Bolivia, a key conditioning factor in the governing of the extractive industries, including local-national relationships, is the need to attract foreign investment and to comply with international treaties and agreements. The TIPNIS project in Bolivia, for example, is part of the region-wide project for energy and transportation integration that includes most governments in South America (*Iniciativa para la Integración de la Infraestructura Regional Suramericana*—IIRSA), an element in a process of increasing regional cooperation in issues of transport, energy sovereignty, and economic development. This process includes a number of regional initiatives, such as UNASUR and ALBA (*Alianza Bolivariana para los Pueblos de Nuestra América*), as well as sector-specific projects such as PetroSur and IIRSA, which are intended to coordinate policy, spur intra-regional investment, and create regional governance mechanisms to promote economic development. This intra-regional orientation is typically understood as a reaction to the international orientation of the neoliberal era, which promoted bilateral and multilateral investment treaties that arguably undermined national sovereignty and democratic accountability. Given the differences in the ideological outlook of their current or recent governments, Peru and Bolivia have divergent positions within these processes. While Bolivia has oriented its interstate relations toward the alliance with Venezuela and Chávez's "oil diplomacy," Peru maintains a closer affiliation to the United States through its free trade agreement.

This chapter problematizes and questions the extent to which the "post-neoliberal" forms of extractive governance emerging at the regional scale reestablish political spaces, or possibilities for actors to influence policy, at the local and national scales. In our perspective, democratically accountable governance of the extractive sector is dependent both on possibilities for local stakeholders to negotiate local impacts and distribution of revenues, and on the ability of national governments to pursue policies in public interests. Conditions for democratically accountable governance are shaped by political and economic processes at a range of scales, and, given the capital intensive and export-oriented character of extractive industries, interstate relations are of particular importance in determining these conditions in that sector. The chapter begins with a discussion of the international regime for extractive governance emerging during the neoliberal era, before it discusses what we call the current "countermovement" of regional initiatives, and the extent to which the countermovement reshapes relationships between communities, citizens, and states. Much of this discussion concerns Latin America as a whole, but we also offer a brief comparative analysis of the regionalization projects of Bolivia and Peru.

Although there has been a discernable reorientation of interstate relations in extractive governance, and an emergence of regional initiatives on energy cooperation, we argue that these do not alter the basic economic realities of extraction, and in turn fail to change the relationships between local communities, citizens, and the extractive strategies of states. The international governance regime based on free trade agreements and arbitration appears to be on the wane in the region as a whole, but as argued here, the countermovement of regional initiatives and ideological alliances has yet to bridge the disconnection between local spaces of participation and states' extractive strategies. The tensions made visible by the TIPNIS and Bagua events appear as enduring characteristics of the challenge faced by Latin American governments trying to use the extractive sector as the engine of national economic development.

The Rise of the International Governance Regime

The extractive industries were at the center of the much-discussed neoliberal governance reforms in Latin America during the 1980s and 1990s. These reforms aimed to make extractive industries more efficient and better managed by reducing the role of the state, placing extraction and energy transport into private hands, and creating incentives for private investments (Brown, 1996; Ward, 2004; Weyland, 2004b). These reforms overturned the "Calvo Doctrine," an anti-interventionist doctrine formulated in the nineteenth century that had been integrated in constitutions and legislation across the region. The Calvo Doctrine stated that international investors could only seek redress in domestic courts in the country in which the investment is located. Laws based on the Calvo Doctrine strengthened national sovereignty in extractive and other sectors, and made it easier for Latin American governments to nationalize extractive industries, which occurred repeatedly in the past century (Cremades, 2006).

Based on the argument that this created significant uncertainties for potential investors and discouraged investment, neoliberal reforms aimed to create a more predictable and stable regime for international trade, investment, and arbitration in the region. Domestic policy changes were part of this effort and were centered on creating the institutional and economic basis for market-based growth with a package of policies to reduce inflation, lower tariffs, sell off state-owned enterprises, and liberalize the financial sector. These reforms were often formulated and pushed by Washington-based institutions, and have been subject to much debate and critique that will not be elaborated here (for a balanced assessment, see Huber & Solt, 2004; Walton, 2004; Weyland, 2004a).

A counterpart to domestic neoliberal reforms was the effort to create an international regime for governance, trade, and transport in the extractive sector, as well as other sectors. This implied replacing the Calvo Doctrine with an extensive regime of bilateral and multilateral treaties, based on principles of free trade, equal protection for national and foreign investors, and integration of energy infrastructure. To encourage foreign investment, Latin American countries radically changed their attitudes to treatment of foreign investors and international arbitration of investor disputes (Brunet & Lentini, 2007). The international regime of governance of the extractive sector was pursued through three concomitant processes: first, the signing of a range of bilateral investment treaties (BITs); second, commitment to binding international arbitration; and third, the gradual development of a region-wide agreement for free trade (the Free Trade Area of the Americas—FTAA).

First, the signing of BITs became increasingly common in the 1980s and 1990s, when there was an "explosion" in the number of treaties signed in comparison to previous decades, with some 2,600 BITs effective worldwide by 2008 (Boone, 2011). BITs proliferated in Latin America during these two decades, and by 2000, the region (including the Caribbean) had produced 366 such treaties (United Nations Conference on Trade and Development [UNCTAD], 2000). BITs typically create safeguards for investors, such as protection against direct, indirect, and regulatory expropriation. The latter means that any type of expropriation, including cases where excessive regulation makes the property of investors useless, subject to adequate and effective compensation. Further, BITs typically mandate national treatment for foreign investors, making it illegal for governments to implement policy that can be seen to favor domestic (including state-owned) companies, and state that investor protection should be no less favorable than that accorded under international law (Boone, 2011). The classic investment treaty provided investors with protection against expropriation of property, like the nationalization of extractive companies to which Latin American governments have been prone.

Second, Latin American countries, during the same era, increasingly committed to international arbitration to signal a legal commitment to the BITs. In brief, international arbitration allows foreign investors to sue domestic governments for passing laws that can be argued to infringe upon investors' rights to protection and equal treatment. Like the BITs, commitments to international arbitration came as part of the bundle of reforms promoted by the Washington Consensus institutions, which saw domestic legal institutions in the region as lacking in independence from the executive branch, lacking in transparency, and being slow and incompetent (Brunet & Lentini, 2007). In turn most Latin American countries signed the Convention on the Settlement of Investment Disputes between States and Nationals of Other States (the ICSID Convention) with the World Bank, as well as the United Nations Commission on International Trade Law (UNCITRAL).

Third, Latin American leaders prepared the ground for integrating bilateral and multilateral treaties into a region-wide free trade agreement that would include the developed economies of the United States and Canada. In 1994, 34 Heads of State signed an agreement to create the Free Trade Area of the Americas (FTAA) by 2005. This process stalled, however, as incoming left or center-left presidents came to view it with skepticism as pushed too heavily by the United States (Kellogg, 2007).

On the basis of privatization of state-owned extraction and energy companies, and a liberalized economic model (*de*regulation at the national scale), combined with international treaties and arbitration mechanisms (*regulation* at the international scale), Latin America was quite successful in gaining foreign direct investment (FDI) throughout the 1990s (see figure 5.1). According to the United Nations' Economic Commission for Latin American and the Caribbean (ECLAC, 2005), most of this FDI was market-seeking and natural resource-seeking, and the latter generated "serious problems" in terms of the following:

> Creating enclave industries entailing few of the types of processing activities that would help integrate these investments into the national economy, as well as for generating low fiscal revenues from non-renewable resources and polluting the environment. (ECLAC, 2005, p. 12)

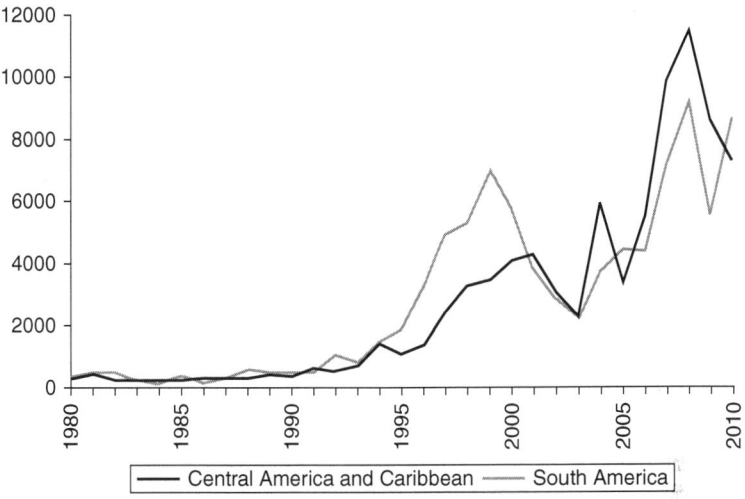

Figure 5.1 FDI in South America, Central America, and the Caribbean, 1980–2010

Arguably, these problems were partly related to the way in which the international governance regime tied the hands of governments in intervening in public interest and limited spaces for domestic and local influence, and in effect embedding extractive interests in international law. There has been a vigorous debate on the extent to which these treaties and the system of arbitration provide governments with adequate powers, for example, in protecting the environment, human rights, and other noneconomic rights, and the system has been criticized for allowing investors from developed countries to file suits against governments in developing countries acting in the public interest (Jacob, 2010; Peterson, 2009). In 2010, 51 developing countries were involved in arbitration proceedings, and the vast majority of cases were initiated by investors from developed countries (UNCTAD, 2011, pp. 101–102).

More recently, treaties have also included protection against "indirect expropriation," which is an ambiguous legal term that has in some instances been interpreted quite broadly to involve almost any government action that infringes upon investors' interests. This has created a degree of uncertainty for governments, and fears that policies to protect public goods like health and the environment might spark claims for compensation from investors (Ancos & Vincente, 2009).

This appears to have motivated a rethinking by certain governments, like Canada and the United States, which have adopted new negotiating templates for their bilateral treaties to strike a balance between protection of foreign investment and the rights of governments to regulate economic activity in the public interest. Peru's investment treaties establish that measures to protect public health, safety, and the environment should not be considered "indirect expropriation." Still, the line between indirect expropriation and legitimate government regulation is blurry, and it doubtful that international arbitration tribunals would accept any form of nationalization in the extractive sector as in the "public interest" (Peterson, 2007). The ambiguity of the "indirect expropriation" clauses is likely to create a "regulatory chill" for public policies that may incite compensation claims (Segrera Ayala, 2009; Zabalo, 2008).

The "equal treatment" clauses embedded in most investment treaties could also limit the abilities of governments of developing countries to create local service industries in the extractive sector, as this involves favoring domestic investors. Encouraging such local industries in extractive sectors has been an important success factor for developed countries (Chang, 2004), as was the case with Norway and many other oil-producing countries that used targeted policy to build domestic industrial capabilities in its petroleum industries in the 1970s (Ryggvik, 2010, pp. 49–52). These policies would likely be considered in violation of current "equal treatment" clauses, unless similar incentives were given to foreign investors (in which case the purpose would be lost).

Others have pointed to the lack of transparency in arbitration proceedings as another factor creating a "regulatory chill" for developing countries. The claimant (usually the foreign investor) can chose between local and international tribunals. The proceedings of the ICSID tribunal in Washington DC take place behind closed doors and are largely secretive, with no accountability to the domestic citizens and no possibility for appeal (Boone, 2011; Mortimore, 2009; Segrera Ayala, 2009). Also, the ICSID Convention is unique in that ICSID decisions do not require domestic enforcement procedures, so an ICSID decision is equivalent to "a final judgment of a court" (Article 54(1) of the Convention) in all participatory states. In other words, decisions taken in Washington are to be directly executed without going through national court systems (UNCTAD, 2010). These arbitrations shift the decision-making sphere from the domestic to the international scale, which makes it unlikely that domestic and governmental developmental strategies for extractive sectors are significant elements in weighing the judgments.

In summarizing the experiences of 15 Caribbean countries in negotiating a trade and investment treaty with the European Union, Girvan (in press) makes some observations that encapsulate much of the critique of the international governance regime. He holds that they are characterized by "technification," by which the language of the agreements and the proceedings are accessible only to professional specialists and not to the broader public, "sweetification," by which potential benefits for developing countries are highlighted and costs understated, and "treatification," by which the actual benefits and costs only become apparent once governments face the task of implementing them in national regulations. He concludes that the "locking in" effect of policies is a problem for the exercise of national sovereignty, but also regarded as their principal virtue by the international actors that promote them.

International treaties have presented legal challenges against government policy of both Bolivia and Peru, including their extractive and energy sectors. Peru has had 10 claims against it admitted into the ICSID, 6 of which are still pending (as of November 2011). Bolivia has had four claims against it in the ICSID tribunal, the latest one initiated by Pan American Energy against the nationalization in 2009 of the Chaco petroleum company. Another arbitration is pending against Bolivia in UNCITRAL for the nationalization of Compañía Logística de Hidrocarburos de Bolivia, and British Petroleum and other companies have indicated that they will pursue claims against Bolivia for various governmental actions related to nationalization (Global Arbitration Review, 2011).

The Regional Countermovement

Since the decade of bilateralism and multilateralism of the 1990s, the specters of "resource nationalism" and a "resurgence of the Calvo Doctrine" have returned to the agenda (Brunet & Lentini, 2007; Cremades, 2006). Closely linked to the rise of new-left governments across the Latin American region, states have to varying degrees attempted to reintegrate active policy and a stronger regulatory rule in the extractive sectors (Stanley, 2009, see also chapter 11 by Nem Singh, this volume). The FTAA process was replaced by an alternative regionalization process that was seen to be more tuned to the development agendas of new-left governments. As part of what we here term the "countermovement" against the international governance regime, there are arguably two complementary or competing regionalization projects under way: ALBA and UNASUR. ALBA came into being through an agreement between Venezuela's Hugo Chávez and Cuba's Fidel Castro in 2004, later joined by Bolivia, Ecuador, Nicaragua, and some smaller Caribbean states. It was explicitly promoted by Chávez as an alternative to the FTAA, and it seeks to develop trade relations on the basis of complementarity rather than competition. Its largest members are governments with leftist platforms (Hörmann, 2010). UNASUR has a longer historical trajectory in that it builds on the older MERCOSUR (Common Southern Market) and the *Comunidad Andina*. In this sense it has its antecedents from the neoliberal era, and it is couched in much less ideological terms compared to ALBA. But it is equally ambitious—it reportedly aspires to be modeled on the European Union. And as with Chávez's ALBA initiative, the UNASUR is understood as reclaiming national and regional sovereignty vis-à-vis multilateral and international governance regimes. To Kellogg (2007):

> The UNASUR represents the assertion of newly confident governments in the region, for the first time in a generation able to envisage economic and social development outside of US hegemony, and looking for an alternative path that will allow them greater room for maneuver. (p. 209)

A significant element of this alternative regionalization process centers on extractive and energy sectors. IIRSA has since its inception in 2000 been a platform for the UNASUR countries to coordinate energy infrastructure development and foster energy integration. And Venezuela has, as part of its active "oil diplomacy," pushed the creation of regional oil initiatives for the Andean region (*PetroAndina*) and South America as a whole (*PetroSur*), under the umbrella of ALBA. The main focus of these initiatives is on long-term regional energy cooperation and integration, for example, not only through cooperation between state-owned energy companies, but they also include bilateral agreements with Venezuela that provide preferential oil loans (Poertner, 2011). Bolivia, Venezuela, Brazil, Argentina, and Ecuador, among other countries, have through nationalization or piecemeal regulations, strengthened the position of state-owned companies in the productive chain.

This shifted focus toward national sovereignty and regional energy integration appears to have been accompanied by an increasing suspicion toward international arbitration and trade and investment treaties with countries from outside the region. The eagerness to enter into BITs has cooled across the globe, it seems, but "the boldest trend is found in Latin America" (Malik, 2008, p. 8). With a high number of disputes arising from the energy and natural resource sectors, it appears that Latin American countries are trying to regain national authority over regulation. To Cremades (2006, p. 59), "the region has witnessed efforts to bring international arbitration under greater control or domestic supervision." He uses Argentina, Brazil, and Venezuela as examples of countries that have increasingly developed a reluctance to accept international arbitration, "particularly when the state's natural resources are at stake" (Cremades, 2006, p. 71). Brunet and Lentini (2007) trace the new policies discouraging use of international arbitration to increased competition for natural resources and states' increasing concern for energy security. According to their data, 40 percent (31 out of 78) of all concluded and pending ICSID cases against Latin American countries as of 2006 were energy related. This proportion is likely to have increased in the years since then, due to stronger energy regulation in Bolivia, Ecuador, Venezuela, and other countries.

Countries in the region have also attempted to terminate BITs created during the 1990s or to withdraw from international arbitration altogether. At an ALBA summit in 2007, Bolivia, Venezuela, and Nicaragua decided to withdraw collectively from ICSID, stating in a press release that they decided to do so "in order to guarantee the sovereign right of countries to regulate foreign investment on [sic] their national territories" (see Committee for the Abolition of Third World Dept [CADTM], 2007). To date, Bolivia is the only country of these three to follow through on this decision, effectively withdrawing in November 2007. The new Bolivian Constitution contains a version of the "Calvo Doctrine," which states that investments in the oil and gas industry are subject to national laws and that no foreign jurisdictions or tribunals are recognized (Article 366). But as several of Bolivia's BITs that offer ICSID arbitration remain active, this has created some legal complexities over whether claims can still be made against Bolivia. States cannot unilaterally change one provision of a BIT without terminating the whole agreement. This issue has not been properly resolved, and Pan American Energy's claim against Bolivia was admitted at the ICSID well after Bolivia's effective withdrawal. Ecuador has announced that its consent to ICSID arbitration is no longer available for any disputes arising from mining and oil contracts, and it has withdrawn from a range of BITs (Malik, 2008). But Ecuador has also experienced how difficult to is to withdraw from investment treaties, as they often contain "survival clauses" stipulating that provisions granted to investments prior to withdrawal "survive" the withdrawal for many years. For example, Ecuador's BIT with the United States has a ten-year survival clause, meaning that the benefits given to US investments under the treaty will be extended for ten years after Ecuador has withdrawn (UNCTAD, 2010). Ecuador has since 2009 led a movement to create a regional arbitration center under the umbrella of UNASUR and ALBA to replace ICSID, which is planned to improve on many of the weaknesses Latin American countries have experienced in the ICSID (Fiezzoni, 2011).

Many of the provisions of the treaties signed during the heyday of economic liberalism will linger on, however, and continue to structure state-investor relations and natural resource governance. Yet the regional trend of pulling back from the international governance regime is clear, particularly in the oil and gas sector. A growing number of investment disputes relating to this sector, as well as a trend toward stronger state regulation and intra-regional energy integration, are important elements of the context. Most commentators would see these trends as indicative of the rise of the new left (Barrett, Chavez, & Rodríguez-Garavito, 2008) in the region, or as signs that the region is distancing itself from its neoliberal past, and as part of an emerging "post-neoliberal" trend that centers on the politics of natural resources and hydrocarbons in particular. Indeed, much of the critique of neoliberal forms of governance has been put forward by popular and social movements, which have protested at what they regard as giveaways of resources inherently belonging to them (Vanden, 2003). These movements have to a large extent been seen as the constituencies for, and the popular force behind, the new-left governments sustaining the post-neoliberal rhetoric. Indigenous movements have pushed for, and in many countries achieved, legislation that grants their communities rights to prior consultation for extractive projects that affect them, in line with the International Labour Organization (ILO) Convention 169. Such legislation has recently been passed in Bolivia, Peru, Ecuador, and Chile, though it differs from one to another (see Haarstad & Campero, 2011). Government policy in the sector has been justified with reference to the need to reassert popular control and democratic forms of governance.

With the TIPNIS and Bagua events as a backdrop, it is reasonable to ask: To what extent does this countermovement, with its rhetoric of "people's ownership" of natural resources and assertion of national democratic sovereignty, provide new conditions for local claims for redistribution, recognition, and representation? If Latin American countries are doing away with the international governance regime that left little political space for governments and granted extensive rights to multinational extraction companies, does this imply the emergence of a model where some of this "surplus sovereignty" is transferred to the local scale? Peru and Bolivia can provide an informative comparison here, as these neighbors are members of several of the same interstate initiatives, but have also oriented these relations in divergent directions.

Post-Neoliberal Extractive Governance—What Difference Does It Make?

Both Peru and Bolivia are members of *Comunidad Andina*, *Asociación Latinoamericana de Integración* (Latin American Integration Association—ALADI), and MERCOSUR, and have signed the Constitutive Treaty of UNASUR. The two countries have also entered into a treaty between themselves to create a common market (2004), which aims to "boost the participation of regional and local authorities, the private sector, and the organizations of civil society in the process of integration and binational cooperation" (Article 1, i). Both countries also have active bilateral treaties, including several with European countries.

However, after Morales came to power, Bolivia reoriented its interstate relations in line with the ideological alliance and "oil diplomacy" objectives of Chávez's Venezuela. In 2006 Bolivia entered into the ALBA-TCP agreement (*Tratado de Comercio de los Pueblos*, People's Trade Agreement) with Venezuela and Cuba, the treaty presented as the alternative to the US-driven FTAA, only days before nationalization was announced. Bolivia under Morales has been one of the countries opposing the FTAA. The new Bolivian Constitution contains provisions that require renegotiation of all the country's previous BITs. Under the ALBA-TCP treaty, Bolivia exports hydrocarbon products to the other participating countries to improve their energy security, and imports fuels and lubricants in return. The treaty has not been a success in trade terms, however. Whereas Bolivia's foreign trade increased by 240 percent between 2006 and 2009, trade with the ALBA partners did not increase, which Hörmann (2010) attributes to the protectionist policy of Venezuela. Under the ALBA umbrella, a treaty was signed in 2007 to promote energy integration between Venezuela, Cuba, Nicaragua, and Bolivia (*Tratado Energético del ALBA*). The treaty gives the signatories participation in a Venezuelan oil block called the "Bloque del ALBA," and it aims to create further interstate cooperation in extractive industries in these countries. Another treaty signed the same year, the

Acuerdo Energético del ALBA, establishes agreement on developing *Petroamerica, Petroandina, Petrocaribe*, and *Petrosur*. It also stipulates an amount of Venezuelan oil to be imported and used only for Bolivia's internal market. Bolivia and Venezuela signed another treaty in 2010, this time bilateral, which is to promote the export of oil-related products from Venezuela to Bolivia, and to promote cooperation between the Venezuelan state company PdVSA and the Bolivian state company YPFB. Worth mentioning is also a treaty between the petroleum ministries in Bolivia and Iran in 2006, for the purpose of installing petrochemical plants in Bolivia. Talks and contracts have also been initiated with China and Russia.

Bolivia has thus attempted to replace the shortage of investment in the wake of its gas nationalization by strengthening ideological ties and entering into agreements, particularly with Venezuela, which appear highly politically motivated. It was likely due to this orientation, as well as what it sees as more difficult conditions for investors, that the US suspended preferential trade status for Bolivia in 2009. Presented as alternatives to US hegemony, the ALBA treaties are underlined by a rhetoric of national sovereignty and "the people," but the economic rationale behind them is less clear and they have yet to be properly filled with economic content.

President García, like most of his predecessors, oriented Peru's interstate relations in the extractive industries in a different direction. He has been much more welcoming to the liberalized, internationalist model. Peru supported the FTAA process, and signed a free trade agreement, the US-Peru Trade Promotion Agreement (PTPA), with the United States in 2007. Ollanta Humala argued strongly against the treaty in the years before he was elected, so its fate remains to be seen. But investment in the Peruvian mining industry tripled in the five-year period after the negotiation of the PTPA (2006–2011) compared with the period before (2001–2005), providing strong arguments in its favor (Andina, 2011). Humala has also stressed that all existing agreements in the mining sector will be respected. The US Department of State evaluates Peru as much more investment friendly than Bolivia, stressing that the PTPA establishes a "secure, predictable legal framework for U.S. investors operating in Peru" (Bureau of Economic, Energy and Business Affairs, 2011). Peru has signed free trade agreements with Singapore, China, Canada, Chile, and the European Free Trade Area. As one of only two countries in Latin America, Peru has become a candidate country in the Extractive Industries Transparency Initiative (EITI). As part of its plan of action to become EITI compliant, Peru has strengthened public access to revenue streams for the extractive industries and involved some NGOs in dialogue on how to further strengthen accountability and transparency. To Klein and Gonzales Espinosa (2011), Peru's main motivation in joining the EITI is to comply with Western expectations and improve the country's standing with donor agencies.

In turn, the "profiles" of interstate relations in the extractive sectors are distinctly divergent. Although Bolivia has increasingly oriented its extractive interstate relations toward ALBA and Venezuela, Peru has during the previous presidencies been clearly oriented toward the liberal policy regimes promoted by the US and multilateral agencies based in the Global North.

To see whether these differences are visible in the extent to which interstate treaties recognize noneconomic rights, we conducted a short review of the treaties, illustrated in table 5.1. We were interested in seeing whether the leftist, "resource nationalist" orientation of Bolivia means that noneconomic rights (environmental protection, stakeholder involvement, and so on) are recognized to a greater degree. The categories are ranked from 1 to 3 ("1" indicating that half or more of the treaties have provisions to protect noneconomic rights, "2" indicating that at least one-third of the treaties have such provisions, and "3" indicating that less than one-third of the treaties have such provisions).

Two things can be read from this review. First, it is apparent that, in either country, most treaties do not contain significant provisions to protect noneconomic rights. Second, it appears that Bolivia's treaties tend to do a little better, in that treaties the country has signed under the umbrellas of CAN and ALBA have some provisions to protect the environment, stakeholder involvement, and sustainable development. While the countermovement does seem to make a difference, however small, to the formation of treaties, these provisions never specify how noneconomic rights should be prioritized in relation to economic imperatives or how to mediate between these concerns when they clash. For Bolivia, it is doubtful that its association with the "countermovement" changes the economic imperatives that bind the government's hands in accommodating local claims. So far, it is concerns for national sovereignty and the development of alternative economic alliance that motivates its interstate relations, but there are no indications that any "sovereignty surplus" is transferred to the local scale.

As the ideological alliance with Chávez's Venezuela and the ALBA treaties appear more politically than economically driven, they do not alter the basic economic realities for Bolivia's extractive sector. Bolivia's primary market for extractive products is actually not Venezuela, but Brazil and Argentina. In 2010, Bolivia exported 27.2 million cubic

Table 5.1 Review of investment agreements and other economic agreements for Peru and Bolivia

	CAN		ALADI		ALBA		MERCOSUR		Bilaterals		FTAs	
	Bolivia	Peru	Bolivia	Peru	Bolivia	Peru	Bolivia	Peru	Bolivia	Peru	Bolivia	Peru
Investment Agreements	X	X			X				X	X		X
Other Agreements	X	X	X	X	X		X	X		X		
Policies to Protect												
Environment	1	3	2	3	1		3	3	3	3	1	1
Stakeholder Involvement	2	3	3	3	2		3	3	3	3	1	1
Transparency	3	3	2	3	3		3	3	3	3	2	2
Democratic Accountability	2	3	3	3	3		3	3	3	3	3	3
CSR	3	3	3	3	3		3	3	3	3	3	3
Sustainable Development	1	3	3	3	2		3	3	3	3	1	1
Indirect Expropriation	3	3	3	3	3		3	3	3	3	1	1

Note: A total of 26 investment agreements and 18 other economic agreements have been reviewed and categorized (see in text explanation). "Other agreements" include economic, energy, and mining cooperation agreements.

meters of natural gas per day to Brazil and 4.8 million m³ per day to Argentina, and the Brazilian Petrobras remains the largest gas producer in Bolivia (*Yacimientos Petrolíferos Fiscales Bolivianos* [YPFB], 2010). So economic realities warrant a stable political relationship to Brazil in particular, who has been less than enthusiastic about nationalization or other policy changes that could affect the stability of supply or the conditions for Petrobras. Shortly after nationalization, Morales pushed out the pro-Venezuelan minister of hydrocarbons Andrés Soliz Rada, apparently due to Brazilian pressure (Calí, 2007).

A scenario drawn up by the YPFB and outlined in its *Plan Estratégico Corporativo 2011–2015* illustrates well the economic imperatives that guide the policy decisions of the Morales government, and in turn the conditions for ceding sovereignty to the local scale. It shows that the country's proven reserves of gas fall way short of the contracted deliveries to the Brazilian and Argentinian markets and domestic demand from 2015 and onward. Even in the best-case scenario (including probable reserves, current exploration prospects, and projections from feasibility studies), available reserves will fall short by 2020 (see figure 5.2). The consequences of falling short will be economically costly compensation payments to Brazil and Argentina

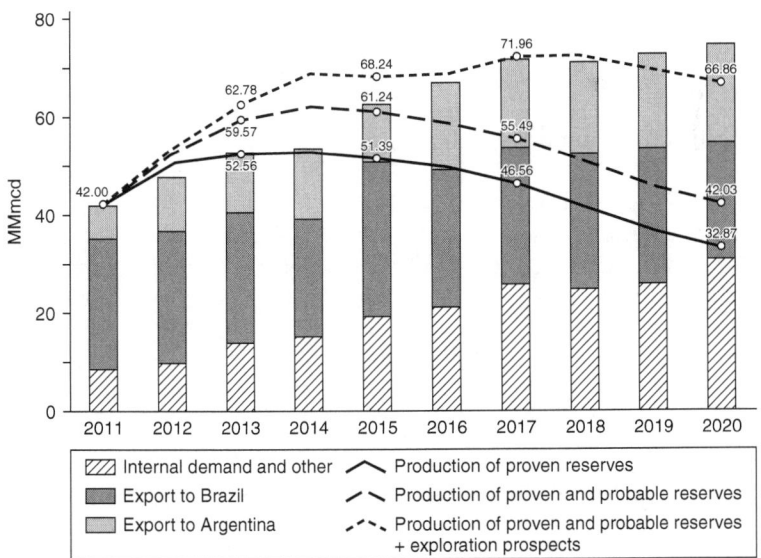

Figure 5.2 Bolivian hydrocarbon production and demand scenario, 2011–2020

and serious damage Bolivia's attempt to become the primary supplier of gas to the region, or the political cost of failing to meet domestic demand, which is a sensitive issue for the Bolivian public. Against this scenario, Bolivia's post-neoliberal project of asserting national sovereignty and economic self-determination is negotiated primarily through its relations with its gas importing neighbors, more so than through the ideological alliance with Venezuela. As the basic economic realities are much the same as for previous governments, so are the conditions for reshaping the relationship between citizens, local communities and the extractive strategies of the state.

This was driven home at the 2010 ALBA summit, where national leaders asserted the right of their states to retain the last word on extractive projects and the importance of overruling local communities to promote the interests of national economic development. They agreed that prior consultation limited the power of the state in unfortunate ways. A report by *Foro Boliviano sobre Medio Ambiente y Desarrollo* (FOBOMADE, 2011) recounts the following exchange between the heads of state:

> How is it possible that territorial administration or national parks pass into the hands of the indigenous, either of the east or the west? The right to consultation creates obstacles for the development of Bolivia," stated Morales. "We will not accept that the Executive has to ask permission from this or that local organization [gremio] to govern," warned [President of Ecuador, Rafael] Correa. Shortly before, the ultraliberal government of Alan García objected to the Law of Prior Consultation because "it implies the risk of turning back to holding up the development of the country." (p. 247)

When Morales found common ground with García in lamenting how the right to consultation for local communities constrained economic development, their ideological differences were less important than their shared role as heads of state for highly resource-dependent countries. This situated them in a complex field between competing economic, social, and political concerns, among which local participation and indigenous rights are not easily reconciled with the economic imperatives of extraction.

The Enduring Problem of Local Political Spaces

Despite a clear countermovement against the neoliberal regime of internationalized governance in the extractive sector, it improbable that this will significantly reshape the conditions for local territorial claims, participation, or citizen attempts to hold governments accountable. The countermovement against the international governance regime is actually characterized by a proliferation of new bilateral treaties and multilateral initiatives, and though they are often couched in more ideological terms, stress national sovereignty, and are more regional in scope, they do not necessarily represent an obvious break from the past in terms of local-national relations. The regional countermovement has to some extent undermined the international governance regime by withdrawing from BITs, challenged international arbitration, and developed regional alternatives. But it appears primarily as a different way for states to relate to each other, rather than a different way for states to relate to local claims. It appears largely political in content, and therefore fails to replace the economic dependence of aligned states in ways that can enable governments to allow political spaces for local actors in governance models. As the TIPNIS protests and the statements of Morales at the ALBA summit indicate, "post-neoliberalism" maintains an uneasy relationship between local territorial claims and the extractive strategies of states.

The rhetoric of national sovereignty, popular ownership of resources, and participation creates expectations that the countermovement fails to fulfill, which sparks tensions and intensified conflict. Bolivia is perhaps the country where this trend is most visible. There, indigenous movements have been emboldened by electoral victories, a new set of rights, and a radical change in the state's discourse. Tensions are generated when extractive activity proceeds without a corresponding change in governing processes or revenue distribution. Movements in Peru, Ecuador and other countries are likely also emboldened by the strengthened rights and sovereignty discourse, which drive higher expectations and demands made against the state. Yet states, including the self-proclaimed "post-neoliberal," have few alternatives to an extractive strategy based on expansion, interstate commitments with national policy constraints and an enduring "disconnect" with local participation.

Does the countermovement make no difference at all? Despite clear implementation problems, the discourse of popular ownership and national sovereignty has still facilitated placing extractive governance on political agendas and made it into a question for legitimate democratic critique. Although the international governance regime sought to remove a range of governance issues from the public agenda, the countermovement and its discourse of national sovereignty have likely expanded the scope of public decision-making. States can now increasingly be challenged on issues of transparency, accountability, environmental impacts, and revenue distribution. Citizens are provided with discursive tools and (limited) legal mechanisms for pressing claims. As Morales suspended the TIPNIS project in Bolivia, and as the *Ley de Consulta* was passed in Peru, it was evident that there are certain spaces within which citizens can influence natural resource governance. But this cycle of rapid project approval–protest–project cancellation is not sustainable, for the state or for its citizens. The challenge for Latin American states is to integrate political spaces for citizens in a stable, institutionalized governance model that can cater both to local claims *and* to national economic development.

References

Achtenberg, E. (2011). Peru's mining conflicts: Ollanta Humala's ticking time bomb. *North American Congress on Latin America*. Retrieved October 12, 2011, from https://nacla.org/blog/2011/7/29/peru's-mining-conflicts-ollanta-humala's-ticking-time-bomb

Aiello, K. (2010, June 25). Bagua, Peru: A year after. *North American Congress on Latin America*. Retrieved October 22, 2010, from https://nacla.org/node/6622

Ancos, H., & Vincente, D. J. (2009, June). *La Promoción de la Responsibilidad Social en los Tratados de Inversión: Los casos de Bolivia y Venezuela*. Avances de Investigación, 30. Madrid, Spain: Fundación Carolina.

Andina. (2011, July 12). Mining Investments in Peru Triple Totalling US$13.7 Billion. *Andina. Agencia Peruana de Noticias*. Retrieved November 28, 2011, from http://www.andina.com.pe/Ingles/Noticia.aspx?Id=xlYSS1io0JM=

Barrett, P., Chavez, D., & Rodríguez-Garavito, G. (Eds.). (2008). *The New Latin American Left: Utopia reborn*. London: Pluto Press.

Boone, J. (2011). How developing countries can adapt current bilateral investment treaties to provide benefits to their domestic economies. *Global Business Law Review, 1*(2), 187–201.

Brown, E. (1996). Articulating opposition in Latin America: The consolidation of neoliberalism and the search for radical alternatives. *Political Geography, 15*(2), 169–192.

Brunet, A., & Lentini J. A. (2007). Arbitration of international oil, gas, and energy disputes in Latin America. *Northwestern Journal of International Law and Business, 27*(3), 591–630.

Bureau of Economic, Energy and Business Affairs (2011, March). 2011 Investment Climate Statement—Peru. *US Department of State*. Retrieved November 28, 2011, from http://www.state.gov/e/eb/rls/othr/ics/2011/157342.htm

Calí, M. (2007). *Why Evo Morales is not going to be the next Hugo Chavez*. ODI Opinion Papers. London, UK: Overseas Development Institute.

Chang, H.-J. (2004). Regulation of foreign investment in historical perspective. *European Journal of Development Research, 16*(3), 687–715.

Committee for the Abolition of Third World Dept (2007, May 2) Bolivia, Venezuela and Nicaragua Withdraw Together From the ICSID. Retrieved March 8, 2012, from http://www.cadtm.org/Bolivia-Venezuela-and-Nicaragua

Cremades, B. (2006). Resurgence of the Calvo Doctrine in Latin America. *Business Law International, 7*(1), 53–72.

Economic Commission for Latin America and the Caribbean. (2005). *Foreign investment in Latin America and the Caribbean.* Santiago, Chile: United Nations Publications.

Fiezzoni, S. K. (2011). The Challenge of UNASUR Member Countries to Replace ICSID Arbitration. *Beijing Law Review, 2*(3), 134–144.

Foro Boliviano sobre Medio Ambiente y Desarrollo. (2011). *Anuario Sena 2010.* La Paz, Bolivia: Foro Boliviano sobre Medio Ambiente y Desarrollo.

García, A. (2007, October 28). El síndrome del perro hortelano. *El Comercio.* Retrieved March 8, 2012, from http://elcomercio.pe

Girvan, N. (in press). Social movements confront neoliberalism: Reflections on a Caribbean experience. *Globalizations.*

Global Arbitration Review (2011). *The arbitration review of the Americas 2012: Bolivia.* London, UK: Law Business Research Ltd.

Haarstad, H., & Campero, C. (2011). *Participation in the Bolivian Hydrocarbons Sector: The "double discourse" and limitations on participatory governance.* URBECO-report 04/11. Bergen, Norway: Center for Urban Ecology.

Hörmann, M. (2010). Regional Integration: Key role for Bolivia. *D+C, 51*(3), 103–105. Retrieved January 8, 2012, from http://www.dandc.eu/articles/168821/ index.en.shtml

Huber, E., & Solt, F. (2004). Successes and failures of neoliberalism. *Latin American Research Review, 39*(3), 151–164.

Jacob, M. (2010). *International investment agreements and human rights.* INEF Research Paper Series on Human Rights, Corporate Responsibility and Sustainable Development. Duisburg, Germany: Institute for Development and Peace, University of Duisburg-Essen.

Kellogg, P. (2007). Regional integration in Latin America: Dawn of an alternative to neoliberalism? *New Political Science, 29*(2), 187–209.

Klein, A., & Gonzalez Espinosa, A. C. (2011). *The EITI transparency standard: Between global power shifts and local conditionality.* Unpublished paper presented at the Politics of Natural Resources in the Global South: Critical International Political Economy Perspectives, Copenhagen, Denmark.

Malik, M. (2008). *Recent developments in regional and bilateral investment treaties.* Background paper for the 2nd Annual Forum of Developing Country Investment Negotiations, November 3–4, Marrakech, Morocco.

Mortimore, M. (2009). *Arbitraje Internacional Basado en Cláusulas de Solución de Controversias Entre los Inversionistas y el Estado en Acuerdos Internacionales de Inversión: Desafíos para América Latina y el Caribe.*

Serie Desarollo Productivo No. 188. Santiago de Chile: Comisión Económica para América Latina.
Peterson, L. E. (2007, February). *Bilateral investment treaties: Implications for sustainable development and options for regulation.* FES Conference Report. Berlin, Germany: Friedrich Ebert Stiftung.
Peterson, L. E. (2009). *Human rights and bilateral investment treaties: Mapping the role of human rights law within investor-state arbitration.* Montreal, Canada: Rights and Democracy.
Poertner, M. (2011). Venezuelan oil diplomacy and voting in the U.N. General assembly. *Journal of International Service, 20*(1), 85–107.
Ryggvik, H. (2010). *The Norwegian experience: A toolbox for managing resources?* Oslo, Norway: Center for Technology, Innovation and Culture (TIK-Centre).
Salazar, C. (2011, July 27). Peru's Garcia leaves conflicts unresolved. *Associated Press.* Retrieved November 15, 2011, from http://www.newsvine.com/_news/2011/07/27/7177164-perus-garcia-leaves-conflicts-unresolved
Segrera Ayala, Y. (2009, December). Restoring the balance in bilateral investment treaties: Incorporating human rights clauses. *Revista de Derecho, 32,* 139–161.
Stanley, L. (2009). Bucking the trend: The political economy of natural resources in three Andean countries. In K. Gallagher & D. Chudnovsky (Eds.), *Rethinking Foreign Investment for Sustainable Development* (pp. 179–200). London, UK: Anthem Press.
United Nations Conference on Trade and Development (UNCTAD). (2000, December 15). Bilateral investment treaties quintupled during the 1990s: New UNCTAD publication releases latest data on the universe of BITs [Press release]. Retrieved March 8, 2012, from http://www.unctad.org/templates/ webflyer.asp?docid=2655&intItemID=2023&lang=1
United Nations Conference on Trade and Development (UNCTAD). (2010). *Denunciation of the ICSID Convention and BITs: Impact on investor-state claims.* International Investment Agreements Issues Note No. 2. New York and Geneva: United Nations Conference on Trade and Development.
United Nations Conference on Trade and Development (UNCTAD). (2011). *World investment report 2011: Non-equity modes of international production and development.* World Investment Report. New York and Geneva: United Nations Conference on Trade and Development.
Vanden, H. (2003). Globalization in a time of neoliberalism: Politicized social movements and the Latin American response. *Journal of Developing Societies, 19*(2–3), 308–333.
Walton, M. (2004). Neoliberalism in Latin America: Good, bad or incomplete? *Latin American Research Review, 39*(3), 166–183.
Ward, J. (2004). *Latin America: Development and conflict since 1945.* Abingdon, UK: Routledge.

Weyland, K. (2004a). Assessing Latin American neoliberalism: Introduction to a debate. *Latin American Research Review, 39*(3), 143-149.
Weyland, K. (2004b). Neoliberalism and Democracy in Latin America: A mixed record. *Latin American Politics and Society, 46*(1), 135-157.
Yacimientos Petrolíferos Fiscales Bolivianos (2010). *Boletín Estadístico Gestión 2010*. La Paz, Bolivia: Yacimientos Petrolíferos Fiscales Bolivianos.
Zabalo, P. (2008). Los Acuerdos Internacionales Sobre Inversión, Otro Obstáculo Para el Desarrollo de América Latina. *Gestión en el Tercer Milenio: Revista de Investigación de la Fac. de Ciencias Administrativas, 11*(22), 27-39.

Chapter 6

Resource Extraction and Local Justice in Chile: Conflicts Over the Commodification of Spaces and the Sustainable Development of Places

Jonathan Barton, Álvaro Román, and Arnt Fløysand

Introduction

As democracy has become more consolidated in Chile, there has been an emergence of socio-environmental conflicts, indicative of the desire of local actors to oppose large-scale projects associated with "national development" that do not satisfy local development needs. This can be seen as a conflict between two different visions of development, one based on local resources and sustainable development of *places*, the other based on nonlocal capital and the commodification of *spaces*. Chile remains wedded to natural resource extraction for its export-oriented economic model, despite its recognition as a Latin American "jaguar" economy since the early 1980s (Borregaard, Volpi, Blanco, Wautiez, & Matte-Baker, 1999). Over 80 percent of its exports are based on minerals, agriculture, and fisheries; most of these have a relatively low level of added value (ProChile, 2010). The intensity of extraction and harvesting to fuel this growth has led to concerns over the sustainability of different sectors and the economy itself. Since the return to democracy in 1990, these criticisms have become more vocal and globalization has facilitated international alliances to channel these claims (Kousary, Murray, & Barton, 2009; Martínez, 2003). These criticisms relate to environmental and social justice issues that can be defined as claims for local sustainable development.

Rather than studying socio-environmental conflicts in isolation, like much of the literature does, this chapter provides a comparative analysis of four different cases. These four cases reveal the diversity of these claims, and the alliances and practices that are employed by different stakeholders in the conflicts that ensue. It also reviews the different governance arrangements that are criticized, and those that are promoted as mechanisms for conflict resolution in these cases.

The first is the environmental conflict over the gold mining project Pascua Lama in the Atacama region. The second is the indigenous conflict relating to plantation forestry in the Araucanía region. The third is the salmon aquaculture industry in the Los Lagos region and the environmental impacts that have been generated. The fourth is the conflict over the HidroAysén dam project in the Aysén region; this project is regarded by its proponents as an essential addition to the energy network to fuel the mining and industry sectors (CNN Chile, 2011). These four case study vignettes will be used to explore a conceptual framework relating to a common construction.

The construction is as follows. Since the 1970s the state has pursued a development model based on an export-oriented economy in which natural resource extraction is the principal motor. Although presented as a "free market" exercise, this neoliberal model is heavily based on public sector orientation: legislation, regulations, rights, and other factors. The model is highly centralized and promoted by a range of sectorial ministries (Daher, 1992). This centralized development model, however, is repeatedly confronted by local justice claims in the areas of extraction and harvesting (Fløysand, Barton, & Román, 2010; Tello, 2010). It is evident that local benefits from these activities are low compared with wider benefits that may accrue, to capital itself and to other fields of the economy. It is for this reason that local public authorities and diverse local civil society actors present a common front against such interventions and make claims for increased participation and increased local benefits, utilizing different strategies and methods in this process. A paradox of state orientation is thus presented with different orientations from above and below, in which the "center" plays the "national development card," to override local interests and commodify these places into "extractive spaces." The chapter argues that effective decentralization is required in order for these types of natural resource conflicts to be resolved, thus increasing the influence of local governance regimes and ensuring more sustainable natural resource-based development that fulfills national and local needs simultaneously.

The Sustainable Development of Places

The Brundtland report of 1987—*Our Common Future* (World Commission on Environment and Development, 1987)—put the concept of sustainable development in the sphere of public policy and social action. Whereas many focused on its orientation in terms of environment and the economy, and an attempt to merge environmental considerations and economic decision-making, others focused on its core definition and primary themes: satisfaction of basic needs, supporting people to meet their own needs in the future, equitable development, empowerment, and the local focus of these activities. In the Brundtland report the importance of equity and justice in meeting needs, generating opportunities, and increasing participation are evident. Furthermore, the emphasis on localizing responses is also part and parcel of sustainable development thinking. Agenda 21 and the promotion of local governments as the coordinating element for local decision-making is a strong theme running throughout, embodied in the popular phrase: "think globally, act locally."

Through the link between local government, local communities, local participation in local resource management, and the idea of "common interest" (as the basis of equity) promoted by the report, it is possible to translate the geography of the concept into the sustainable development of places. These places, according to Yi Fu Tuan (1977) are "centers of felt value where biological needs, such as those for food, water, rest, and procreation, are satisfied" (p. 4), and "what begins as undifferentiated space becomes place as we get to know it better and endow it with value" (p. 6).

Whereas the national level of administration and orientation remains important for reasons of international security and governance, it is at the level of places that meaning is generated and at which people experience development. This is where (in)justice is experienced and where people enter into conflict over what is "just development" (as opposed to interstate conflict, war, and diplomacy, the focus of international relations specialists).

In the Chilean case, the claims for justice that appear in the cases reviewed in this chapter emerge from changes in the "places-spaces" in which people are able to exercise these claims for "just development." "Just development" is understood here as a synonym for sustainable development since it infers justice within the current generation and intergenerationally, across different spaces (nation-state and global) and places (localities). It refers not only to basic needs satisfaction and opportunities for creating better lives as a social endeavor, but also the demands on nature that these processes require and the importance of recognizing their interactions, as a socioecological complex (Gallopín, 2003). Just development refers to a process by which people are able to secure their well-being and adapt it over time. It is a quest for security, for survival and then for fulfillment. This quest is pursued in specific places, with which we identify ourselves. Following Tuan (1977): "Place is security, space is freedom: we are attached to the one and long for the other" (p. 3). This longing for freedom has inherent risks, as Tuan (1977) adds: "To be open and free is to be exposed and vulnerable" (p. 54).

Claims for just development emerged more strongly during the 20 years of the *Concertación* center-left coalition (1990–2010) as democracy became more consolidated, the civil-military balance of power was renegotiated, and the divisions of the dictatorship increasingly reconciled (principally via legal processes and "dialogue roundtables"). It is this deepening of democracy following the transition that has been at the heart of the emergence of socioecological conflicts. The term "socioecological conflict" relates to the point that the issues are neither social nor environmental in a fragmented sense (Sabatini, 1997), but combined in terms of pretensions of local development based on people and their local resource base.

The deepening of democracy refers to democracy not only as a formal, liberal democratic process of suffrage but rather a process of participation in, and control over decision-making. In this sense there is a complement of formal representative democracy with participative democracy, the latter referring to a binding rather than consultative notion of participation (Tedesco & Barton, 2004). The rise of socioecological conflicts in different locations around the country is a sign of the deepening of democracy and the desire of different local coalitions to emerge and oppose specific projects generated centrally by large-scale, nonlocal capital in collaboration with ministries pursuing "national development." These conflicts constitute the interface between the two visions of development.

The Chilean Development Model

The recent conflicts over local sustainable development in Chile are embedded within a context that can be defined as the Chilean development model. This model has its roots in the dictatorship of 1973–1990 and is grounded in neoliberal economics supported by a strong legal system that defends private property. The current Chilean Constitution (*Constitución Política de la República de Chile de 1980*, 2005), approved in 1980 by plebiscite in undemocratic circumstances, cements this foundation (Article 24 in particular).

The "Chicago Boys" economists formed in the University of Chicago and Catholic University in Chile were the principal architects of the model, which was introduced in 1975 as a form of liberalizing the economy while labor rights and political representation were repressed (Chonchol, 1996). This particular economic liberalization founded on classic economic orthodoxy was accompanied by a particular version of conservative nationalism based on the thinking of Jaime Guzmán; just after the return to democracy (April 1, 1991), Guzmán was gunned down outside one of the campuses of the Catholic University where he was a lecturer in constitutional law. Together, a traditional view on social development, the family and property were married with a view of economic organization that favored private interests over the state, and individualism over collective interests.

One of the most important consequences of the consolidation of this model from the mid-1970s was that the actions of the private sector in the field of productive activities were to be supported in different regions of the country by the central administration: the junta and its technocrats. The goal was to shift toward an export-oriented economy, not only based on mineral exports, principally copper. Despite the existence of a discourse that favored decentralization and the creation of a new political and administrative geography, in terms of the creation of regions (Boisier, 2000), the dictatorship demanded a tight administration of the country in order to curb opposition.

This level of centralization of decision-making, centrifugally flowing out to the regions, provinces, and municipalities through officials selected by the junta, embedded this highly centralized model, for example, high-ranking military officers as regional *intendentes*. While decision-making around government was highly concentrated and restricted forms of political and social activity, the scope for investment and operation of the private sector was increased significantly. Limitations on productive investments were few, and these were heightened further by the sale of state assets that were priced attractively for the private sector, particularly the larger national economic groups. In this scenario, the condition of the state copper firm CODELCO remained an anomaly. To this day it remains in state hands (see chapter 11 by Nem Singh, this volume). The explanation for its survival under neoliberalism is that 10 percent of its sales go directly to the coffers of the military under the *Ley Reservada del Cobre* (Law 13.196 of 1958 with important modifications to the military's benefit in 1973 and 1986) (Ley 13.196, 1975).

Although the Chilean economy experienced a major shock in the early 1980s with the international recession, it was also an opportunity to diversify the export base of the country. Nontraditional agricultural exports (NTAX) were added to the traditional mining products as an important new element of the productive structure. These exports included cellulose, fruit, wines, and salmon. Although mining exploitation had a long history in the country dating to nitrate boom in the second half of the nineteenth century, these NTAX led to increasing demands for productive spaces in different areas of the country, away from the traditional copper mining regions in the north and center near Rancagua, or the coal mines of Coronel, Lota, and Magallanes to the south.

Commodification of land and sea to generate products for export became the logic of the development model during the 1980s. Increasingly intensive use of land and increasingly extensive areas converted to production were core to this process. Although these investments gave rise to new labor opportunities, there were no local, vocal opposition to these transformations of the land- and seascapes of Chile (Barton & Murray, 2009). Dictatorship, and the consolidation of a strong discourse of neoliberalism (through government, the private sector, and the press) as the way for Chile to flourish through exports within a scenario of contemporary globalization, had led to a fait accompli. This situation was widely known as "the Chilean miracle" (Schurman, 1996). This miracle was micromanaged from Santiago (Boisier, 2000), whereas the other regions of the country were converted into productive landscapes—extractive spaces—that would fuel capital accumulation in the metropolitan region, increasing investment in construction, in investment overseas, and in increased consumption for a national business elite.

The process of commodification of land and sea for export production, supported by the military-technocratic alliance based in the capital gave rise to a notion that investment should be encouraged at all times and in all locations. Local autonomy, local decision-making, and local sustainable development were not considerations within this market-based logic. "Trickle down" from exports, through wages principally (rather than tariffs for government coffers, which were gradually dismantled in the drive to liberalize trade) was supposed to open the door to local development opportunities, for individual advancement, and consumption of material goods and private services, including health and education. Although overall poverty rates in Chile decreased considerably under democracy from 1990, concerns over the equitable distribution of the economic "miracle" remained (Kousary et al., 2009). A further concern was the degree of centralization of the model and the failure to change the primate city model of Chilean growth, accumulating capital generated in the other 12 regions (14 from 2005). Rather than a notion of development based on aggregate national data and a national model within which all would be subsumed for a concept of common good, defined and communicated from the center, there was a strong sense of injustice in terms of the geography of capital generation and its accumulation. During the first decade of the twenty-first century, these concerns would be converted into calls and claims for greater autonomy from Santiago and local justice in the face of the commodification of Chilean places into productive spaces.

National Neoliberal Development versus Local Sustainable Development: Four Case Studies

The selected case studies have constituted the principal conflicts over development futures during the last decade. Although the 1990s was a decade during which the country was consolidating democracy and the menace of the military was ever-present in the character of General Pinochet (as commander in chief of the armed forces to 1998, then senator prior to his arrest in London and return to Chile, allegedly infirm). During this time, the most well-known conflicts were those relating to the Pangue and Ralco dam projects. Both of these projects were finally approved but opposition, from environmental groups and *Mapuche* indigenous communities, revealed the possibilities of social mobilization in the face of centrally generated territorial transformations (Carruthers & Rodríguez, 2009). This revelation would return with added momentum in 2011 with the conflict relating to the HidroAysén project in the south of the country. HidroAysén, a project cofinanced by the firms Endesa and Colbún, aims to create the largest hydroelectric project in the country across the Baker and Pascua rivers (HidroAysén, 2011). This energy will then be transported along one of the longest transmission lines in the world to the main centers of demand toward the center of the country. In May 2011, following several years of conflict, the project was finally approved by the Regional Environment Commission. However, the conflict and the principal opposition organized under the movement *Patagonia sin Represas* (Patagonia without Dams) revealed a new standard of organization, international financing, and capacity for mobilization of social opposition to major development projects (Toledo, Aravena, & Olivares, 2009).

It has been common for individual cases of environmental conflicts to be studied in isolation. There is a dominant notion in much of the literature that each has its specificities and trajectories and this requires a focus on the internal machinations. The assumption is that there is little to gain from comparative analysis, or simply that all of these cases are examples of neoliberal exploitation. Another common feature of writing on these conflicts is that they are often quite descriptive and chronological, with the objective of presenting the conflict, its roots, and outcomes. However, the question remains: What can we learn from these conflicts, to reduce future conflicts and to promote socioecological justice?

In this chapter, comparative analysis is provided by viewing these conflicts through a specific lens. The lens is the relationship between local actors and nonlocal actors, particularly the role of government institutions, and the ways in which the national development agenda is placed in opposition to a local justice agenda. What this situation generates in all of the case studies is a tension in terms of democracy, between different institutional levels and their legitimacy in representing people in different places and with different objectives.

The Gold Mining Project Pascua Lama in the Atacama Region

Chile is a mining country. The nitrate boom from the late 1800s until the German synthetic nitrate replacement during the First World War, then the rise and consolidation of the copper industry from the interwar period, have defined Chilean development. The current success of the Chilean export model is based on Chinese demand for copper and the role of the national firm CODELCO and a handful of large private firms, headed by the large BHP Billiton's Escondida mine.

This mining dependence, and the Dutch disease that it has generated in the mining regions and also for the national economy, has defined the country and its role in the global economy. Diversification from copper into other products, whether nontraditional agricultural exports from the early 1980s, or more recently alternative mining products such as molybdenum, lithium, and increased gold extraction, have dominated discussions of how the future of the country is to pan out as copper reserves run down during the current century. Consequently, it came as no surprise when, during the government of Ricardo Lagos, a Binational Mining Treaty was signed between Chile and Argentina to provide concessions to firms to mine in the transboundary zone of the high Andes, to exploit new deposits, of gold, in particular. The major beneficiary of this initiative was the Canadian firm Barrick Gold, and the specific project Pascua Lama would come to dominate socioecological justice issues during the mid-2000s. The project was located at high altitude and would be defined by three specific conflicts. The first of these was the removal of glaciers in order to mine beneath them. The second was the downstream impacts in the Valle del Huasco, where agriculture dominated local economic activity (Urkidi, 2010). A further dimension would be provided by the different positions of the indigenous community in the watershed as opposed to the *mestizo* settlements.

The first of the themes would be resolved after a long struggle relating to the environmental impact assessment (EIA) process. The final decision of the Regional Environmental Commission (COREMA) was that the glaciers could not be removed and the firm would have to find alternative; more costly forms of mining to access the deposits (Resolución exenta n° 24/2006). The other two aspects of the conflict would be bound up together through community conflicts regarding acceptance or rejection of the project, also the role of external actors, such as the state (as supporter of transboundary mining) and an alliance of NGOs, led originally by the Latin American Environmental Conflicts Observatory (OLCA), then including conflict-specific groups such as "No a Pascua Lama" (Observatorio Latinoamericano de Conflictos Ambientales, n.d.).

As with other mining projects around the world, apart from the formal EIA process, the firm sought an informal social license that would invoke a situation of relative lack of conflict at the local level (Urkidi, 2010). Given the major impacts generated by the project, such as road infrastructure, water use, tailings, and changes in local employment structure and economic culture, this need to engender support for the project became a major social strategy of the company, waged at local and national levels. As with the other conflicts that have defined more contemporary socioecological conflicts in the country, such as HidroAysén and the Arauco cellulose plant contamination in Valdivia, the role of the firms in media campaigns to offset environmental group criticisms has been a significant development (Sepúlveda, 2011; Toledo et al., 2009).

Unlike the indigenous conflict around forestry and HidroAysén, the case of Pascua Lama is closer to the experience of the archipelago of Chiloé and salmon farming since the centers of location and influence are clearer. In the case of Barrick Gold, the role of the town of Vallenar and the municipality of Alto del Carmen would become central to the conflict. Divisions would appear within the municipal authorities, with a range of other stakeholders, and local indigenous groups as Barrick Gold became increasingly influential in local politics and communications. In order to secure its social license, Barrick targeted this locality with several millions of dollars of support. It was precisely this injection of capital into a relatively low-income municipality that led to splits and different positions emerging. Perhaps the most emblematic development at the municipal level was the support for the campaign of Nora Rojas Ardiles to become mayor of the Alto del Carmen municipality. A former secretary of Barrick, it was argued that her campaign was bank-rolled by the company, also that there were irregularities in the voting (with the electoral register soaring between municipal elections as new voters were enrolled, rising from 2,989 votes cast in 2004 to 3,329 in 2008) (Maldonado, 2011). In the municipal elections of 2008, Rojas ran as a right-wing independent, and won 45.36 percent of the vote; the 2004 election had been won by the previous right-wing candidate—Carmen Bou Bou—by a single vote. The final environmental approval was granted in February 2006 (Resolución exenta n° 24/2006); an inspection by the Regional General Water Directorate in December 2009 revealed that many of the considerations of the Environmental Qualification Resolution (defined by the EIA evaluation) were not being met, however (Comité Operativo de Fiscalización, 2009).

The Indigenous Conflict Relating to Plantation Forestry in the Araucanía Region

The indigenous conflict in Chile is without doubt the longest and most intractable. Indigenous peoples in Chile have been progressively displaced, then urbanized during the postcolonial periods. Over time, issues that have generated conflict have changed, shifting between identity themes, diverse rights, and benefits expected from the Chilean state. However, all of these issues can be subsumed within the overarching theme of land rights (Carruthers & Rodríguez, 2009). The struggle of the *mapuche* people in particular, the dominant indigenous group in Chile principally located in the south of the country (Región de la Araucanía), has been the most potent since the return to democracy in 1990. The claims for socioecological justice have been framed in particular with regards to the use of their ancestral lands by plantation forestry activities.

In 1974, the Decree Law 701 declared by the dictatorship promoted plantation forestry activities (Decreto Ley 701, 1974). It is this piece of legislation that gave rise to this sector becoming the leading nontraditional export sector (alongside salmon farming, fruit, and wine). As a consequence of the growth of these exports, increasingly large areas of land were converted to plantation forestry, radiata pine in particular (Departamento de Economía, 2009). As demand for land increased, these firms were able to expand into areas over which indigenous land claims existed (Llancaqueo, 2006; Navarro & Henríguez, 2005). Although these claims were repressed during the dictatorship, they would be ignited following the return to democracy. In 1993, the Indigenous Law (Ley 19.253, 2008) would seek to redress injustices in terms of the relationship of the Chilean state and indigenous peoples, whereas the 1994 Environmental Law would also be relevant given its definition of environment (including impacts on different groups and cultures) and the initiation of new mechanisms such as EIA for large projects in indigenous territories (Carruthers & Rodríguez, 2009), hydropower in particular. Although EIA would only come into force in 1998, the Ralco dam project led to one of the first major standoffs between large-scale investment and indigenous claims for socioecological justice.

Although the state sought to channel claims through formal systems, such as the new institutionality of the National Corporation for Indigenous Development (CONADI) from 1993, direct action would increasingly accompany this process (Llancaqueo, 2006). By the 2000s, this direct action would be organized within radical groups such as the *Coordinadora Arauco-Malleco* (CAM), with attacks on plantation forestry installations and also farms. One of the most emblematic targets of these conflicts has been the farm of René Urban. Since 2002, the farm has been attacked more than hundred times (El Mercurio, 2011b), requiring a permanent police response. During this period, the conflict between *mapuche* and police has led to three deaths (Alex Lemún in 2002, Matías Catrileo in 2008, and Jaime Mendoza in 2009) and the use of the antiterrorist law to attempt to control the increasing violence. At the same time, the formal system of state-indigenous cooperation has led to more land transfers to recognized indigenous communities, more intercultural education initiatives (Richards, 2010), and major development programs such as the *Programa Orígenes*.

The role of local governments in this process has been complex. In many cases, mayors and local councilors who are closely tied to indigenous interests lead these municipalities, in rural areas in particular. However, their role in trying to balance formal channels and direct action has been outweighed by national-level interventions in indigenous territories based on logic of national security. Regional

CONADI institutions make direct links to recognized indigenous communities that have been institutionalized under the Indigenous Law. However, these community institutions are not necessarily the same as the traditional authorities of *loncos* (chiefs) and *machis* (healers); the new institutions have presidents and other representatives (Parra, Simon, & Villegas, 2008), and only through state recognition of the community can it access state benefits and subsidies.

The current picture of conflict and justice relating to the territorial transformations generated by the forestry plantation and processing activities, involves multiple actors and positions. It is also spread unevenly over the territory where the activity is concentrated. Although the CAM and similar radical movements make claims for land against the colonial *winka* state, other *mapuche* communities and organizations have accepted land transfers from state agencies, thus meeting their demands (Carruthers & Rodríguez, 2009). Consequently, the *mapuche* do not share one voice and do not mobilize as one force. This is similar to their historical organization in small isolated communities—*lofs*—which restricted the creation of a singular *mapuche* nation.

Local socioecological justice in areas of traditional *mapuche* settlement, and where forestry has a strong role, has positioned identity issues against the national export-oriented model and the idea of a common national development project (Richards, 2010). The case of forestry in Araucanía provides a stark case of these contrasting positions and claims, with the added dimension of interethnic historical and contemporary differences that accentuate the lack of a common perspective. Justice is constructed differently by these different ethnic peoples across different time frames, cosmovisions, and value systems, with widely differing notions of nature and its possible commodification. In particular, the construction of a national project that fails to consider the different peoples with claims over the territories within the national jurisdiction, points openly to the difficulties of equating positions. The International Labour Organization (ILO) 169 Convention that supports indigenous claims in this regard, ratified by the government of Michelle Bachelet in September 2008, goes someway to recognizing this diversity and different claims however it is unlikely to revert centuries of injustice by the *winka* against the *mapuche*.

The Salmon Aquaculture Industry in the Los Lagos Region

As with other initiatives for national development, the emergence of the salmon aquaculture industry in Chile is a product of national government collaboration with international development, then private, organizations. The salmon aquaculture project of the Japan International Cooperation Agency (JICA) in the early 1980s led to the recognition that the Región de Los Lagos had both freshwater and saltwater conditions that were ideal for salmonid aquaculture (both trout and salmon) (United Nations Conference on Trade and Development, 2006). This project gave rise to the Salmones Antártica company and a rapid increase in domestic and foreign investment in the sector. Given the specific conditions for salmon production, from eggs, lake cages, sea cages to harvesting, sea production was concentrated on the eastern coast of the island of Chiloé.

The region was one of the poorest in the country when this economic alternative was generated (División Social de MIDEPLAN, 2004). The new investment reduced out-migration, increased public investment in infrastructure and social infrastructure, and gave rise to a new wave of development in the province of Chiloé (Fløysand et al., 2010). With salmon products destined almost exclusively for export, the province became closely connected to the export development model associated with the NTAX, promoted for the national economy to recover from the international recession of 1982–1983 (Barton & Murray, 2009).

Whereas these exports fuelled the Chilean economic "miracle," generating parallels with the southeast Asian tiger economies, the impacts in the province were both positive, including labor opportunities for men and women, and negative, in terms of environmental impacts (with effects on preexisting economic activities such as finfish and shellfish extraction), changes in local culture, and certain labor conditions associated with these new opportunities. The need to recognize these negative impacts and address them was consistently overlooked, whereas the positive impacts were hailed as an example of how rural economies could be reoriented (Amtmann & Blanco, 2001; Buschmann & Fortt, 2005; Cárdenas, Melillanca, Durán, & Medina, 2005; Claude & Oporto, 2000). Although the socioeconomic indicators for the province improved considerably from the early 1980s, this was not only due to job opportunities and the guarantee of the minimum wage, but also due to considerable flows of public investment.

The velocity of change in the province generated by the private and public investments was not supported by changes in local public institutions to cope with the new conditions and to mitigate the most negative effects. Local government was not regarded as a key actor in this NTAX development model. The principal movers behind the sector were the firms, led by the larger foreign businesses (primarily Norwegian), with support from the Under-Secretariat of Fisheries (production authorizations), the Regional Government (economic promotion), and other related state agencies, for example, public works (infrastructure and port facilities) and the Navy (marine site concessions). The ten local governments in the province were not regarded as relevant public intermediaries since they had no administrative responsibilities over marine areas, and land-based production facilities only had to meet basic construction norms (Fløysand et al., 2010). Nevertheless, these localities would be subject to a complete overhaul of their local conditions. At the same time, flows from these new companies to the municipalities would be limited to small amounts paid in commercial taxes (*patentes comerciales*), insufficient to account for the demands of new migrant workers, including pressures on local public infrastructure (roads, schools, educational establishments, water supply and sanitation, and housing).

Despite the sector being presented as a savior of the local and regional economies, it also brings with it important environmental and social impacts. Local justice issues have been overridden by a national-level demand for export-led development, and the attraction of foreign direct investment and domestic investment to achieve this. National-level production and trade organizations have promoted the sector and its potential whereas local authorities, civil society groups, and productive organizations not dependent on aquaculture have made claims for socioecological justice in attempts to ground more of the value of the sector in the areas of production and processing, and to reduce the associated negative impacts (Barton & Murray, 2009).

The "boom" of the sector would be accompanied by a "bust" in 2007 with the emergence of the ISA virus. The severe impact of the virus led to a renegotiation of the social contract of this productive activity, and a new Fisheries and Aquaculture Law (approved in 2010) (Ley 20.434, 2010), including a range of new instruments to ensure more sustainable development of the sector. This response was too late for many workers and other local people who are not directly employed but are indirectly linked to aquaculture. The "security of their places" has been compromised in the "boom and bust" process, in spite of their persistent claims for more sustainable development in the face of the voracious expansion of the sector since the early 1980s (Barton & Fløysand, 2010).

The Conflict over the HidroAysén Dam Project in the Aysén Region

Energy demand in Chile is met principally by imports. With limited fossil fuel in the Magallanes region and a decision not to continue with the traditional coal industry in the area of Lota and Coronel during the 1990s, heavy emphasis has been laid on imported fossil fuels (gas and coal) and the use of hydroelectricity. Megahydro has been part of the national energy agenda since the second half of the twentieth century and it is well established; hydropower now contributes 22.5 percent of the national supply (2008) (Comisión Nacional de Energía, 2009). However, since the return to democracy in 1990, there has been increasing opposition to megahydro.

The forerunner to the more recent conflict—the current HidroAysén project in the Region de Aysén in Chilean Patagonia—was the Ralco dam project. During the second half of the 1990s, the construction of the Ralco dam on the Biobío river became emblematic for two reasons. The first involved the environmental impacts of large-scale damming on one of the country's principal rivers. The second involved the displacement of an indigenous Pehuenche community (Bauer, 2009; Carruthers & Rodríguez, 2009). It was only sometime after the decision had been taken to construct the dam that the final settlement was made with the last remaining inhabitants: the Quintremán sisters (during the presidency of Ricardo Lagos at the end of 2002) (Goméz, 2002). Effectively, this acceptance of relocation by Endesa to other land in the Biobío valley marked the end of the indigenous-environmentalist opposition. However, what this struggle revealed was that local, national and international organizations were able to mobilize around megaprojects and bring pressure to bear, both on the developer—the energy firm Endesa—and the Chilean government that sponsored the project (Bauer, 2009).

Although without the immediate indigenous dimension, the struggle over the HidroAysén project in the Aysén Region has dominated the Chilean socioecological justice agenda over the past five years, alongside the Pascua Lama mining project. As with the other projects noted in these vignettes, the HydroAysén initiative emerges as a response to the energy deficit in Chile. During the early 2000s, much store had been put in gas supply from Argentina. However, a lack of investment in supply infrastructure and rising domestic demand in Argentina led to shortages in the two gas pipelines built to connect the Argentinian and Chilean systems (Bauer, 2009). As a response, different private initiatives came to the fore that would reduce the geopolitical vulnerability of this situation and the fact that Bolivia will only trade some of its gas with Chile if a resolution is found to their claims for access to the sea. Given this situation, three major solutions emerged, two driven by private actors, the other by the state. The state initiative involved the construction of a gas terminal in Quinteros in 2009 to reliquidify gas transported by ship from sources in Asia and elsewhere, whereas the private initiatives revolved around new thermoelectric power stations and a major new hydroelectric project in the south of the country. The HidroAysén project involved the creation of a new company by the same name, which merges investment by the international firm Endesa and the national firm Colbún. The project seeks to dam the Baker and Pascua rivers with five dams to generate 2,750 MWh of power for the main interconnected energy supply system (SIC) that supplies the lion's share of Chilean industrial and residential energy demand (Comisión Nacional de Energía, n.d.). Whereas the areas of intervention are not inhabited, the main issues to be raised by environmental groups has been the transformation of a habitat that is regarded as valuable given its relative lack of intervention to date, outstanding natural beauty, and other benefits that can be generated in the area, tourism in particular. The standoff between environmental opposition and the firm began early in the process once the project came light. *Patagonia sin Represas* and the *Consejo de Defensa de la Patagonia* were the NGO response to the project: financed by US environmental groups and led by two of the leading environmental voices in Chile—Juan Pablo Orrego of the NGO *Ecosistemas* (also a veteran of the Ralco conflict) and Douglas Tompkins (US owner of the Pumalín ecological reserve in the south of the country), among others (Toledo et al., 2009). Tompkins would become a key actor in the subsequent discussions relating to the route of the high-tension cables that are projected to link the dams with the main centers of demand further north, since they would have to traverse his land at some point.

Early in 2011, after years of conflict, the project was finally approved by the COREMA for Aysén (El Mercurio, 2011a). This approval marked a turning point for the project; however the definition of the energy distribution routes will lead to further conflicts, given that these will pass through indigenous land and numerous other private holdings. To get to this point, and with a controversial final decision-making process under the right-wing government of Sebastián Piñera, considerable pressure was brought to bear on different officials and community groups. Basically, the 2011 approval had to overturn a previous decision on the EIA of the project that had generated over 2,700 objections by 33 different government agencies and services only a year and a half earlier (Valencia, 2009). The change of government (March 2010), and the consequent changes in the leadership of the local and regional government agencies and services (posts that are filled directly by presidential mandate), were instrumental in this change of technical evaluation. On April 27, 2011, the head of the EIA service in the region resigned for "personal reasons"; the vote in favor of the project took place on May 9, 2011, with ten of the 11 committee members approving it (one abstention). Environmental NGOs challenged the conflicts of interest of some COREMA members, also the influence of national-level authorities in their clear support of the project during the evaluation process ("HidroAysén: Intenso Debate", 2011).

A further element of the HidroAysén intervention in the region was its support for activities in the municipalities of Cochrane, Aysén, and Coyhaique. Via submissions to the national financial controller, NGOs criticized these agreements between the firm and local governments, deeming them to be illegal ("HidroAysén: Intenso debate", 2011). Nevertheless, these NGO arguments and the majority rejection of the project by local people (persistently in opinion polls), has failed to carry the day. As with other projects of this nature, the local and regional environments are now part of a commodification process, as valleys are converted into energy storage and generation units for consumption principally in minerals processing and industrial development further north.

Locating Justice: Local Places, National Spaces

The struggles for socioecological justice in Chile that were effectively silenced under dictatorship have flourished under democracy. The dominance of the national-level development discourse—based on the export-oriented model and a neoliberal framework of market mechanisms—put in place by the Chicago Boys in the mid-1970s—has persisted. Consequently, major productive and services investments are justified at the national level and pursued by the productivist hierarchy of the central administration. The lead organizations of this hierarchy—the ministries of economy, agriculture, mining, foreign relations (ProChile and the Foreign Investment Committee), and justice in particular—have brought pressure to bear on regional- and local-level public sector organizations, for example, CONAMA (now Ministry of Environment) and the COREMA, the *Dirección del Trabajo,* and Municipal authorities, to accede to these national-level demands. This is evident in the case of the HidroAysén EIA approval for instance, with centrally selected regional representatives dominating the Regional Environment Commission that approved the project. The firms are supported and protected by these productivist authorities in the face of local opposition and social and environmentally oriented NGOs. They also operate with their own communicational and investment strategies to win support for their projects and the relevant approvals. Investing in local activities through municipalities, reportedly supporting local political candidates, and local and national media campaigns are some of the measures employed, as the vignettes illustrated.

The outcome has been the approval of these projects and the development of "extractive spaces" that follow a logic of commodification of local territories, whereby their resources are valorized through processing and sales in export destinations. These extractive spaces are therefore converted into national spaces of development generation, according to this overriding development discourse that focuses on comparative natural advantage, as opposed to building competitive advantage. There is also evidence that the counterlogic of the "sustainable development of places," including participation and equity considerations at the local level, has failed in replacing the hegemony of territorial transformation under dictatorship and, subsequently, democracy. Opposition has been increasingly vociferous as NGOs have created more international alliances during the 2000s (Barton & Fløysand, 2010), however almost all of the major projects in conflict, and the productive sectors that have generated most opposition, are operating. This is not specific to Chile, however. The fact that the Chilean model has defined neoliberalism in Latin America helps to explain why localities across the region have been subjected to "placeless" extractive processes that override local considerations and local claims for decision-making over territorial transformations.

Chile is also defined by its high degree of political centralism. This is evident in the overriding of local decision-making bodies by centrally appointed representatives within regional settings (*Intendentes* and regional ministerial secretariats in particular), also the political affiliations of local mayors and councilors, and their alignment with national-level party political mandates. The outcome is a national-level development discourse that is able to convert any selected resource-rich place into commodified space understood in terms of its contribution to the export-led development model. Justice is thus defined also at the national level, through GDP growth and aggregated notions of poverty reduction principally. Yet justice is experienced more closely at the level of place, by people in the places that undergo these transformations. It is at this level, more than the national level (via presidential and Congressional elections) that people attempt to construct more sustainable development through participation that seeks to redress problems of equity and promotes claims for justice. For these types of natural resource conflicts to be resolved, and for ensuring more sustainable natural resource-based development that fulfills national and local needs simultaneously, effective decentralization is required. However, strong resistance to decentralization is part and parcel of the conflicting visions of development in Chile. Effective decentralization assumes that a focus on more sustainable development of places is fundamental for the promotion of equity and justice considerations (as emphasized in *Our Common Future*). In contrast, the hegemony of the commodified and centralized export-oriented development logic, with its insistence on "trickle down," regards these considerations as secondary, as possible outcomes rather than primary goals of capital accumulation.

References

Amtmann, C. A., & Blanco, G. (2001). Efectos de la salmonicultura en las economías campesinas de la Región de Los Lagos, Chile. *Revista Austral de Ciencias Sociales, 5*, 93–106.

Barton, J. R., & Fløysand, A. (2010). The political ecology of Chilean salmon aquaculture, 1982–2010: A trajectory from economic development to global sustainability. *Global Environmental Change, 20*(4), 739–752.

Barton, J. R., & Murray, W. E. (2009). Grounding geographies of economic globalisation: Globalised spaces in Chile's non-traditional export sector, 1980–2005. *Tijdschrift voor Economische en Sociale Geografie, 100*(1), 81–100.

Bauer, C. J. (2009). Dams and markets: Rivers and electric power in Chile. *Natural Resources Journal, 49*(3/4), 583–651.

Boisier, S. (2000). Chile: la vocación regionalista del gobierno militar. *EURE (Revista Latinoamericana de Estudios Urbano Regionales), 26*(77), 81–107.

Borregaard, N., Volpi, G., Blanco, H., Wautiez, F., & Matte-Baker, A. (1999). *Environmental impacts of trade liberalization and policies for the sustainable management of natural resources: A case study on Chile's mining sector.* New York & Geneva: United Nations.

Buschmann, A. H., & Fortt, A. (2005). Efectos ambientales de la acuicultura intensiva y alternativas para un desarrollo sustentable. *Revista Ambiente y Desarrollo, 21*(3), 58–64.

Cárdenas, J. C., Melillanca, P. I., Durán, P. C., & Medina, I. D. (2005). *Las directrices de la OCDE y la salmonicultura en Chile.* Santiago de Chile, Puerto Montt: Centro Ecocéanos.

Carruthers, D., & Rodríguez, P. (2009). Mapuche protest, environmental conflict and social movement linkage in Chile. *Third World Quarterly, 30*(4), 743–760.

Chonchol, J. (1996). Reflexiones sobre Chile: ¿hay alternativas al modelo neoliberal? *Estudos Avançados, 10*(27), 141–162.
Claude, M., & Oporto, J. (Eds.). (2000). *La ineficiencia de la salmonicultura en Chile: Aspectos sociales, económicos y ambientales*. Santiago de Chile: Fundación Terram.
CNN Chile. (2011, May 10). Hidroaysén va a abastecer a la gran minería privada en Chile. Retrieved from http://www.cnnchile.com
Comisión Nacional de Energía. (2009). *Balance nacional de energía, 2008* [Excel workbook]. Retrieved February 1, 2012, from http://www.cne.cl/ cnewww/ opencms/ 06_Estadisticas/Balances_Energ.html#;
Comisión Nacional de Energía. (n.d.). *Sistema Interconectado Central (SIC)*. Retrieved February 1, 2012, from http://www.cne.cl/cnewww/opencms/ 03_Energias/ Otros_Niveles/Electricidad/Sistema_Electrico/sic.html
Comité Operativo de Fiscalización. (2009, December 22). *Informe técnico: Visita inspectiva del Comité Operativo de Fiscalización: RCA COREMA Atacama N° 24/2006*. Dirección General de Aguas. Retrieved January 31, 2012, from http://www.e-seia.cl/archivos/Inf_Tec_DGA____COF_-_ EIA_Modificaciones_Proyecto_Pascua_Lama__Dic_09_.pdf
Constitución Política de la República de Chile de 1980. (2005, September 22). *Fija el texto refundido, coordinado y sistematizado de la Constitución Política de la República de* Chile. Santiago de Chile: Ministerio Secretaría General de la Presidencia. Retrieved from http://www.leychile.cl/Naveg ar?idNorma=242302&tipoVersion=0
Daher, A. (1992). Ajuste económico y ajuste territorial en Chile. *EURE, 18*(54), 5–13.
Decreto Ley 701. (1974, October 28). *Fija régimen legal de los terrenos forestales o preferentemente aptos para la forestación, y establece normas de foment sobre la material*. Santiago de Chile: Ministerio de Agricultura. Retrieved from http://www.leychile.cl/Navegar?idNorma=6294
Departamento de Economía. (2009). *Análisis de la cadena de producción y comercialización del sector forestal chileno: estructura, agentes y prácticas*. Concepción: Universidad de Concepción.
División Social de MIDEPLAN. (2004, September). *Pobreza y distribución del ingreso en las regiones*. Serie CASEN 2003, Volumen 2. Ministerio de Planificación y Cooperación. Retrieved from http://www.archivochile. com/Chile_actual/ 11_econom/chact_econ0022.pdf
El Mercurio. (2011a, May 10). Comisión aprobó HidroAysén, pero empresa deberá cumplir exigencias en beneficio de la región. *El Mercurio*.
El Mercurio. (2011b, July, 30). Ercilla: donde la tierra se siembra con balas y lacrimógenas. *El Mercurio*.
Fløysand, A., Barton, J. R., & and Román, Á. (2010). La doble jerarquía del desarrollo económico y gobierno local en Chile: El caso de la salmonicultura y los municipios chilotes. *EURE, 36*(108), 123–148.
Gallopín, G. (2003). *Sostenibilidad y desarrollo sostenible: un enfoque sistémico*. Santiago de Chile: Naciones Unidas.

Goméz, P. (2002, December, 19). Nicolasa Quintremán cede y firma con Endesa. *El Mercurio*. Retrieved January 31, 2012, from http://www.mapuche.info/news/ merc021219.html

HidroAysén. (2011). Descripción del Proyecto. Retrieved from http://www.hidroaysen.cl/que-es-hidroaysen/descripcion-del-proyecto/

HidroAysén: Intenso debate sostuvieron Sara Larraín y Daniel Fernández. (2011, April 16). *La Tercera*. Retrieved from http://latercera.com

Kousary, L., Murray, W. E., & Barton, J. R. (2009). Land of miracles? A critical analysis of poverty reduction strategies in Chile, 1975-2005. *International Development Planning Review*, *31*(2), 127-163.

Ley 13.196. (1975). *Reservada del Cobre*. Santiago de Chile: Ministerio de Hacienda.

Ley 19.253. (2008, May 9). *Establece normas sobre protección, fomento y desarrollo de los indígenas, y crea la Corporación Nacional de Desarrollo Indígena*. Santiago de Chile: Ministerio de Planificación y Cooperación. Retrieved from http://www.leychile.cl/Navegar?idNorma=30620

Ley 20.434. (2010, April 8). *Modifica la Ley General de Pesca y Acuicultura en materia de acuicultura*. Santiago de Chile: Ministerio de economía, foment y turismo; subsecretaría de pesca. Retrieved from http://www.leychile.cl/Navegar?idNorma=1012014

Llancaqueo, V. T. (2006). El enclave forestal chileno en territorio mapuche. *Asuntos Indígenas*, *4*, 44-50.

Maldonado, R. A. (2011, April 15). Ecocidio en el Valle del Huasco. *Punto Final*, *731*. Retrieved from http://puntofinal.cl/731/ecocidio.php

Martínez, R. Q. (2003). *Comercio, inversiones y sustentabilidad: el caso de Chile*. Santiago de Chile: Programa Chile Sustentable.

Navarro, R. M., & Henríquez, N. C. (2005). ¿Desarrollo sostenible o eco-etnicidio? El proceso de expansión forestal en territorio mapuche-nalche de Chile. *Ager. Revista de Estudios sobre Despoblación y Desarrollo Rural*, *4*, 101-133.

Observatorio Latinoamericano de Conflictos Ambientales. (n.d.). Proyecto minero de Pascua Lama. Retrieved from http://www.olca.cl/oca/chile/pascualama.htm

Parra, C. G., Simon, J., & Villegas, K. (2008). Respondiendo a un mundo globalizado: Cambios en la estructura de autoridad de los pehuenche de Alto Biobío, Chile. *Sociedad Hoy*, *15*, 55-66.

ProChile. (2010, April). *Análisis de las exportaciones chilenas, 2009*. Dirección General de Relaciones Económicas Internacionales. Retrieved February 1, 2012, from http://www.prochile.cl/regiones_pro/archivos/region_IV/documentos/analisis_exportaciones_chilenas_2009.pdf

Resolución exenta n° 24/2006. (2006, February 15). Copiapó: Comisión Regional del Medio Ambiente, Región de Atacama.

Richards, P. (2010). Of indians and terrorists: How the state and local elites construct the Mapuche in neoliberal multicultural Chile. *Journal of Latin American Studies*, *42*(1), 59-90.

Sabatini, F. (1997). Chile: conflictos ambientales locales y profundización democrática. *Ecología Política*, *13*, 51–69.
Schurman, R. A. (1996). Chile's new entrepreneurs and the "economic miracle": The invisible hand or a hand from the state?" *Studies in Comparative International Development*, *31*(2), 83–109.
Sepúlveda, C. (2011, April 11). Celco y el desastre de Valdivia: la hora de la verdad." *El Mostrador*. Retrieved January 31, 2012, from http://www.elmostrador.cl/
Tedesco, L., & Barton, J. R. (2004). *The state of democracy in Latin America: Post-transitional conflicts in Argentina and Chile*. New York: Routledge.
Tello, M. D. (2010). Del desarrollo económico nacional al desarrollo local: aspectos teóricos. *Revista CEPAL*, *102*, 51–67.
Toledo, H. R., Aravena, H. R., & Olivares, X. T. (2009). Agua, poder y discursos: conflictos socio-territoriales por la construcción de centrales hidroeléctricas en la Patagonia Chilena. *Anuario de Estudios Americanos*, *66*(2), 81–103.
Tuan, Yi-Fu. (1977). *Space and place: The perspective of experience*. Minneapolis, MN: University of Minnesota Press.
United Nations Conference on Trade and Development. (2006). *A case study of the salmon industry in Chile*. New York & Geneva: United Nations.
Urkidi, L. (2010). A glocal environmental movement against gold mining: Pascua-Lama in Chile. *Ecological Economics*, *70*, 219–227.
Valencia, A. (2009, November 11). Plantean duras objeciones a HidroAysén. *La Nación*. Retrieved from http://www.lanacion.cl
World Commission on Environment and Development. (1987). *Our common future*. UN Documents. Retrieved from http://www.un-documents.net/wced-ocf.htm

Chapter 7

Territorializing Resource Conflicts in "Post-Neoliberal" Bolivia: Hydrocarbon Development and Indigenous Land Titling in TCO Itika Guasu

Penelope Anthias

Introduction

For lowland indigenous peoples in Bolivia, neoliberalism brought both threats and opportunities. On the one hand, neoliberal economic restructuring intensified the incursions of extractive industries in their lands, producing profound social and environmental impacts. On the other hand, multicultural reform created a new package of cultural rights for indigenous peoples, among them the opportunity to gain collective title to their ancestral territories, recognized in 1996 as Original Communal Lands (TCOs). Less than a decade later, a neoliberal government was swept aside by a wave of popular mobilization, heralding the beginning of a new era of cultural and resource politics. Yet, for all the transformations of the Morales era, this double movement—the expansion of an indigenous rights framework accompanied by the advance of the extractives frontier—has continued.

This chapter explores the dynamics produced when these two logics, of extractive development on one hand, and cultural rights on the other, collide in particular territories. It does so by focusing on one indigenous group's struggle to gain legal title to their TCO territory in the midst of a new wave of hydrocarbon development. This is a struggle that began in the late 1990s but continues under the current government of Evo Morales. By examining these parallel struggles over land and gas as they have unfolded in one territory, the chapter aims to provide a territorialized reading of contemporary resource conflicts in Latin America, which tempers optimism about "post-neoliberal" resource governance and highlights the continuing challenges faced by indigenous populations engaged in struggles for territorial control and resource justice.

As the introduction to this book makes clear, any discussion of resource justice must take into account questions of redistribution, recognition, and representation. Yet, as well as considering how effectively these "three Rs" are addressed by specific resource governance regimes, it is important to reflect on how resources figure within broader postcolonial struggles for social justice. Although extraction creates new dynamics, it also maps onto existing geographies of power produced through uneven processes of colonization, nation building, and social struggle. Across Latin America, these racialized geographies are being challenged and transformed in a variety of ways by indigenous movements. How is the "new extraction" (Bebbington, 2009b) affecting these broader transformations? This question is particularly pertinent in Bolivia, where state-led hydrocarbons development is now framed as the basis for "plurinational" and "decolonizing" development. By placing a recent hydrocarbons conflict in the context of a broader indigenous struggle for land and territory, I aim to provide some initial reflections.

The chapter is structured as follows. It begins by placing the *guaraní* land struggle in Itika Guasu in two key contexts: the postcolonial and the neoliberal. It then describes how hydrocarbons development in the TCO shaped—and ultimately jeopardized—indigenous land rights, by mapping onto a racialized geography of rights at the very moment that this faced transformation. It then explores why this occurred, arguing that indigenous land rights became intimately connected with a series of other indigenous claims in the context of extraction. The chapter then goes on to describe how the dynamics of this conflict have shifted under the Morales government (since 2006) and what resources the *guaraní* have drawn on to achieve recognition of their demands. The chapter is based on fieldwork conducted in Tarija department in 2008–2009 and 2011. Key methods include in-depth interviewing, community-level participant observation and analysis of documents, and cartographic data.

Postcolonial Territory: The Struggle for Land Rights in Itika Guasu

The *guaraní*, Bolivia's largest lowland indigenous group, continue to live primarily within their ancestral lands in the Chaco, a semi-arid but biodiverse plain extending over parts of Bolivia, Paraguay, Argentina, and Brazil. In Bolivia, *guaraní* communities live in parts of Santa Cruz, Chuquisaca, and Tarija departments. Itika Guasu is the largest *guaraní* area in Tarija, located in a transitional zone between the sub-Andean valleys and the Chaco. Although the *guaraní* were not defeated militarily until the 1890s, the following century proved devastating, as waves of colonization left them dispossessed, marginalized, and, in many cases, trapped in exploitative labor relations. Although initially driven by an expanding cattle ranching economy, the colonization of the Chaco was consistently aided by state attempts to "seat sovereignty" in this resource-rich region. In the period after the Chaco war with Paraguay (1932–1935), which is still framed in Bolivia as an oil conflict, excombatants were encouraged to occupy gas-rich lands, whose dispersed and largely indigenous population was seen as insufficient to guard against future incursions. Early hydrocarbons development, which began in the 1920s, assisted this process of colonization by opening up roads into formerly inaccessible areas of the Chaco and facilitating their settlement (Octavio, 2008). During the 1952 agrarian reform, which had an explicit agenda of lowland colonization, many of these new settlers acquired land rights, leading to a more aggressive occupation of indigenous lands and the spread of exploitative labor practices.

By the 1980s, most *guaraní* of Itika Guasu, who had not migrated to Argentina, were either enslaved under a system of debt bondage on *haciendas* or living a precarious existence on marginal land. It was in this context that these communities began to organize in 1987, following contact with *guaraní* leaders from the neighboring department of Chuquisaca. In 1989, the *guaraní* of Itika Guasu established their own territorial organization, the *Asamblea del Pueblo Guaraní Itika Guasu* (Guaraní People's Assembly Itika Guasu—APG IG). Land rights were quickly identified by the new organization as key to breaking dependency on *patrones* and establishing the basis for alternative livelihoods. In 1996, the APG IG's territorial demand was among those presented by the *guaraní* following the lowland indigenous March for Territory and Dignity, which took place as a new agrarian reform law, the INRA Law (which established TCOs), was being debated in Congress. A year later, Itika Guasu was formally recognized as a TCO and began the long and complex titling process, known as SAN-TCO. Among other stages, this process involves the evaluation of private "third-party" claims within the TCO, which may be recognized alongside the collective land rights of indigenous claimants. The state is obliged to compensate indigenous claimants for any privately titled land, either with land adjacent to the TCO or by expropriating private land owners.

Although there is not space here to do justice to this history of indigenous dispossession and resurgence, this brief description gives an indication of what was at stake in TCO titling for the *guaraní* of Itika Guasu. Beyond its legal complexities, TCO titling promised a radical transformation of ethnic power relations in a region where indigenous people had never before been imagined as rights-bearing citizens. As various scholars have noted, "maps and indigeneity are not alone sufficient for transforming [colonial] power relations" (Bryan, 2009, p. 31; see also Sletto, 2009). Indeed, as a tool for realizing indigenous aspirations for "territory," TCO titling has received numerous critiques, mainly from indigenous peoples themselves (Almaraz, 2002; Paredes & Canedo, 2008). However, in a context where indigenous peoples had few options available to them, TCO titling did become a central, if imperfect, tool within a broader decolonizing project.

Two Faces of Neoliberalism: The INRA Law and the Law of Capitalization

If the land struggle in Itika Guasu emerged from a specific regional history of colonization, then it must also be placed in a broader context: that of neoliberalism, implemented in Bolivia from the mid-1980s. The general characteristics of neoliberalism and the specific ways in which it played out in Bolivia have been described in detail elsewhere (see especially Kohl & Farthing, 2006; and Perreault, 2006). Here, it is sufficient to note a few of the ways in which neoliberal reform enabled, motivated, and ultimately conditioned the *guaraní* struggle for land rights in Itika Guasu.

Guaraní organization in Itika Guasu was part of a wave of indigenous resurgence throughout lowland Bolivia (and Latin America more broadly) from the late 1980s, which emerged through articulation with emergent transnational networks of development actors promoting indigenous rights (Andolina, Radcliffe & Laurie, 2005; Gustafson, 2009; Valdivia, 2005). At the same time, lowland indigenous mobilization for land rights occurred in a context where these peoples were facing increasing incursions from extractive industries in their lands, as a result of neoliberal economic restructuring. These reforms, which began in 1985, included the gradual privatization of state-owned companies and measures to promote foreign direct investment, particularly in extractive industries.

These new threats and opportunities were of course not unrelated, as Hale's (2002) concept of "neoliberal multiculturalism" makes explicit. According to Hale, "proponents of the neoliberal doctrine pro-actively endorse a substantive, if limited, version of indigenous cultural rights, as a means to resolve their own problems and advance their own political agendas" (p. 487). Indeed, the INRA Law formed part of a package of multicultural reforms implemented during the mid-1990s, alongside a second wave of neoliberal reform, which included the capitalization and restructuring of the hydrocarbons sector (Hindery, 2004; Kohl & Farthing, 2006). These investment-friendly policies fuelled a boom in hydrocarbons development, particularly in Tarija where key gas reserves are located beneath indigenous ancestral lands.

I have referred to these two contexts, the postcolonial and the neoliberal, because the story that follows is partly about the "contingent articulations" (Tsing, 2005) that emerged between cultural rights, extractive development, and the racialized geographies of one territory. As the following sections show, these articulations created a set of contradictory, and at times explosive, dynamics that emerged during the late 1990s and have continued to play out under the government of Evo Morales.

TCO Titling and Hydrocarbons Development in Itika Guasu 1996–2006

"Recalcitrant Elites," Intransigent Institutions

In a context where colonial discourses and power structures remained largely intact, TCO titling faced multiple obstacles from the outset. During the early years of the titling process, *guaraní* leaders were met with violent threats from local cattle ranchers, which evolved into coordinated actions to obstruct the progress of land titling by exerting pressure on regional institutions. The effectiveness of this opposition was aided by the fact that regional institutions, including the land reform agency, INRA, remained governed by elites who were generally hostile to indigenous land rights. Equally obstructive was a lack of political will to recognize indigenous territorial claims at the national level. The incorporation of TCOs within the INRA Law had been a reluctant concession to indigenous and donor pressure by the neoliberal government of Gonzalo Sanchez de Lozada, which remained ideologically committed to a market-led model of agrarian reform.

These obstacles at least partly account for the poor results of TCO titling in Itika Guasu. Today, 14 years after the TCO was legally established, the *guaraní* of Itika Guasu have received title to 90,539.9 hectares, 38 percent of the total TCO area (see figure 7.1). This area is discontinuous, interspersed with private properties, and generally the least productive land in the TCO. These obstacles and results echo those witnessed in other TCOs in Bolivia during this period (Guzmán et al., 2007).

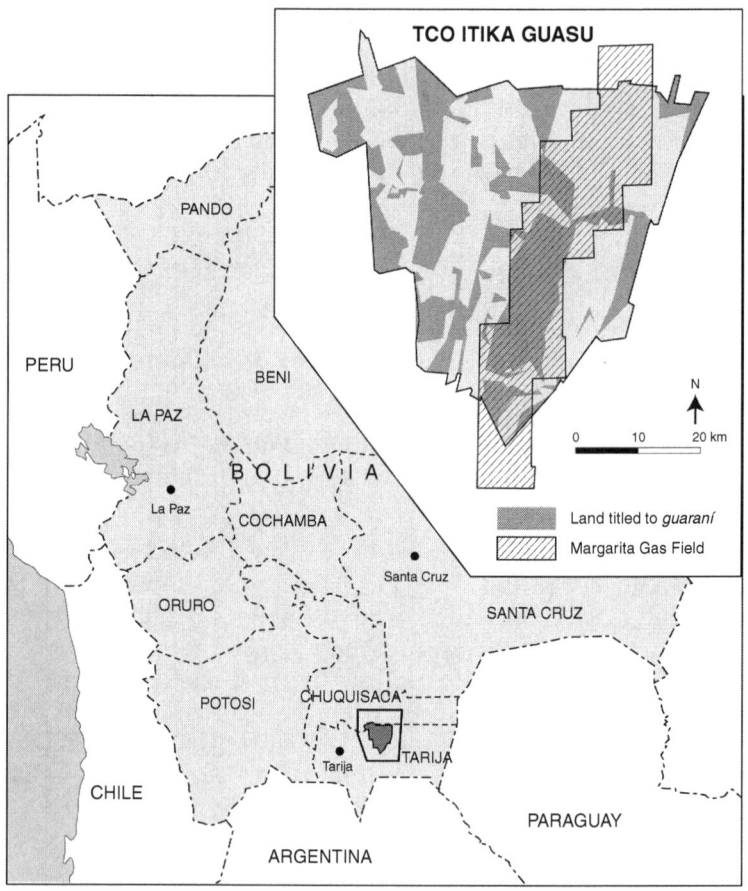

Figure 7.1 Location of TCO Itika Guasu and Margarita Gas Field in Bolivia

Securing Rights for Capital: Repsol's Arrival in TCO Itika Guasu

There was the TCO but inside there was a third party who said "this is my property: here is your property, here is mine." What Repsol did is enter this property, measured but still without title, entered and said, "I want to work in your property. That is to say, renting a part of your land, I'm going to work here, I want to live here." Repsol settles there, was a tenant . . . INRA legally certified this case. I told them clearly that they were concentrating on conserving the huge interests; INRA knew, loads of people knew, but they preferred not to admit it, to let [Repsol] settle, and give them security of where to live. (APG IG leader, interview with author, April 2009, Tarija)

TCO Itika Guasu overlies Margarita Gas Field, which forms part of what is undisputedly Bolivia's largest gas field (indicated in figure 7.1). Beginning in 1997, Margarita Gas Field (or Campo Margarita, part of the Caipipendi Block) has been operated by the Spanish company Repsol YPF, which shares the concession with its partners British Gas and Pan American Energy (a subsidiary of BP).

Repsol signed a mixed-risk contract with YPFB (*Yacimientos Petroliferos Fiscales Bolivianos*) for activities in Caipipendi Block on May 14, 1997, nearly two months after the TCO was officially recognized. Shortly afterward, the company began its operations in Campo Margarita, including the drilling of four gas wells and the construction of a processing plant, airstrip, and access roads. This meant that the TCO was in a legal state of "immobilization" throughout the course of Repsol's activities. Under this status, all property rights within the TCO are subject to revision and indigenous claimants have priority rights until private titles have been awarded.

In spite of this, when Repsol entered TCO Itika Guasu in 1997, the APG IG were not informed of planned activities. Instead, the company established its operations within properties claimed by non-indigenous cattle ranchers, with whom it signed land-use agreements and negotiated compensation payments. Legally, these contracts must be negotiated with the legal proprietor of the required land. In this case, however, they were made with third-party claimants within the TCO whose land rights had not been established. It is important to note that, during the course of the TCO titling process, third-party claimants may be awarded titles or may have land confiscated or reduced, depending on a variety of factors, including whether land is used productively (fulfills an Economic Social Funcion, or FES).

Evaluating these claims requires extensive fieldwork; for example, in a cattle ranching region like Itika Guasu, evaluation of the FES requires the rounding up, marking, and counting of cattle, a time-consuming process carried out with participation of indigenous monitors. Predicting the final results of TCO titling without conducting fieldwork activities is impossible.

In fact, official documentation from INRA's fieldwork (conducted in 2000) suggests that several claimants with whom Repsol negotiated were ultimately unable to prove productive use of their properties. Although the titling process highlighted problems faced in justifying these claims, so far none of this land has been awarded to the *guaraní*. Not only did the land-use agreements preempt the results of land titling, but there is also evidence that in at least one case Repsol's presence influenced them. In the case of an airstrip, it appears that infrastructure built by Repsol was used as evidence of productive land use, thereby legitimizing the individual claimant's property rights (fieldwork interviews, see also *Asamblea del Pueblo Guaraní de Itika Guasu*, 2005).

Having heard varying accounts of INRA's collusion in legally validating these land-use contracts, I asked the agency's former director on what legal basis this occurred. He explained that the agreements had been validated on the basis of titles awarded following the 1952 agrarian reform. Beyond the fact that all preexisting titles were legally subject to revision under the SAN-TCO titling process, their existence in these properties is noteworthy. INRA documentation produced at the start of the TCO titling process suggests that a minority of nonindigenous inhabitants of Itika Guasu possessed formal land titles in 1997. Those that did so, represent the longest-standing and most powerful landowning families of the region. In fact, almost all Repsol's infrastructure is located in what were formerly two of the region's largest *haciendas*.

As noted above, the awarding of titles to *mestizo* settlers in this region after the first agrarian reform was instrumental to *guaraní* dispossession, and based on colonial discourses that excluded them from citizenship rights. It is precisely this geography of rights that the TCO titling process set out to transform. However, just at the moment when these ethnoterritorial power relations were set to be reconfigured, the emergent geography of extraction mapped onto and secured them. For the *guaraní*, INRA's willingness to sacrifice their rights to provide legal security for Repsol represents the latest link in a chain of historical collusions between the state and local elites in this region.

Land Rights as a Basis for Other Indigenous Rights

What [Repsol] said is: "If you're not owners of the territory, while you're not owners of the territory, you can't question the work we're doing." It couldn't be clearer. (Representative of CERDET, interview with author, May 2009, Tarija).

Whereas the land-use agreements described above initially took place without the knowledge of the *guaraní*, the agreements were to become subject to extensive scrutiny and contestation in the context of an ensuing conflict over indigenous rights and hydrocarbon development in TCO Itika Guasu. As the social and environmental impacts of extraction became apparent (see *Asamblea del Pueblo Guaraní de Itika Guasu*, 2005; Perreault, 2008), the *guaraní* began to make sustained claims for the recognition of their rights. These claims were articulated with reference to the International Labour Organization (ILO) Convention 169 (ratified by Bolivia in 1991), which requires governments and companies to consult with the peoples living on the land prior to permitting resource exploitation, and states that they should participate in the benefits of such activities and receive "fair compensation" for any damages they sustain as a result of these activities (Articles 6 and 15). In 2003, the APG IG complained about their lack of consultation and demanded land-use payments, compensation for social and environmental impacts and measures to monitor and address these impacts. This was the beginning of a long and bitter dispute that was not resolved until late 2010 (discussed below).

It was in this context that the APG IG began to scrutinize the means by which Repsol had established itself in the TCO and identified the legally dubious land-use contracts as a means by which the company had sought to avoid recognizing their rights. The *guaraní* first raised the issue of the land-use contracts in a meeting with Repsol's subcontractor, Maxus, in February 2003, where they demanded land use payments. According to an activist who participated in this meeting:

> [Maxus said:] "We've sorted it out; we've paid land use payments to the owners." And there the answer was: "There are no owners precisely because all rights are under a process of revision. And the preferential right is with the [guaraní] people, with the TCO. So if you've paid, you've paid wrong, you've paid before knowing who is the final owner, you've paid wrong." And if in the end they determine that the owner is different from who they paid, the company would have to pay again. Because to pay wrong is to pay double, isn't it? (Activist, interview with author, May 2009, Tarija).

In March, Maxus flatly rejected this claim in a letter to the APG IG. Later that month, another meeting was held, this time between the APG IG, Maxus, and INRA, in which INRA officials were called upon by the APG IG "to explain the situation of the land titling process in Itika Guasu, through which companies should respect the preferential right of the APG and mitigate the environmental impact" (CERDET, 2003). In April, following a complaint by the APG IG to the ministry of hydrocarbons, Maxus agreed to fund a development plan proposed by the APG IG and to make payments based on the market value of land. However, the agreement was framed as a goodwill gesture and explicitly rejected the *guaraní's* rights to consultation or compensation.

These concessions failed to satisfy the *guaraní* and on May 28, 2003, they blockaded the Margarita Bridge, bringing extractive activity to a halt. Within days, the government had ordered a military division from Villamontes to break up the demonstration. In the months that followed, the APG IG and Maxus reached a compromise over land-use payments and signed the final version of the first development plan, which remained a voluntary agreement.

However, the APG IG's battle with Maxus and Repsol for recognition of its rights continued in the years that followed and the land-use agreements continued to resurface as a pretext for defending or contesting other *guaraní* claims. In 2006, an APG IG environmental monitoring team sent to inspect the four gas wells concluded in a report: "This terrain is property of the TCO, for which reason they should have consulted, given that it is in a process of land titling and therefore immobilized" (*Asamblea del Pueblo Guaraní de Itika Guasu*, 2007). Repsol responded with a document entitled "Social-environmental development in Caipipendi Block," in which it claimed:

> All the contracts made with proprietors of the zone, called third parties by the indigenous were made following verification of their property rights, certified by the same National Institute of Agrarian Reform, so that the air strip, the gas wells, the Margarita plant and other installations are found in properties that will be titled to the said third parties. (Repsol, 2006)

This letter explicitly rejects the APG IG's claim to consultation on the basis that the properties hosting its operations belonged to third parties and not to the *guaraní*. In the years that followed, Repsol continued to refuse to recognize either *guaraní* land rights or their right to consultation and compensation.

Cultural Rights versus Neoliberal Capitalism?

That Repsol's demand for legal security should trump the *guaraní's* still unconsolidated territorial claim may not appear surprising. Recent political ecology literature has provided numerous examples of how processes of capitalist territorial restructuring shape the rules and institutions that govern access to and control of natural resources, often to the detriment of poor resource-dependent communities (Bebbington 2009a; Bury, 2005; Holt-Giménez, 2007; Le Billon, 2001; Peet & Watts, 2004; Sawyer, 2004; Tsing 2005). The above discussion echoes these accounts, revealing how a neoliberal state ultimately privileged the territorial requirements of transnational capital over the *guaraní's* legally recognized rights to their TCO. However, this was not simply a case of the state enacting policies and laws that from the outset favored private companies; what we see instead is the flexible implementation of a legal norm originally designed to recognize the cultural rights of indigenous peoples. This is important because recent critiques of cultural rights have tended to rest on their assumed compatibility with neoliberal economic development (Hale, 2002; 2005). According to Hale (2005), "collective land rights actually help advance the neoliberal model by rationalizing land tenure, reducing the potential for chaos and conflict" (p. 13). The case of Repsol in Itika Guasu suggests that, as a governmental fix, indigenous land rights may work better in theory than in practice. In terms of limiting the destructive effects of neoliberal development on indigenous peoples, it is in territories targeted for extraction that indigenous land rights are most needed. However, it is precisely in these territories, like TCO Itika Guasu, that these rights are most likely to be subordinated to economic development.

The above account of neoliberal resource governance in Itika Guasu provides an important counterpoint to the discussion that follows. As has been well documented (Kohl & Farthing, 2006; Perreault 2006; Postero, 2010), the election of Evo Morales as Bolivia's president in 2005 was, broadly speaking, the product of a social responses to neoliberalism and, more specifically, popular demand for a more just regime of hydrocarbons governance. At the same time, however, Morales's election was the product of a broader set of indigenous demands directed at addressing Bolivia's colonial legacy. These demands centered on the vision of a "plurinational" state, which would offer new forms of participation and more substantive rights for indigenous peoples. How have these two shifts—from multicultural to plurinational governance, and from private to state-led extraction—affected the way resource conflicts are managed? By describing how the intertwined struggles over land and gas in Itika Guasu continued to unfold under Morales's Movement to Socialism (MAS) government (2006–2011), the next section highlights some of the changes, continuities, and contradictions that this project has entailed.

Extraction, TCO Titling and Indigenous Rights Under the MAS Government 2006–2011

Frustrated Hopes, Mounting Tensions

Part of the dispute cited above, over land rights as a basis for other rights, occurred in 2006—that is, after Morales took office. As this example suggests, the election of an indigenous president did not bring an immediate resolution to the APG IG's unfulfilled demands. To the contrary, the early years of the Morales government saw an intensification of this conflict, as the *guaraní* became increasingly impatient at the new state's apparent reluctance to recognize their rights. *Guaraní* leaders describe how their repeated appeals to the Morales government for support in their ongoing battle with Repsol were consistently met with silence or evasion. As one *guaraní* leader complained in 2009:

> To date, [the government] haven't reached any conclusion about who is right, the APG or the company – they keep telling us: "No, we haven't reached a conclusion." We've already shown them all the documentation, but all the government has done is to remain silent. How can they say they guarantee indigenous rights when there are guilty parties who have committed violations and contamination, social and cultural impacts? (APG IG leader, interview with author, April 2009, Tarija)

The *guaraní* were told by the government that their negotiation with Repsol was between "private parties" and that the state could not intervene. Another leader described the exchange as follows:

> In negotiations [the government says]: "You are the people of Itika, you're a private people, it's a negotiation between the oil company and you." The reply of the organization: "No, you're the father of the nation; you have to comply with the law, not the oil company." (APG IG leader, interview with author, April 2009, Tarija)

In July 2010, the APG IG sent a letter to Morales, who they addressed as "the President of the Plurinational State," expressing their anger at the granting of 20 new environmental licenses to companies to operate in the TCO, without prior consultation. Despite significant progress at a national level (Fundación Tierra, 2011), land titling in Itika Guasu has remained practically paralyzed since 2006, partly due to ongoing funding shortages. The APG IG's attempts to secure a share of departmental gas rents for TCO titling in 2009 were thwarted by regional opposition, while attempts to release money from an Indigenous Fund, which receives 5 percent of IDH, were blocked due to the Fund's committee's failure to reach consensus. This Fund was originally demanded by the *guaraní* as direct compensation for the disproportionate effects they suffer from gas extraction. The fact that it came to be shared between indigenous and peasant organizations nationally, with MAS ministers on its committee, is cited by APG IG leaders as an example of this government's betrayal.

Other indigenous territories in Tarija have faced similar problems regarding land titling since 2006 and have become increasingly vocal in expressing their disillusionment (see chapter 2 by Humphreys Bebbington & Bebbington, this volume). This is revealed by the following passage from a statement issued during a recent assembly of Tarija's three indigenous groups:

> With the new governmental administration we held the hope of a better tomorrow for our children, but until now we don't feel a real change in our lives. Even worse, our communities are threatened by the growing advance of the oil and gas industry, the extension of the agricultural frontier, the formation of new elites that take advantage of the gas rents that come from our territories, without us until now having been able to achieve the titling of our lands and territories, and a direct benefit from the resources exploited. (Third Departmental Assembly of the Tapiete, Weenhayek and Guaraní Indigenous Peoples, 2011)

As this passage highlights, indigenous land rights continue to be imagined both as a means of protection from the territorial impacts of extraction and as the basis for claims to participate in its economic benefits. Frustration about the partial implementation of these rights is compounded by the fact that, under the 2009 Constitution, "consolidated indigenous territories" (i.e., titled TCOs) provide what is often to only viable route to indigenous autonomy (Albó & Romero, 2009).

Gas As An Obstacle to TCO Titling Under Morales

In recent years, the frustrations described above have been a subject of extensive debate and analysis by the *guaraní* of Itika Guasu.

In 2008–2009, numerous assemblies were held to discuss the "land issue," which had been the APG IG's main priority over the previous decade. During these discussions, participants often arrived at the same question: "What is the obstacle?" As noted above, obstacles to TCO titling over the previous decade had been numerous. By this point, however, a single explanation had come to the fore. As an APG IG leader explained in 2009:

> If we review the UN Declaration, the ILO, the New Constitution of the current government, the Hydrocarbons Law 3058, it's clear . . . before the government or someone wants to intervene or exploit those resources, they must go through a process of consultation, because it's inside a TCO. And that is not foreseen in the new contracts . . . the reason why we don't advance with the consolidation of the TCOs is that we are going to directly intervene, we're going to demand that they comply with the norm and go through a consultation process, and if it's going to affect us directly, we can say that we don't agree and they're not going to exploit. (APG IG leader, interview with author, April 2009, Tarija)

By 2009, the idea that gas interests represented the main obstacle to the conclusion of TCO titling had gained widespread currency in Itika Guasu. On the one hand, this theory can be seen as emerging from lessons learned over the previous decade: that land rights strengthen other claims in the context of extraction and that transnational companies can gain state collusion to influence the outcomes of titling. In that sense, it points to the *guaraní's* recognition of the *continuity* in state behavior under Morales.

At the same time, however, the above quotation reflects the *guaraní's* understanding of the particular, indeed exacerbated, contradictions between indigenous rights and extraction under the Morales government. As this leader notes, the MAS government has strengthened indigenous rights in the context of extraction in important ways. In 2007, Morales passed decrees to implement the 2005 Hydrocarbons Law, which reaffirms indigenous peoples' right to prior and informed consultation, participation in the benefits of extraction, environmental monitoring in TCOs, and compensation for direct, cumulative, and long-term social, cultural, and environmental impacts. The same year, Bolivia signed up to the United Nations Declaration on the Rights of Indigenous Peoples, which recognizes indigenous peoples' right to not only consultation but also consent in the context of development projects in their lands. The 2009 Constitution also recognizes indigenous peoples' right to prior consultation and participation in the benefits of exploitation of nonrenewable hydrocarbons resources that are found in their territories (articles 30.2, 352, and 403).

As the above quotation also highlights, these changes have been accompanied by the implementation of a new hydrocarbons regime. On May 1, 2006, Morales passed his "Heroes of the Chaco" decree officially "nationalizing" Bolivia's hydrocarbons reserves. Essentially, the new regime consists of higher taxes, the renegotiation of contracts with private companies, and the rebuilding of the state hydrocarbons company, YPFB. Under the new contracts, the remaining 50 percent of revenues, after the royalty (18 percent) and IDH (32 percent), is split evenly between YPFB and the private company, resulting in an overall government share of about 54 percent. These changes have substantially increased national revenue from gas, which now funds a range of social programs, including old-age pensions and benefits for students and expectant mothers. Not only is Bolivia under Morales more dependent than ever on gas revenue, but the state is also committed to bearing the cost of any delay to planned extraction; under the new mixed contracts, YPFB must cover the recoverable costs of private companies operating in Bolivia (Kaup, 2010).

In this context, the implementation of indigenous rights presents a conflict of interest for the Morales government. For example, a consultation process requires the diffusion of detailed information on planned developments and a series of meetings with affected communities and indigenous authorities, which themselves require logistical support, such as transport of people from dispersed and often inaccessible areas. Furthermore, reaching agreement may itself require a lengthy process of negotiation. Given the tight time-frames of contracts with transnational oil companies and gas-receiving countries, this process could easily delay the granting of environmental licenses and ultimately jeopardize production and export targets, the cost of which would be borne by the Bolivian state.

The government's position is made more awkward by the fact that, unlike in the past, it must now negotiate directly with affected communities over planned extraction. As one *guaraní* leader explained, this puts the state in a difficult position regarding compliance with norms on indigenous rights:

> There was a moment when it seemed that it was more the transnationals that were the owners, but now when they sign a contract they are partners, so the moment we consolidate our lands we are going to demand that they comply with the norms. And the government will have to respect that decision, and that creates an internal conflict

between the oil companies who are going to exploit, and the national government, because we [the indigenous people] should come first. (APG IG leader, interview with author, April 2009, Tarija)

That is not to say that state involvement in these negotiations always brings greater accountability. As he went on to explain:

> It's worse talking of Evo Morales being a partner . . . now the oil company says, "we're not alone anymore," it says, "you have to talk directly with the government" and if they authorize [extraction] we have to accept it. (APG IG leader, interview with author, April 2009, Tarija)

This statement, read in conjunction with Morales's reported assertion that "it's a negotiation between the oil company and you," suggests that the new "mixed" contracts may be a pretext for a dual evasion of responsibility for indigenous rights by both transnational oil companies and the Bolivian state.

Shifting Discourses of Land, Gas, and Nation

As the above quotations reveal, in making their claims the *guaraní* have been quick to draw on the new state language of plurinationalism, to cite new legal and constitutional norms guaranteeing their rights, and to point out the reasons why in practice these rights are not implemented. In doing so, they expose fundamental contradictions within the MAS development agenda, undermining the official discourse of a "post-neoliberal" *and* "plurinational" Bolivia. It is perhaps because of this that their demands have provoked an intolerant response by the government. In private negotiations and public discourse, leading figures of the Morales government have repeatedly accused the *guaraní* of Itika Guasu of being "a threat to the country's energy development" and dismissed claims to consultation and compensation as *chantaje* (blackmail).

Although this is not the first time a state has sought to delegitimize indigenous claims in the context of extraction, the tone of this discourse has shifted. In a context where nationalized gas reserves are portrayed as the basis for social development, those who contest extraction are increasingly framed as a threat, not only to the state, but also the Bolivian people. For a people whose claims to rights are an expression of a fragile and recently granted citizenship, these accusations are particularly difficult to absorb. Increasingly, the *guaraní* have sought to defend themselves from such allegations, often by emphasizing that they do not oppose extraction per se. As an APG IG leader insisted:

> The underlying fear is that . . . if they give us the TCOs with our resource wealth we´re not going to give them permission to explore the natural resources. And that's a lie . . . if the project guarantees, respects indigenous rights, the peoples are always going to say "go ahead, work" because its development for the country. (APG IG leader, interview with author, April 2009, Tarija)

However, this has not discouraged the *guaraní* from making claims; for it is precisely through the act of claiming rights that the *guaraní* experience and reaffirm their citizenship; as one *guaraní* leader put it, "If you don't make them comply with the law, no one else will; you as a citizen have to say: '*Compañeros*, I have a law'." In doing so, they defend a vision of plurinationalism, positioning themselves among the true architects and beneficiaries of this national project, which is being undermined not by their claims, but by the state's denial of their rights. This is often frequently conveyed through an analogy of denied paternity; as another leader concluded: "what the government is doing is as if you had a son and you don't want to defend him."

Shifting Strategies of Land and Gas

I have already provided some indications of how land titling and hydrocarbons development began to converge in indigenous-state negotiations under the Morales government. First, the *guaraní* now found themselves negotiating more directly with the state over the terms of extraction (or at least attempting to do so) at the same time their demands for TCO titling were being increasingly scaled-up from a regional to a national level. Second, the *guaraní* became increasingly convinced that hydrocarbon development was preventing the titling of their TCO, as part of a company-state conspiracy to evade recognizing their other rights. In light of this, it is perhaps not surprising that the APG IG began to strategically link the land and gas issues in their negotiations with the state.

The first attempt came in the form of an ultimatum. In February 2009, the APG IG sent a letter to Evo Morales relating the decision that no type of operations in *guaraní* territory would be allowed until titling of the TCO was completed. The letter was discussed in a departmental assembly held in April. Although the APG IG had not received a reply from Morales, it was claimed by the leaders at the meeting that the letter had succeeded in delaying the granting of authorization to two other oil companies for operations in the TCO. Based on this achievement, participants reflected on the success of this approach. As one leader concluded: "it is necessary to reach decision-making political bodies, and finally realise that the hydrocarbons issue is intimately linked to the titling issue" (APG IG minutes). However, whatever ripples of unease it generated for the government, this ultimatum did not succeed in achieving either an advance on TCO titling or a cessation of hydrocarbon development in the TCO.

A few months later, the two issues were once again brought together. In May 2009, the APG IG wrote to the ministry of land requesting the *suspension* of the TCO titling process. Ironically, this occurred just as INRA Tarija had secured funding to continue with the SAN-TCO process following several years of paralysis. The letter provides some insight into the reasons for this sudden u-turn. It begins by criticizing INRA's failure to provide requested information on land titling and expresses frustration over the fragmentary effects of partial titling. The next passage is worth quoting at length:

> [The APG demands] the annulment of all the assignments to irregular third parties, that is, those who have violated their resource rights and/or [expressed] opposition to the APG IG and, the priority in this annulment should be all the assignments that coincide with the oil and gas exploitation or transport pipelines that pass through the TCO, making clear that none of the companies that are found operating in the TCO have complied with the rights to prior consultation, nor with the procedures for calculation of damages, for which reason ALL are operating illegally and don't have the corresponding environmental licences . . . all this demonstrates the total lack of defence of, and permanent violation of, our most elemental rights, including to property.
> (*Asamblea del Pueblo Guaraní de Itika Guasu*, 2009)

This passage reveals that the APG IG's decision to paralyze the land titling process was at least partly driven by concern that the process would consolidate third-party claims within gas-rich areas of the TCO and, in doing so, weaken indigenous claims in the context of new and ongoing hydrocarbons projects. The resurgence of this issue (who owns land demarcated for extraction) points to striking continuities in resource conflicts under the Morales government, where the territorializing effects of extraction continue to collide with indigenous rights, and potentially jeopardize their implementation. The APG

IG's decision can be read as an attempt to preempt a repeat of the experiences of 1997–2003, when third-party land rights were used by Repsol as a basis for denying the *guaraní's* claims to compensation. At the same time, however, this change is framed by APG IG leaders as an important shift in strategy on land titling, based on the possibilities of the new political context. Rather than simply waiting in vain for INRA to complete the legal titling process, APG IG leaders now believe that they can get faster and surer results by purchasing private properties within the TCO. The potential for success of this strategy remains unclear, as do the possible terms of negotiations over land purchases. However, it does represent an important departure from the recent history of TCO titling in Itika, where an imperfect law (the INRA Law) was tirelessly wielded by *guaraní* leaders as the only means of extracting rights from hostile regional elites and an ambivalent neoliberal state.

Of course, the crucial issue that arises is: How does the APG IG propose to pay for these properties? The answer is also provided in the letter. The cost of purchasing land, it proposes, will be met by a loan to the APG IG from the Indigenous Fund (see above), which "will be underwritten by the nationalised oil companies present in the TCO, that is, Transredes and YPFB." The repayment of these loans, the letter proposes, should be deducted from the payments that (the companies) should make to the APG IG for environmental licenses and compensation for damages. In other words, the proposal is that land titling be *overseen by* the APG IG and *funded by* a combination of gas rents (distributed to the APG IG) and anticipated compensation payments from ongoing hydrocarbons development in the TCO. Paradoxically, while hydrocarbon development has consistently been identified by APG IG leaders as the single biggest obstacle to the consolidation of their territorial rights, it is increasingly through negotiations over extraction that it seems possible to advance with the land struggle.

Extracting Justice? The *Acuerdo de Amistad*

The above account has described how the APG IG have sought to defend their rights under the Morales government in ways that make explicit the links between land titling and hydrocarbons development. However, this is only one part of the story. Parallel to their negotiations with the state, the APG IG was engaged in a process of negotiation with Repsol that took place in a transnational arena. As I have described, the APG IG's battle for recognition of their rights began with support from two Bolivian nongovernmental organizations (NGOs), *Centro de Estudios Aplicados a los Derechos Económicos Sociales y Culturales* (Centre for Applied Studies of Economic, Social and Cultural Rights—CEADESC), and *Tarijeño Regional Research Centre* (Centre for Regional Studies of Tarija—CERDET). In 2006, these NGOs and the APG IG participated in an international campaign led by INTERMON-OXFAM entitled *"Repsol mata"* (Repsol kills), which sought to publicize the social and environmental impacts of Repsol's activities in Bolivia (see *Asamblea del Pueblo Guaraní de Itika Guasu*, 2005). As part of this campaign, NGO representatives accompanied APG IG leaders to Madrid, where they visited Repsol's international headquarters. Although no agreement was reached between the APG IG and Repsol in the subsequent negotiations, the trip led to the forging of new transnational alliances and an important shift in the APG IG strategy. Shortly afterward, the APG IG began a formal relationship with two European legal advocacy groups, who waged an international legal campaign against Repsol that played out over the next four years.

The negotiations described above, including the paralysis of TCO titling, occurred while this legal campaign was still underway and its outcome uncertain. This situation changed in December 2010, when the APG IG and Repsol signed a historic *Acuerdo de Amistad* (Agreement of Friendship). This agreement, which coincided with the beginning of a new wave of hydrocarbon development in the TCO, includes the payment of USD14.8 million into an "Investment Fund" for indigenous development coadministered by Repsol and the APG IG. Under the terms of the agreement, Repsol has for the first time recognized the APG IG's rights under international law, *and*— something APG IG rarely omit to mention—their property rights to the entire area of the TCO. Speaking at the APG IG's twenty-second anniversary in March 2011, the president of the organization claimed:

> We have signed without renouncing our rights and achieving full legal recognition of our property rights to the TCO and of the existence of the APG IG. We are proud of this agreement, which brings together some special conditions that makes it unique in Bolivia and even in Latin America . . . [Its principles] will serve as an example to other indigenous communities. (Speech by President of APG IG, 22nd anniversary of the foundation of APG IG, Ñaurenda, 23 March, 2011)

There is not scope here for a discussion of all aspects of this agreement, or the dynamics it has created within and beyond TCO Itika

Guasu. What is important to note here is the continuing importance of "scale-jumping" as a strategy for indigenous rights advocacy under the Morales government. That this struggle for indigenous rights should be resolved in an international arena, without participation of the Bolivian state, is perhaps surprising. It certainly runs counter to official discourse of a "post-neoliberal" Bolivia, where "an empowered state" (empowered by its sovereignty over the nation's gas wealth) was to "provide a protective shield for the social movements, an international armour for the growth of the social struggles" (Bolivian Vice President Garcia Linera, see Garcia, 2007).

And yet, even if this agreement was reached through transnational legal advocacy, it is in the context of the APG IG's relationship with the state and regional actors that it acquires meaning. APG IG leaders frequently frame the Investment Fund as a route to achieving not only territorial development, but also political autonomy. By establishing a degree of economic independence, they hope to transcend the kinds of co-optation and conditionality that have characterized their relationship with the state and regional elites—not least under the Morales government. Perhaps even more powerful is the question of recognition. By engaging with international law and acting through transnational alliances, the APG IG leaders feel they have found a way to force other actors to respect their rights, and to transcend the colonial power dynamics that have defined their engagements with the *karai* (non-*guaraní* people).

Ultimately, then, it is through their transnational alliances, and not through trade-offs with the state, that the APG IG have advanced furthest in securing recognition of their rights. In doing so, they have established a new and uncharted course for territorial development in Itika Guasu—a concept that has been redefined by and partially reconciled with, the reality of ongoing hydrocarbon development in the TCO.

Conclusions

This chapter has drawn attention to the continuities, as well as the novel characteristics, of resource governance under the Morales government. There is little doubt that this government is delivering, as promised, a very different regime for distributing gas rents and a renewed role for the state in the extractive process. And, of course, state-led extraction is only one aspect of a multifaceted "process of change" currently taking place in Bolivia. Yet, it is important to be attentive to the challenges and contradictions that this project is giving rise to.

Through an examination of the *guaraní* struggle for land rights in Itika Guasu amidst ongoing hydrocarbons development, I have shown that indigenous rights—both to territory and to meaningful participation in hydrocarbons governance—continue to be subordinated to the territorial and temporal demands of natural gas extraction. This subordination becomes ever more visible and contested in a political context that combines an official discourse of plurinationalism with increased state dependence on, and state involvement in, extraction. This is not simply a conflict between local claims and transnational, or more recently national-transnational, capitalist interests. From the outset, indigenous demands for territory have been framed with reference to global legal norms, which were translated into national policy in the 1990s in the form of TCOs and other multicultural rights. On the other hand, transnational companies do not merely swoop down from above to extract gas; they must navigate existing geographies, negotiate land use with local actors, and establish legal security from the state, represented by whatever individuals happens to occupy state functions within a specific regional context. It is in this process of territorialization that colonial geographies of power become enlisted, reproduced, and potentially reworked.

As I have shown, in their struggle to establish their territorial rights and negotiate participation in the benefits of extraction, the *guaraní* have employed diverse strategies and acted at multiple scales. Under the Morales government, they have grounded their claims with reference to new national legal norms and discourse on indigenous rights, defending a vision of a plurinational citizenship that they themselves helped to construct. Furthermore, by demanding direct negotiations with central government over land and gas, they have shifted the scale of both these struggles, circumventing elite-controlled regional institutions in the case of land titling, and seeking to bring the state to account for the actions of a transnational oil company. Ultimately, however, it is by acting through transnational networks and outside of the state that the APG IG leaders believe they have finally succeeded in "extracting justice" in their decade-long battle with Repsol. How far this success will redefine aspirations or strategies for territorial development in TCO Itika Guasu, and whether it will become a precedent for other indigenous struggles over territory and natural resources, remains to be seen.

References

Albó, X., & Romero, C. (2009). *Autonomías Indígenas en la Realidad Boliviana y su Nueva Constitución*. La Paz, Bolivia: Vicepresidencia del Estado Plurinacional de Bolivia.

RESOURCE CONFLICTS IN BOLIVIA 151

Almaraz, A. (2002). *Tierras Comunitarios de Origen: Saneamiento y titilación: Guía para el patrocinio jurídico.* Santa Cruz, Bolivia: Centro de Estudios Jurídicos y Investigación Social

Andolina, R., Radcliffe, S., & Laurie, N. (2005). Development and culture: Transnational identity-making in Bolivia. *Political Geography, 24,* 678–702.

Asamblea del Pueblo Guaraní de Itika Guasu. (2005, December). *Impactos Ambientales, Sociales y Culturales de REPSOL YPF en Territorios Indígenas de Bolivia.* Programa de Vigilancia Socio Ambiental de las Industrias Extractivas. Santa Cruz, Bolivia: CEADESC.

Asamblea del Pueblo Guaraní de Itika Guasu. (2007). *Inspección in Situ de las Operaciones de Repsol YPF en el Campo Margarita del 11 al 14 de Octubre de 2006.* Programa de Vigilancia Socio Ambiental de las Industrias Extractivas. Santa Cruz, Bolivia: CEADESC.

Asamblea del Pueblo Guaraní de Itika Guasu. (2009) *Letter to Alejandro Almaraz, Minister of land, Bolivia,* 27 August. Unpublished. Entre Rios, Bolivia: APG IG.

Bebbington, A. (2009a). Latin America: Contesting extraction, producing geographies. *Singapore Journal of Tropical Geography, 30*(1), 7–12.

Bebbington, A. (2009b, September/October). The new extraction: Rewriting the political ecology of the Andes? *NACLA Report on the Americas, 42*(5), 12–20, 39–40.

Bryan, J. (2009). Where would we be without them? Knowledge, space and power in indigenous politics. *Futures, 41,* 24–32.

Bury, J. (2005). Mining mountains: Neoliberalism, land tenure, livelihoods, and the new Peruvian mining industry in Cajamarca. *Environment and Planning A, 37,* 221–239.

CERDET. (2003). *Memoria de las Negociaciones Entre la Asamblea del Pueblo Guaraní y la Empresa Petrolera Maxus con el Asoramiento de CERDET.* Unpublished note.

Fundación Tierra. (2011, July). *Territorios Indígena Originario Campesinos en Bolivia: Entre la Loma Santa y la Pachamama.* Informe 2010. La Paz, Bolivia: Fundación TIERRA.

Garcia, A. (2007, January 15). Neo-liberalism and the new socialism—Speech by Alvaro Garcia Linera (W. T. Whitney Jr., Trans.). *Political Affairs.* Retrieved February 9, 2012, from http://www.politicalaffairs.net/neo-liberalism-and-the-new-socialism-speech-by-alvaro-garcia-linera

Gustafson, B. (2009). *New languages of the state: Indigenous resurgence and the politics of knowledge in Bolivia.* Durham: Duke University Press.

Guzmán, I., Núñez, E., Pati, P., Urapotina, J., Valdez, M., & Montecinos, A. (2007). *Saneamiento de la Tierra en Seis Regiones de Bolivia 1996-2007.* La Paz, Bolivia: Centro de Investigación y Promoción del Campesinado (CIPCA).

Hale, C. R. (2002). Does multiculturalism menace? Governance, cultural rights and the politics of identity in Guatemala. *Journal of Latin American Studies, 34,* 485–524.

Hale, C. R. (2005). Neoliberal multiculturalism: The remaking of cultural rights and racial dominance in Central America. *PoLAR: Political and Legal Anthropology Review, 28* (1), 10–28.
Hindery, D. (2004). Social and environmental impacts of restructuring in Bolivia: An analysis of Enron and Shell's hydrocarbons projects. *Singapore Journal of Tropical Geography, 25*(3), 281–303.
Holt-Giménez, E. (2007). La Reestructuración Territorial y las Bases de la Reforma Agraria: Comunidades indígenas, minería aurífera y el Banco Mundial. In A. Bebbington (Ed.), *Minería, Movimientos Sociales y Respuestas Campesinas: Una ecología política de transformaciones territoriales* (pp. 81–114). Lima, Peru: Instituto de Estudios Peruanos.
Kaup, B. Z. (2010). A neoliberal nationalization? The constraints on natural-gas-led development in Bolivia. *Latin American Perspectives, 37*(3), 123–138.
Kohl B., & Farthing, L. C. (2006). *Impasse in Bolivia: Neoliberal hegemony and popular resistance.* London, Uk: Zed Books.
Le Billon, P. (2001). The political ecology of war: Natural resources and armed conflict. *Political Geography, 20,* 561–584.
Octavio, M. (2008). *Problemas Socio-ambientales de Hidrocarburosgas en Bolivia.* La Paz, Bolivia: Liga de Defensa del Medio Ambiente (LIDEMA).
Paredes, J. & Canedo, G. (2008). *10 Años de SAN-TCO: La lucha por los derechos territoriales indígenas en tierras bajas de Bolivia.* Santa Cruz de la Sierra, Bolivia: La Rosa Editorial.
Paye, L., Arteaga, W., Ramírez, N., & Ormachea, E. (2011). *Compendio de Espaciomapas de TCO en Tierras Bajas: Tenencia y aprovechamiento de recursos naturales en territorios indígenas.* La Paz, Bolivia: Centro de Estudios Para el Desarrollo Laboral y Agrario (CEDLA).
Peet, R., & Watts, M. (Eds.). (2004). *Liberation ecologies: Environment, development, social movements* (2nd ed.). London, UK: Routledge.
Perreault, T. (2006). From the Guerra del Agua to the Guerra del Gas: Resource governance, popular protest and social justice in Bolivia. *Antipode, 38*(1), 150–172.
Perreault, T. (2008). Natural gas, indigenous mobilization and the Bolivian state. *Identities, Conflict and Cohesion Programme Paper Number 12.* United Nations Research Institute for Social Development (UNRISD).
Postero, N. (2010). Morales's MAS government: Building indigenous popular hegemony in Bolivia. *Latin American Perspectives, 37*(3), 18–34.
Repsol. (2010). *Desarollo Socioambiental en el Bloque Caipipendi.* Unpublished document. Santa Cruz, Bolivia: Repsol.
Sawyer, S. (2004). *Crude chronicles: Indigenous politics, multinational oil, and neoliberalism in Ecuador.* Durham, NC: Duke University Press.
Sletto, B. (2009). "Indigenous people don't have boundaries": Reborderings, fire management, and productions of authenticities in indigenous landscapes. *Cultural Geographies, 16*(2), 253–277.

Third Departmental Assembly of the Tapiete, Weenhayek and Guaraní Indigenous Peoples. (2011, 4-6 May). Public statement, unpublished. Villamontes, Bolivia.

Tsing, A. L. (2005). *Friction: An ethnography of global connection*. Princeton, NJ: Princeton University Press.

Valdivia, G. (2005). On indigeneity, change, and representation in the northeastern ecuadorian amazon. *Environment and Planning A, 37,* 285–303.

Chapter 8

The Governing of Extraction, Oil Enclaves, and Indigenous Responses in the Ecuadorian Amazon

María Antonieta Guzmán-Gallegos

Introduction

This chapter discusses the governing of oil extraction in Ecuador, the formation of oil enclaves, and indigenous responses to the establishment and operation of oil fields. It focuses on a specific case; the exploration and exploitation of oil by the Consortium Arco Oriente, later AGIP, in Oil field 10 in Pastaza province, part of Ecuadorian Amazonia. Oil exploration and production in this part of Ecuadorian Amazonia have prompted different types of indigenous responses; organized indigenous resistance on the one hand, and a parallel cooperation between certain communities, newly established indigenous organizations, and the oil company on the other.

My analysis combines two different theoretical approaches. The first deals with enclave formation related to extractive industries and focuses on three interlinked aspects. The first aspect of this approach concerns the establishment of a partnership between the state and transnational corporations through the granting of specific concessions (Reed, 2009; Sawyer, 2004). The second aspect concerns the physical/geographical separation of oil extraction activity and its organization through the building of a proper delimited space of operation (Guzmán-Gallegos, 2009; Little, 2001). The third aspect concerns the economic and political structuring of extraction activity through mechanisms of detachment. Various new studies (Appel, 2010; Ferguson, 2006; Reed, 2009) describe "detachment" as the companies' systematic disentanglement from responsibility for the negative effects of oil operations, in combination with "deep entanglements" or "unruly engagements" with significant other actors. In the discussion I use especially the notion of deep entanglements or unruly engagements. Deep entanglements or unruly engagements refer to the messy interactions between oil companies, state institutions, local populations, and the environment; interactions that make possible the establishment and maintenance of enclaves (see also chapter 9 by Okamoto and Leifsen, this volume).

The second theoretical approach in this chapter deals with the rationale of local actors and the dynamics of local social organization that exist prior to the presence of oil companies and the state's intervention. It focuses on value(s) and the circulation of resources. Value(s) refers first to culturally and socially defined needs, wishes, and goals associated with the procurement, production, or control of vital resources such as land, forests, and other resources, and of cherished goods coming from external sources. Second, value(s) refers to the relations that constitute vital resources for actors. These relations can be kinship relations or those established with external actors (Graeber, 2001; Munn, 1986; Turner, 1979). Hence, value refers, first, to obtaining what makes life worth living and, second, to the creation and recreation of social relations and, thereby, to the reproduction of people.

Value is closely connected to the circulation of resources, which occurs within certain relations and networks, and has spatial effects. Places become linked to each other through the transference of values and the circulation of resources (Law & Hetherington, 2000). In these networks, there are certain nodes, certain persons that constitute themselves as privileged points of passage (Callon, 1986). These are points that are unavoidable and that control the circulation of resources. By controlling such circulation, they constitute particular power configurations.

By combining these two theoretical approaches, I aim to grasp better the importance that local agencies and local histories of differentiation and conflict have for the establishment of oil fields, both socially and politically, and for indigenous resistance to this establishment. As we shall see in the following sections, oil extraction in Ecuador is based on a specific state-company partnership where the Ecuadorian state's licensing policies facilitate the establishment of enclaves as operational spaces. The establishment of enclaves implies delegation to private companies of the provision of public services, construction of infrastructure, and the access to and control of rivers and aviation space.

In spite of the unequal power relations determined by the state's often unconditional support for the oil companies, oil companies also depend on the collaboration and acceptance of indigenous communities in the areas in which they operate. A main feature of the company-indigenous population relationship is that only communities within and near to the oil field gain access to the companies' resources such as health services, education, scholarship possibilities, and other "public" services. Hence, the establishment of the enclave economy creates an exclusionary field of company support in a situation where state provision of public welfare is inadequate if not totally lacking.

Oil fields juxtapose already existing spaces of local social organization characterized by specific dynamics of family groups and communities, with internal rivalries, conflicts, and differing interests. By taking advantage of preexisting dynamics and logics of social formation and political conflicts, the oil company contributes to the formation of new settlements, and new local power configurations that are maintained by an exclusionary circulation of resources. By the establishment of oil fields, geographies are changed and already populated areas reshaped due to differences created between those on the inside and those on the outside of these fields.

The excluding character of oil extraction, together with its transformative and polluting effects inside as well as outside of the enclaves, increases indigenous resistance and processes of contestation. The struggle for legal recognition of indigenous territories forms part of the resistance to state policies of internal colonization and to extractive industries. This resistance has established new local-to-global alliances between indigenous political leaders and organizations, on one hand, and national and international development NGOs and activist organizations, on the other. Alliances between indigenous ethnopolitical groups and NGOs create networks that put resources into circulation and give access to political possibilities to those communities that are opposed to oil extraction, creating an alternative flow of wealth. Paradoxically, I argue, this alternative flow of resources (modest in relation to that flowing from the oil economy) contributes to maintaining an unjust distribution of resources that, at the end of the day, results in strengthening enclave formation.

The analysis presented in this chapter is based on data produced during 12 months of fieldwork in Pastaza province in the period 2002–2003. It combines information produced during visits to several communities within Oil field 10, where I stayed with different families, with data from meetings in different communities that participated in an evaluation carried out by an independent consultancy firm concerning the relations between the oil operator and the communities.

The analysis also builds upon several interviews with two mid-level managers in AGIP and on written documentation made available to me through members of the Environmental Technical Commission (TCA), a commission constituted by representatives of the state, the oil operator, and indigenous organizations.

The Structuring of Oil Extraction in Ecuador

Ecuador's oil history started as early as 1878, when the first offshore oil fields were established on the Pacific coast. This history may be divided into three main periods, in which there are significant differences regarding the roles assigned to the state, the transnational corporations, and the local populations (Wray, 2000). In the first period, from the 1870s to the 1960s, oil extraction was conceived of and organized as a completely private enterprise. Oil companies had almost unlimited possibilities to carry out their exploratory activities, and the state gave huge concessions even without signing contracts. One of the biggest was a concession received by Royal Dutch Shell in 1937, which covered 10 million hectares, half of Ecuadorian Amazonia at that time. In this period there was not just a total absence of state control, but the state's economic participation was also significantly low. The royalty rates charged by the state on oil production amounted to approximately 6 percent of oil revenues (Martz, 1987).

The second period started in 1972, five years after the announcement of oil finds in the northern part of Ecuadorian Amazonia. Stronger state control and nationalization of the oil industry, both of upstream and downstream activities, characterize this period. A main objective was to reinstate state ownership over subsoil riches, which was central in the legislation approved after Ecuador's independence. New oil legislation was adopted, and the role of public institutions, such as the Ecuadorian State Petroleum Corporation, was reinforced. Existing contracts with oil companies were renegotiated and 80 percent of the areas given in concession were transferred back to the state (Martz, 1987; Wray, 2000). The liberalization of the country's economy and, as part of it, the promotion of private investments, especially in the oil sector, initiated the third period. In 1987, almost 15 years after the nationalization of the oil industry, oil legislation was amended anew and the functions of the state corporation were severely reduced. The participation of the state in oil revenues was diminished to 15–30 percent, depending on the contracts signed with the different oil companies (Llanes Suárez, 2006). The liberalization of oil policies entailed the organization of several bidding rounds leading to the division of 67 percent of Ecuadorian Amazonia into oil fields (Finer, Jenkins, Pimm, Keane, & Boss, 2008). The role assigned to local populations during these three periods has varied. In the two first periods, official imagery portrayed Amazonia as consisting of immense areas of vacant and uninhabited lands. Public discourse negated the existence of indigenous populations, or at best considered them to be irrelevant. With the discovery of oil and its exploitation, roads and oil pipelines were built, favoring massive migration of impoverished peasants, and thereby intensifying the colonization of Amazonia. The granting of land titles to new settlers legalized the displacement of the indigenous populations from areas they had occupied hitherto (Guzmán-Gallegos, 1997; Trujillo, 2001; Whitten, 1976). During the last period, the relations between the state and the indigenous population changed substantially, leading to the recognition of the indigenous citizens as important political actors who could no longer be ignored. Indigenous mobilization, the strengthening of environmental organizations, alliances between these two actors, nationally and globally, and paradoxically enough, the World Bank's policies seeking to smooth the effects of economic liberalization, resulted in significant legal improvements. The last two Constitutions, of 1998 and of 2008, and the International Labour Organization (ILO) 169 Convention, ratified by Ecuador in 1998, guarantee specific collective rights to the country's indigenous peoples. The most important are the rights to ancestral lands and the right to prior consultation concerning plans or programs that could affect their lands and ways of life. Moreover, environmental legislation, aimed to guarantee every citizen's right to a healthy environment, was also approved.

Although the implementation of these legal instruments is deficient, they do constitute a legal framework that influences the state's responsibility, corporations' strategies, and indigenous responses. The establishment of Oil field 10 is interesting in this regard. Oil field 10 was given in concession before the approval of the indigenous legal reforms of the late 1990s, reforms that, as we shall see in the next section, influenced the ways this oil field was established as an enclave.

The Establishment of an Enclave: Oil Field 10

In 2000, there were 15 oil fields in Ecuadorian Amazonia, five of them in Pastaza province. One of these was Oil field 10, which as of 2009 was the only oil field in operation in this province (see figure 8.1).

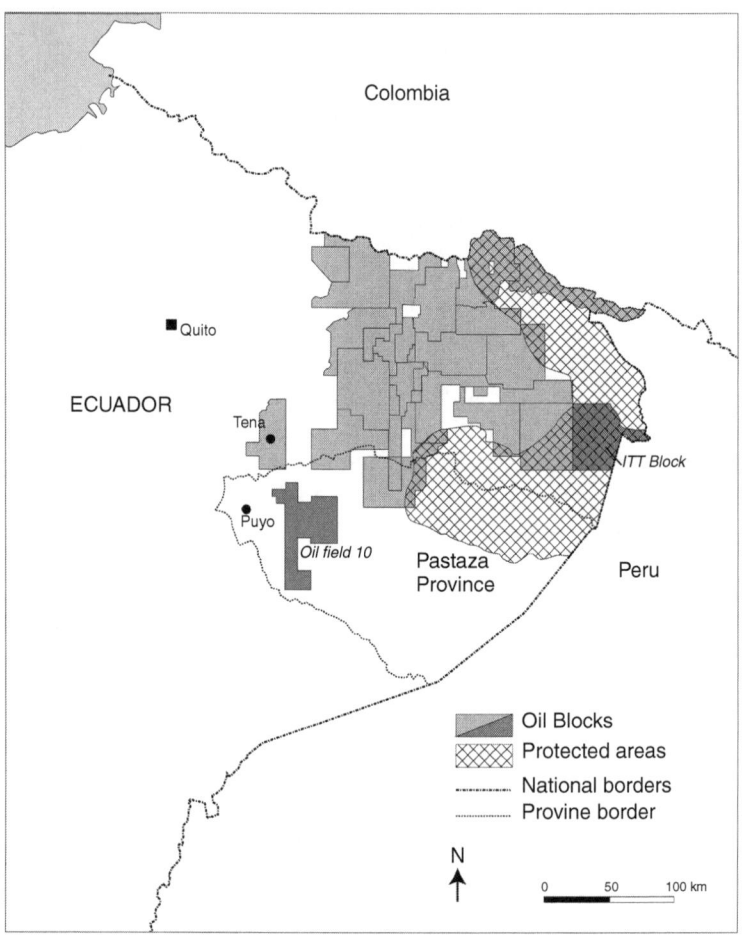

Figure 8.1 Oil concessions in Amazonian Ecuador

Oil field 10 was established in 1988 when the Ecuadorian state licensed it to Arco Oriente Co., a transnational corporation that participated in Ecuador's fifth round of petroleum licensing. Arco Oriente Co., a subsidiary of the US Arco International Company of Plano, Texas, was the majority holder in a consortium that included AGIP, owned by the Italian state corporation Eni. In 2000, Arco Oriente transferred all its rights and obligations to AGIP Oil Ecuador, making AGIP the sole operator company of Oil field 10 (Melo, Ortiz, & López, 2002; Wray, 2000).

Arco Oriente began the first exploratory phase of seismic explorations in the Villano Basin in 1988. According to Melo et al. (2002), these entailed laying out 36 seismic lines that crossed each other, forming a grid that covered part of Oil field 10. Along these lines, 1,200 kilometers of trails, each one to three meters wide, were cleared. Holes, some 2–5 meters deep, were drilled every hundred meters, and varying amounts of dynamite were detonated in each hole. In all, 39,000 explosions were registered. In addition to the clearing of trails and the drilling of holes, the company built 1,500 heliports. Between 1989 and 1994, Arco Oriente carried out the second exploratory phase. In approximately the same area where Royal Dutch Shell had carried out exploration activities in the 1940s, Arco drilled three exploratory wells. In 1998, Arco Oriente started extraction activities and built its first production facilities.

By 2003 these included the Villano Production Field, a 4-hectare area where the oil wells are located, the Central Processing Facility (CPF), where oil is separated from residual gases and formation water and which is located outside the Oil field, and an oil-flow line that connects the production field with the Central Processing Facility. From the latter runs the secondary oil pipeline, operated by AGIP, which cuts across various indigenous villages. This pipeline connects to the Trans-Ecuadorian Pipeline System (SOTE). In addition, AGIP operates the Baeza Terminal, in Napo province, where the oil produced in the Villano Field is stored. By 2003, there were 11 perforated wells; seven were production wells. Arco Oriente conducted its exploration activities and later on built the Villano Production Field and the oil-flow line without constructing roads. This decision was taken partially to meet the demands of the Organization of Indigenous Peoples of Pastaza (OPIP), one of the most important indigenous organizations in Pastaza province.

A risk-service contract signed between the Ecuadorian state and Arco-AGIP regulates Arco-AGIP's activities in Oil field 10. A risk-service contract implies that the oil company renders its services to the Ecuadorian state for a profit share from any oil discovered. This means that the oil company covers the expenses of all exploration activities, and if the oil company finds reserves of crude oil, the Ecuadorian state reimburses all exploration costs and pays the company a share of the profits. When extraction activities start, the oil company is obliged to cover the expenses of certain economic and environmental investments in the communities located within the oil field. According to the 1995 Environmental Regulations for Hydrocarbon Activities, amended in 2001, all oil companies are required to present a detailed environmental management plan. This plan is to contain a program for community relations to be developed in consultation with local residents. The program should include environmental and development activities such as providing environmental information about oil operations to the villages affected by exploration and extraction activities, establishing a participative environmental education system, financing compensatory and sustainable development projects, and providing basic services to the communities. In Oil field 10, as in most of the oil blocks in Ecuadorian Amazonia, investments in villages have not corresponded to what the law stipulates (see Kimerling, 2001; Llanes Suárez, 2006). From 1998 to 2003, the years when the company's investments increased significantly, they were still low in relation to the oil company's total investments, representing barely 0.76 percent. From 1998 to 2003, the company's community investments fluctuated between USD209,109 and USD787,311 per annum (ILAM, 2003).

The risk contract and the environmental management plan—and the program for community relations in particular—thus constitute the legal framework for the oil company's investments in the indigenous communities affected by its activities. These legal instruments are also constitutive for the establishment of Oil field 10 as an enclave. Both the contract and the environmental management plan entail the absence of the state and the transference to the oil operator of the state's responsibilities toward its citizens. For people living within Oil field 10, AGIP has become the main external actor to which they relate. AGIP is the only provider of health and welfare services and education that in other parts of Ecuador are guaranteed—though poorly—by the state. People do not relate to local and provincial authorities, as other communities outside the oil field do.

Enclave formation implies also the creation of a bounded and topographically arbitrary space. Oil field 10 is a quadrangular area of 200,000 hectares whose borders, defined by the state, only take into account the existence of previously licensed blocks, with no reference either to any actual topographic feature or to previously existing inhabited spaces. Until 2011[1] the oil field, located between the Curaray and Pastaza Rivers, cut across the lands and territories of *kichwa, zapara,* and *waorani* people.[2] However, in 2003, both exploratory and exploitation activities were confined mainly to the basins of the Villano, Liquino, and Conambo Rivers and their tributaries, and affected mostly *kichwa* settlements located in these areas. These were the only settlements that benefitted from the oil company's diverse investments.

Although the enclave is an arbitrary space whose limits ignore and cut across inhabited spaces, its establishment does not stand apart and is not disengaged from previously existing social and spatial dynamics. These dynamics are not the product of the state's or corporation's intervention, but they intertwine in contradictory ways with enclave formation. Local histories and social and political processes which are constitutive for the foundation of indigenous places, together with the legal instruments already described, are central for the relations and interactions the operator and indigenous peoples established and for the ways in which unruly engagements come into being. The next section focuses on local dynamics in the settlements within Oil field 10 and the way the *kichwa*, whose settlements are most affected by oil extraction, socially organize space.³

Indigenous Lands, Kinship, and Colonization

For the *kichwa*, a settlement is the product of kinship relations. It is also the product of the presence of powerful external actors and of the relations the *kichwa* historically have established with them. Hence, *kichwa* social organization of space is characterized by a duality. A *kichwa* settlement consists of a village and of *purinas*.⁴ Villages have often been located nearby nonindigenous institutions; in the past this could be a mission post, a rubber *hacienda* or a military post, a school, or, in recent times, an oil production site. Purinas are, on the contrary, places located several hours or even days journey from the village, in areas where forest resources are more abundant.

Kichwa settlements are always inhabited by people who are kin. People tend to live together with their own family group or settle in the lands of their extended families. Depending on its size, a settlement may consist of several family groups. Thus, villages and purinas are identified with particular family groups, and people identify themselves with particular settlements. A settlement should be maintained. Family groups do this by living there and by periodically transforming forests into cultivated gardens (Guzmán-Gallegos, 1997, 2010; Uzendonsky, 2005; Whitten, 1976). In this continuous process of maintenance and transformation, collective work based on reciprocal exchanges between family groups is essential. To be able to have enough land and forests to guarantee the well-being of one's kin people is central to what the *kichwa* conceive as a good and valuable life.

Settlements change constantly, houses may be moved, gardens may be abandoned, or regenerated as forests. The right a family group has to a particular place is a product of their work. When they leave a place and the forest takes over, their right may gradually fade away. Abandoned places within a village or, in particular, within purina areas, are always a cause of dispute. Internal conflicts may lead people to move out and resettle, or, with enough support from close kin (either of their own or of their spouse's siblings), to found a new settlement (Guzmán-Gallegos, 1997, 2010; Uzendonsky, 2005; Whitten, 1976). *Kichwa* settlements have been influenced by the relations and contacts people have established with a wide range of external actors. Through these relations, often asymmetrical in character, the *kichwa* have sought to obtain a diversity of desired goods, services as schools, and opportunities such as paid jobs. Family group leaders play a central role in establishing and managing these relations by acting as mediators and by channeling the wealth of powerful actors to their own family groups and settlements (Guzmán-Gallegos, 2009).

Alliances with powerful external actors have also been central in times of interethnic and internal conflicts. Fleeing from attacks from other groups, such as the *waorani, kichwa* family groups moved closer to mission posts in search of protection. When a group moves out of a settlement due to increasing internal conflicts, and decides either to resettle or to found a new place, they seek to strengthen their position by establishing alliances with missionaries, or, in recent times, by establishing contact with local authorities in order to achieve the official recognition of a new village, through, for instance, the establishment of public institutions such schools.

Needless to say, the presence of external actors has not just been instrumental to local social and power dynamics. Their presence, always connected to colonization processes, has led to the loss of ancestral lands and forests, and the establishment of asymmetrical, exploitative relations, that have put the existence of the *kichwa* as a people at risk. Obtaining valued goods and entering into alliances with powerful actors, such as landlords, rubber patrons, or missionaries, led to debt-peonage relations and enslavement. The coercive control these powerful actors had over the *kichwa* and their work diminished the *kichwa*s' capacities to produce for their own kin, and in their own eyes, to have a valued life. Family group leaders, as mediators of these relations, entered into these power structures, occupying leading positions assigned by local authorities, landlords, and missionaries. While they attempted to better their people's life conditions, they also contributed to the organization of indigenous labor as required by these actors (Guzmán-Gallegos, 2010; Muratorio, 1987; Whitten, 1976, 1985).

There have been different waves of colonization in Pastaza province. In the 1930s and 1940s, the approval of new legislation and the construction of roads, one of them by the Shell Dutch company, led to the establishment of new *haciendas*, of tea and sugar plantations, and to massive migration of impoverished peasants from the Andean Highlands. The presence of the Shell Dutch company and the start of exploratory activities also led to the relocation of indigenous settlements and the foundation of new ones in the province. Family groups living along the Villano River moved close to the company's installations in search of work opportunities (Trujillo, 2001).

The *kichwa*'s response and resistance to colonization has been diverse. To secure access and control to land and forest resources has however been a shared concern. Family groups used different strategies. They attempted either to obtain land titles as private owned lots, termed *colonias*, or used existing legislation, the *Ley de Comunas* of 1937, which stipulated that people of indigenous origins could established *comunas*, areas which are collectively owned (Guzmán-Gallegos, 1997; Perrault, 2003; Ruiz, 1993; Whitten, 1976). Thus, family groups attempted to secure as much land as possible, either as private or as collective owners.

By the late 1970s and in the 1980s indigenous resistance toward the ongoing colonization of indigenous lands took a new turn with the emergence of ethno-political organizations. In Pastaza province, the OPIP, founded in 1979, was the most important. OPIP aimed to represent Pastaza's different indigenous groups and demanded the legalization of ancestral lands. Until 2003 OPIP helped different settlements, especially those localized along the roads, to obtain the status of *comuna*. By 1992, after Oil field 10 was given in concession, OPIP started demanding the legalization and control, not of communal lands, but rather of autonomous territories that belonged to indigenous peoples (see also Sawyer, 1997). As an organization representing indigenous peoples, OPIP's demands went beyond territorial claims based on kinship bonds, and new forms of leadership emerged.

The emergence of indigenous organizations and new forms of leadership, based on ethnic belonging, does not mean, however, that kinship is less central in the *kichwa* social organization of space. Kinship and belonging to particular villages are crucial in the very functioning of indigenous organizations as well. For instance, most of the people living in the 17 villages located in the basins where oil extraction activities are carried out within Oil field 10 are related to each other by kinship bonds or have moved in because of marriage. Processes of relocation and the foundation of new places by people who are close kin are still continuing. In the late 1990s, a new village, Paparahua, was founded within Oil field 10. Three brothers, who had experienced conflicts in the villages where they were living, promoted and participated in the foundation of Paparahua in an area where there were supposed to be unoccupied lands and forests. They built new houses and invited other couples to settle there. As in the past, the presence of external actors played a role. Paparahua became a village due mainly to AGIP's support. Since the brothers were active supporters of the company and leaders of the organization it had helped to create, the company provided, surprisingly quickly, a schoolroom, a communal house, and some water pipes (Guzmán-Gallegos, 2009).

Territorial claims and spatial organization based on kinship bonds made up an important background for the contrasting and conflicting responses to the establishment of Oil field 10. In its engagement with local communities, the oil operator's officials took advantage of internal disagreements to strengthen the position of some actors and to weaken claims based on ethnic or national belongings as those presented by OPIP. Internal disagreements thus favored the establishment of the enclave, as we will see in the next section.

Indigenous Demands and Unruly Engagements

When Oil block 10 was licensed in 1988, most of the lands the *kichwa* inhabited in the basins of the Villano, Liquino, and Conambo Rivers were not titled, with the exception of an area that already was titled as a *colonia*, composed of privately owned lots. To obtain the title to ancestral lands had been, for at least a decade, one of the most important demands of the OPIP and of the indigenous people living there. This demand came to be instrumental in establishing the enclave and in indigenous responses and resistance to it.

When Arco Oriente-AGIP announced that the *Compagnie Generale de Geophysique* (CGG) were to conduct the first exploratory phase of seismic exploration, existing local conflicts worsened and the contested process of legalization of ancestral lands started. The CGG planned to drill an oil well in an area disputed by the settlements of Sarayaku and Moretecocha. The people of Sarayaku were against oil extraction, and claimed that this area was part of their purinas. The residents of Moretecocha argued the same. In order to prevent the CGG from drilling the well and at the same time defending the land they saw as theirs, the people of Sarayaku started clearing and planting gardens in the disputed area, only to see them destroyed by the people of Moretecocha. Family groups of Moretecocha allied with family groups of the Pandanuque settlement who also maintained strained relations with Sarayaku, and started working to get their lands legalized. They demanded that the state recognize them as *comunas*, that is, as indigenous people who had collective property rights to their land. In 1991, Pandanuque and Moretecocha were recognized as *comunas* with the assiduous help of Arco Oriente-AGIP field officials and the unusual efficacy of *Instituto Ecuatoriano de Reforma Agraria y Colonización* (Ecuadorian Institute for Agrarian Reform and Colonization—IERAC), the state institution in charge of legalizing indigenous lands.

One year later, in 1992, OPIP organized a march from Puyo, the provincial capital of Pastaza, to the national capital, Quito. OPIP demanded the legalization of indigenous territories, a demand the government rejected. After hard negotiations, the government gave property titles over 1,115,472 hectares, divided into several blocks that did not coincide with but rather cut across the lands used by the different settlements. At the same time, the government allocated 44,810 hectares to the Colonia Liquino, which grouped 11 communities within Oil field 10. As Sawyer (2004) asserts, with the demarcation of Pandanuque and Moretecocha as *comunas* and of the Colonia Liquino, the Ecuadorian state created pockets of pro-oil communities in this part of Pastaza province. It also made possible the physical establishment of the enclave. Indeed, Arco Oriente-AGIP planned to drill oil wells in Moretecocha and Pandanuque and to construct an oil-flow line that would run through the lands of the Colonia Liquino.

From the perspective of local leaders and inhabitants of Moretecocha, Pandanuque, and of the Colonia Liquino, the land titles they obtained, however, secured at least part of their lands from new nonindigenous settlers. The titles also secured in their favor disputed purina lands. At the same time, the titles defined a bounded space within which cherished values could be fulfilled and obtained by controlling the resources coming from the oil company. Sarayaku and other villages outside Oil field 10 were excluded from this space. The people of Moretecocha and Pandanuque saw no possibilities to stop the state's concession. However, they were not willing to let exploratory activities start without receiving something in compensation. They decided thus to cooperate with the oil company, a decision influenced by their desire to obtain goods and services they lacked in exchange for what they thought they would lose.

The announcement of seismic exploration initiated, indeed, a series of dubious exchanges between several settlements within the oil field, and the different subcontracting firms hired by Arco Oriente-AGIP. The subcontracting firms that had time-limited contracts with the oil operator were willing to provide the villages with a variety of goods and limited services to ensure that exploratory operations could proceed without delays. By fulfilling their activities within the agreed time, they avoided having to pay Arco Oriente-AGIP financial compensation. As a crew chief put it: "we would walk in and ask them what they wanted. Whatever they asked for we would do: hire a few local people, fix the airstrip, maybe even build a school or a clinic, or give them school supplies or medicines. As long as it was reasonable, we just gave it to them" (cited in Mendez, Parnell, & Wasserstrom, 1998, p. 5).

In 1998, the practice of establishing contact with settlements through casual gifts of goods and services changed in character. This year Arco Oriente-AGIP started exploitation activities, which meant that the operator needed to establish long-term agreements that could ensure good relations with local communities for longer periods. Arco Oriente-AGIP started operating with long-term agreements that centered mainly on better health care, education, and transport, and the construction and maintenance of communal buildings. Through the provision of goods and services, the consortium came to occupy the position of a wealthy provider, a position that could be compared to that of the landlords or the rubber patrons in the past. The villagers within the oil field were fully aware that the consortium's position depended on indigenous goodwill and help. The settlements allowed—and by doing this helped, in their view—the operator to be able to conduct its activities on community land. They perceived their relations and collaboration with the operator in terms of exchange with connotations of reciprocity. At the same time, they resented the asymmetries that characterized these exchange relations. After many years of disappointments, as they said, they had come to understand that what they had received from the company was much less that what the company had obtained from their lands. For this reason they welcomed the legal dispositions, such as the environmental management plan and the community relation program, that oblige the operator to compensate the communities that might be affected by their activities.

The circulation of resources coming from AGIP, however, followed a particular spatial ordering that responded to corporate interests. According to AGIP's community relations office, the company gave priority to those villages situated close to its production facilities, the wells, and the oil-flow line, and to those villages that had more people and political capacity to advance their demands (ILAM, 2003, p. 185). AGIP also tended to give priority to the demands of local leaders who supported their actions, strengthening both their position as leaders in the eyes of their followers and the possibilities (of education, of better health care) for these leaders' family groups. The leaders became mediators par excellence between AGIP and the settlements, channeling resources to the settlements and to their own groups. The ways these value and resources flowed both created new inequalities and reinforced those already existing.

The practice of strengthening supportive leaders was not new. Arco-AGIP supported the creation of a new organization, DICIP (later ASODIRA[5]) in the Villano area as early as 1988. By 2003 AGIP continued to pay all ASODIRA's fixed and current expenses, and provided its leaders with better transport and job possibilities (access to pick-up trucks, small airplanes, and scholarships). This strategic funding, however, produced discontent and resistance within the less favored settlements in the oil field, resulting in the formation of new organizations. AGIP here followed a practice that is common among oil operators in Amazonia, and part of the unruly engagements operators use to facilitate the establishment of the enclaves. AGIP hence contributed to a dynamic of fraction, which built upon and reinforced local differences, and weakened the possibility of constituting a broader organization that could represent most of the villagers within Oil field 10.

OPIP and Organized Indigenous Resistance

The land titles, the provision of goods and services, and AGIP's differentiated support to settlements, leaders, and family groups, contributed to establishing Oil field 10 as an enclave, and were part of the unruly engagements that severely weakened OPIP's representation within it. Indeed, in the early 1990s OPIP was the main and strongest organization in this part of Pastaza province. One decade later, none of the villages within the field recognized OPIP's representation.

OPIP's leadership and most of its constituency had always been against oil extraction. They first attempted, through different actions, to hinder the establishment of Oil field 10, and later they called into question the boundedness of this enclave. OPIP, supported by Confederación de las Nacionalidades Indígenas de la Amazonia Ecuatoriana (Confederation of the Nationalities Indigenous to the Amazon of Ecuador—CONFENIAE) and *Confederación de Nacionalidades Indígenas del Ecuador* (Confederation of Indigenous Nationalities of Ecuador—CONAIE), the regional and national indigenous organizations of which OPIP is part, demanded from the state the assessment of environmental impacts of exploratory activities on all indigenous lands, not just on the settlements which happened to be within the field[6]—a demand the state eventually accepted. In alliance with national and international actors such as Rainforest Action Network, OPIP also forced Arco Oriente-AGIP to create an environmental technical commission, consisting of representatives from the consortium, from Ecuador's state company, Petroecuador, and from three indigenous organizations, OPIP, ASODIRA, and AIEPRA,[7] to monitor and assess all of Arco Oriente's activities in Oil field 10. OPIP argued that oil exploitation concerned all the indigenous villagers of Pastaza province, not just the communities within the oil field. They also reasserted the importance of indigenous participation, not just as recipients of the company's random favors, but as actors who could exercise control and take part in making vital decisions affecting their communities. OPIP framed the existence of a unitary *kichwa* territory in the province and posited that all its inhabitants, not just the villagers living within the oil field, should be entitled to assess the effects of oil exploitation and take part in determining the benefits it might generate. OPIP's positioning and the wide support it enjoyed nationally and abroad had tangible effects: they influenced Arco Oriente's agreement to important environmental measures, such as not building any road to its production facilities within the oil field.

The villagers, local leaders, and even the leadership of the organizations within Oil field 10 recognized OPIP's political capacity for mobilizing people, and for establishing useful political alliances within the country and abroad. In the many periods of conflict they had with the operator over the operator's failure to fulfill previous agreements, they always allied with OPIP, knowing that OPIP would be able to press the operator. Moreover, they agreed and supported OPIP's territorial and autonomy claims. The villagers saw themselves as the owners of the lands and forests in which, in their view, there were abundant traces of their work as well as that of their family groups. They insisted, however, on the differences in the interests and priorities of the various settlements. They could not accept that the *kichwa* territory was one unit, a whole that OPIP leaders alone could represent and manage. They questioned OPIP's leadership and highlighted their close relations with particular settlements and family groups.

OPIP's leadership balanced between being representatives of the *kichwa* as an ethnic group or as a nation, and as representatives of their own settlements and family groups. As an ethno-political organization, OPIP received support from national and international

NGOs, and from public actors, to carry out a wide range of projects that in different ways supported OPIP's political goals and territorial demands. From the early 1990s and up to the late 2000s, OPIP received financial support to create environmentally sustainable economic alternatives, manage a credit cooperative and operate a small airplane company, among other projects (see Guzmán-Gallegos, 2009). These interventions benefitted villages that were already part of OPIP's constituency. The distribution of project resources also depended on OPIP's leadership in the sense that the leaders' settlements and their family groups often tended to benefit from project resources more than others. Hence, OPIP's leaders were mediators in relation to NGOs controlling the circulation of project resources. The periodical election of OPIP's leaders contributed though to a wider distribution of project resources and wealth. However, there were some family groups and some settlements that dominated OPIP's leadership, a fact that was often pointed out by OPIP's own constituency, and which provoked internal conflicts. A shared perception was that the settlements of Sarayaku, Arajuno, Union Base, and San Jacinto, and the leaders coming from these places, had led and contributed substantially to the indigenous struggles and victories. These settlements and these leaders had at the same time accumulated resources and power.

The concentration of resources and power in certain settlements and family groups were favored and sometimes promoted by the supporting NGOs. From a project management perspective, it was important to support the villages and the family groups that were able to comply with the projects' goals and results. Those who were not, who often were weaker groups in terms of economic and social capital, did not participate in the projects. NGOs also tended to favor those settlements and local leaders that could articulate clear political positions that agreed with the NGO's own political agenda and views. Elected leaders that showed ambiguous positions toward extractive industries risked losing financial support, and becoming isolated (Guzmán-Gallegos, 2009).

OPIP was recognized as a powerful political actor in Pastaza province. However, the closed and unequal circulation and distribution of project resources and of political power within its constituency contributed to weaken its legitimacy. In the eyes of its followers, and for those who were not part of OPIP's constituency, OPIP's leadership supported certain family groups and certain villages to obtain and fulfill values that, according to local expectations, made their life better. These families and settlements became stronger as groups, and wealthier, getting better possibilities to continue with *kichwa* ways of life and, at the same time getting access to other external goods.

By strengthening certain family groups and certain settlements, OPIP's leaders weakened the organization's role as the representative of a whole ethnic group. The spatial distribution of project resources and of political power led to power configurations that privileged certain settlements and certain families, contributing as well to isolate those settlements and family groups who did not share OPIP's political agenda. The exclusion of settlements such as those within Oil field 10 came to reinforce indirectly the consolidation of this field as a bounded space in which AGIP was an uncontested wealth provider of a diversity of goods and, in the absence of the state, of welfare services that the villagers of Oil field 10 perceived as necessary for their well-being and for their survival as a people.

Conclusion

In Ecuador, oil extraction has been regulated by legislation that, except for a short period in the 1970s, has promoted the delegation of state functions to oil operators. Regulations and contracts approved in the 1980s and 1990s as part of neoliberal reforms strengthen the constitution of oil enclaves as exclusionary bounded operational spaces in which oil operators have territorial control. Hydrocarbon extraction legislation obliges oil operators to elaborate environmental impact assessments, environment management plans, and programs for community relations. These regulations contribute to consolidate oil operators in the role of providers of welfare services and cherished goods, reinforcing at the same time the absence of the state.

Through the concepts of "disentanglement" and "unruly engagements" proposed by new studies of extractive industry, I have discussed how oil enclaves are established. Such enclaves are arbitrary spaces disentangled from their surroundings both topographically and socially. Once established, certain power relations and distributive patterns emerge internally. In defining the enclave borders, the state only takes into account previously licensed oil blocks, with no reference to any actual topographic features or previously inhabited spaces. Oil field 10 cuts across the lands of the *kichwa*, the *waorani*, and the *zapara*, and its establishment has reshaped geographies and local dynamics by creating differences between communities inside and outside the oil field.

Although the establishment of an oil field entails the constitution of an exclusionary field characterized by unequal power relations, oil companies still depend on having collaborative relations with local people—disentanglement therefore entails deep and unruly engagements. Through supporting new indigenous organizations, establishing strategic alliances with state institutions both to deal with and undermine local territorial claims, and through the uneven distribution of wealth, the oil operator has succeeded in establishing a set of relations that make the maintenance of the enclave possible.

Local power configurations related to the creation of the enclave are based on exclusionary circulation of resources. The ways resources circulate may be better understood if we consider not solely the operator's unruly engagements, but also the actual social organization of space in which kinship relations and perceptions of belonging to particular places are central. Local processes of differentiation and conflict, considered also over a longer historical time frame, are important. Historically, the *kichwa* in Pastaza province have related to and depended on a wide range of external actors. Managing the asymmetric and exploitative relations established with these actors has always implied maintaining a difficult balance. Functioning as mediators, local leaders have often become "privileged points of passages" (Callon, 1986) by controlling the circulation of resources, balancing between channeling resources to their own family groups and settlements, and risking strengthening patronage-client relations.

Kinship, local differentiation, and the management of asymmetrical relations are central not only in the context of enclave formation, but also in the building of ethno-political organizations to negotiate territorial claims and collective rights. Oil operators, in this case Arco Oriente-AGIP, systematically take advantage of local dynamics, conflicts and value, and wealth expectations in the unruly engagements they establish with local people. Through exclusionary circulation and flows of resources to certain settlements, oil operators manage to consolidate oil enclaves as bounded, exclusionary spaces. Indigenous resistance organizations, through alliances with national and international actors, have opposed processes of enclave formation. An unexpected outcome is the emergence of an alternative and more moderate—but still exclusionary—circulation of resources within the indigenous-global civil society networks. The NGO economy operates on the side of the oil economy in enclaves, but an important observation in my analysis is that the former may contribute to maintain and solidify the latter. Thus, NGOs may end up weakening indigenous struggles and their possibilities for territorial consolidation. As long as the state is not able to ensure that its indigenous citizens have possibilities to reproduce themselves as peoples, oil extraction in the context of enclave formation will continue to weaken any possibility of improving justice and democracy.

Notes

1. In 2011, as part of the renegotiation of AGIP's contract, the state redefined the area of Oil field 10. It was extended to the south, to include several other *Kichwa* communities.
2. There are six indigenous peoples living in Pastaza province: the *Kichwa*, the *Waorani*, the *Shiwiar*, the *Zapara*, the *Andoas*, and the *Achuar*.
3. *Kichwa* refers in this chapter exclusively to the people living in the provinces of Pastaza, Napo, and Sucumbios, who in the literature are also known as *Quijos* and *Canelos Kichwa* respectively.
4. *Purinas* refer to areas composed of dispersed houses, gardens and hunting tracks that belong to different families. These families usually lived in the same village (Guzmán-Gallegos, 1997; Whitten, 1976).
5. DICIP means the Inter-communitarian Directive of Independent Communities in Pastaza, whereas ASODIRA stands for Association for Indigenous Development in the Amazonian Region.
6. CONAIE, which means *Confederación de Nacionalidades Indígenas del Ecuador* (the Confederation of Indigenous Nationalities of Ecuador), is a national umbrella organization. It groups three regional organizations. One of these is the CONFENIAE, *Confederación de Nacionalidades Indígenas de la Amazonía Ecuatoriana* (Confederation of Indigenous Nationalities of the Ecuadorian Amazon).
7. AIEPRA, founded in 1981, means Association of Evangelical Indians of Pastaza—Amazon Region.

References

Appel, H. (2010). Offshore work: Oil and the making of modularity in Equatorial Guinea [Conference Presentation]. *American Anthropological Association 109th Annual Meeting*, November 17–21, New Orleans, LA.

Callon, M. (1986). Some elements of a sociology of translation: Domestication of the scallops and the fishermen of the St. Brieuc Bay. In J. Law (Ed.), *Power, action and belief: A new sociology of knowledge* (pp. 196–233). London, UK: Routledge & Kegan Paul.

Ferguson, J. (2006). *Global shadows: Africa in the neoliberal world order*. Durham, NC: Duke University Press.

Finer, M., Jenkins, C. N., Pimm, S. L., Keane, B., & Boss, C. (2008). Oil and gas projects in the Western Amazon: Threats to wilderness, biodiversity and indigenous peoples. Plos ONE, 3(8), e2932 doi: 10.1371/journal.pone.0002932

Graeber, D. (2001). *Toward an anthropological theory value: The false coin of our dreams*. New York, NY: Palgrave.

Guzmán-Gallegos, M. A. (1997). *Para qua la Yuca Beba Nuestra Sangre: Trabajo, género y parentesco en una comunidad quichua de la Amazonia Ecuatoriana.* Quito, Ecuador: Abya Yala.

Guzmán-Gallegos, M. A. (2010). *Conflicting spatialities: Networks, mediation and alterity in the making of indigenous territories in Ecuadorian Amazonia.* Oslo, Norway: UNIPUB.

Guzmán-Gallegos, M. A. (2009). Identity cards, abducted footprints, and the book of San Gonzalo: The power of textual objects in Runa worldview. In F. Santos-Granero (Ed.), *The Occult Life of Things: Native Amazonian theories of materiality and personhood* (pp. 214–234). Tucson, AZ: The University of Arizona Press.

ILAM (2003). *Informe de Evaluación del Programa de Relaciones Comunitarias de AGIP Oil Ecuador B.V. en el Bloque 10 (Pastaza).* Quito, Ecuador: ILAM Ecuador S.A.

Kimerling, J. (2001). Uncommon ground: Occidental's land access and community relations standards and practices in quichua communities in the Ecuadorian Amazon. *Law and Anthropology, 11,* 179–247.

Law, J., & Hetherington, K. (2000). Materialities, spatialities, globalities. In J. R. Bryson, P. W. Daniels, N. Henry & J. Pollard (Eds.), *Knowledge, Space, Economy* (pp. 34–49). London, UK: Routledge.

Little, P. E. (2001). *Amazonia: Territorial struggles on perennial frontiers.* Baltimore, MD: Johns Hopkins University Press.

Llanes Suárez, H. (2006). *Oxy, Contratos Petroleros, Inequidad en la Distribución de la Producción.* Quito: Artes Gráficas Silva.

Martz, J. D. (1987). *Politics and petroleum in Ecuador.* New Brunswick, NJ: Transaction Books.

Melo, M., Ortiz, P., & López, V. (2002). *Petróleo, Ambiente y Derechos en la Amazonía Centro Sur.* Quito, Ecuador: CDES/OPIP/IACYT-A.

Mendez, S., Parnell, J. & Wasserstrom, R. (1998). Seeking common ground: Petroleum and indigenous peoples in Ecuador's Amazon. *Environment, 40*(5), 13–40.

Munn, N. (1986). *The fame of Gawa: A symbolic study of value transformation in a Massim (Papua New Guinea) society.* Durham, NC: Duke University Press.

Muratorio, B. (1987). *Rucuyaya Alonso y la Historia Social y Económica del Alto Napo, 1850–1950.* Quito, Ecuador: Abya Yala.

Perrault, T. (2003). Making space: Community organization, agrarian change and the politics of scale in the Ecuadorian Amazon. *Latin American Perspectives, 30*(1), 96–121.

Reed, K. (2009). *Crude existence: Environment and the politics of oil in Northern Angola.* Berkeley, CA: University of California Press.

Ruiz, L. (1993). *Estado, Movimiento Indígena y Conflicto en la Amazonia: El caso de Pastaza.* Quito, Ecuador: Facultad Latinoamericana de Ciencias Sociales.

Sawyer, S. (1997). The 1992 Indian mobilization in Lowland Ecuador. *Latin American Perspectives, 24*(3), 65–82.

Sawyer, S. (2004). *Crude chronicles: Indigenous politics, multinational oil, and neoliberalism in Ecuador.* Durham, NC: Duke University Press.
Trujillo, J. (2001). *Memorias de Curaray.* Quito: Fondo Ecuatoriano Populorum Progressio.
Turner, T. (1979). Anthropology and the politics of indigenous peoples' struggles. *Cambridge Anthropology,* 5, 1–43.
Uzendonsky, M. (2005). *The Napo Runa of Amazonian Ecuador.* Urbana, IL: University of Illinois Press.
Whitten, N. (1976). *Sacha Runa: Ethnicity and adaptation of Ecuadorian jungle Quichua.* Urbana, IL: University of Illinois Press.
Whitten, N. (1985). *Sicuanga Runa: The other side of development in Amazonian Ecuador.* Urbana, IL: University of Illinois Press.
Wray, N. (2000). *Pueblos Indígenas Amazónicos y Actividad Petrolera en el Ecuador: Conflictos, estrategias e impactos.* Quito, Ecuador: Oxfam America & IBIS.

Chapter 9

Oil Spills, Contamination, and Unruly Engagements with Indigenous Peoples in the Peruvian Amazon

Tami Okamoto and Esben Leifsen

Introduction

This chapter explores unruly engagements in the case of an onshore oil spill in Amazonia. "Unruly engagements" refers here to the oil company's strategies for handling knowledge, information, participation, resources, and relationships in irregular ways in order to manage the effects of contamination and to remain detached from its social and environmental responsibilities. Currently, in the Peruvian Amazon, these strategies reinforce a form of extraction that enables the oil company to operate relatively undisturbed from the critique of public entities and civil society, and their calls for remediating action.

Mainly based on qualitative data collected during four month of fieldwork, we discuss the dynamics between *Kukama-Kukamiria* and riverine communities, state institutions, and the largest hydrocarbon producer company in Peru, Pluspetrol, in the aftermath of an oil spill in the country's northeastern region in June 2010 (the Marañón case). The oil spill, of approximately 400 barrels of crude oil, affected numerous *Kukama-Kukamiria* and riverine communities—located along the lower Marañón river—whose livelihoods and cosmologies are directly dependent on the river's water and resources. After the oil spill, several negotiations as well as mobilizations by the affected communities and associations took place, contesting the ways in which contamination from the oil was being handled.

Analyzing these strategies of detachment, we draw on recent innovative theoretical approaches used in studies of the extractive sector in West Africa (cf. Appel, 2010; Ferguson, 2006; Reed, 2009). These studies focus on the economic and political structuring of extraction activity through mechanisms of disentanglement. Disentanglement refers here to the detachment of the "production of profit from the place in which the industry happens to find itself, to structure liability and responsibility in such a way that the industry can remove itself from the social, legal, political, and environmental chaos it creates in its wake" (Appel, 2010, p. 8). This "exclusionary structure of petrocapitalism" (Reed, 2009, p. 15) is made possible by disentanglement in combination with deep entanglements or unruly engagements of the oil industry in people's lives, institutions, and environments. We adapt the concept of "unruly engagements" to analyze the oil company's strategic handling of oil spills and indigenous responses. In adapting this conceptual approach to the Amazonian context of onshore oil extraction, it has been necessary to undertake modifications that account for, among other things, the complexity of interrelations between actors and processes of governance in Peru.

Pluspetrol's oil blocks (like most extraction sites in the Peruvian Amazon) are located in areas considered semiremote, and thus weakly governed by the state, with limited public services available. Comparable to offshore facilities in Angola, almost no rights are enforced in these areas and the impacts of extractive activities are infrequently inspected or regulated. In that sense, the extraction site's strategic goal in the Amazonian context seems to be what Ferguson (2006) highlights, based on African experiences, as "the endeavour to make onshore extraction as offshore as possible" (p. 61). In Amazonia, the spatial disconnection between the extractive industry, and the surrounding communities and local conditions can be depicted in the way barges filled with crude oil come and go across the river, delivering oil from remote wells directly into the market, undisturbed, regardless of the extent of contamination.

Unruly engagements and the situations in which they are played out also open political spaces for contestation. This space is used by affected groups and actors in different ways and in different combinations of confrontation, playing by the rules, and building alliances. Nonetheless, the degree of contestation appears to be relatively stronger in the Amazonian than in the West African context. Unruly engagements in Amazonia could be seen as products of contestation and conflict that are on the rise. As claims and negotiations, blockades, and disputes intensify, the company's strategies for handling responses multiply, and the engagements among industry, state, and communities proliferate.

Moreover, we hold that an element of state heterogeneity hinders a *complete* detachment of the oil industry from extraction sites and local conditions. This state heterogeneity is characterized by the contradictory ways that Peruvian state institutions relate to the extractive sector, and local and indigenous peoples. On the one hand, Peru has ratified the International Labour Organization (ILO) 169 Convention in 1994, was one of the main proposing countries for the United Nations Declaration on the Rights of Indigenous Peoples (UNDRIP) in 2007, and has recently approved a Law of Consultation. State institutions and civil society make use of these legal tools in favor of indigenous rights. On the other hand, however, hydrocarbon governance in Peru is marked by the importance of the extractive industry to the current booming economic growth. The present political economic-model equates development to natural resource extraction at the expense of overriding the rights of local communities and populations. State-corporate partnerships support this particular model, both legally as well as through corruption. Moreover, the long history of discrimination against *kukama-kukamiria* and indigenous peoples in general remains entrenched among Peru's dominant society and is manifested, among other ways, in debates over sovereignty. A paternalistic inclusion of indigenous people in the national political sphere, and narratives portraying them, their organizations, and allies as "manger dogs," "backwards," and "radicals" are recurrent themes in public discourse (see newspaper op-ed by former president Alan García [García Pérez, 2007]).

In the Marañón case, state heterogeneity was evident in the public stance taken by the minister of energy and mines (MINEM) and the minister of the environment (MINAM) compared with other state institutions. As two of the central institutions dealing with the extractive sector, MINEM and MINAM alleged that "it is a very small amount [400 barrels of crude oil]. Actually, compared with what has happened in the Gulf of Mexico, it is a small issue that should not be reason for alarm" (El Comercio, 2010), and "The emergency system [Pluspetrol's contingency plan] worked adequately and fast, so the impact has been minimal" (Univisión 2010). Although MINEM, MINAM, and several regional authorities openly denied there had been any mishandling after the oil spill, other state institutions (mainly regional) took a more vigilant stand. Among them were the regional Ombudsman, the semi-independent and respected environmental regional entity IIAP (Research Institute of the Peruvian Amazon), and to a lesser extent, DICAPI (the General Directorate for Harbor and Coast Guards) ascribed to the ministry of defense. The paradoxical approaches and conflicting interests encapsulated within what represents the Peruvian state in its relations to indigenous and environmental issues create a particular context that it is crucial to take into account.

The Marañón Case and Its Unruly Engagements

The oil spill in the Marañón river and smaller tributaries resulted from an accident involving an oil-barge leaving Pluspetrol's installations near the community of San José de Saramuro in the Loreto region on the afternoon of June 19, 2010. One day after the oil spill, leaders from most nearby communities, together with the heads of the *Kukama* Association ACODECOSPAT[1] (also representing some of the affected communities), traveled to the city of Iquitos with the purpose of disseminating videos and photographs taken as the crude oil reached their communities. Soon after hearing the denials of the MINEM and MINAM, based in Lima, the indigenous associations together with other local civil society organizations publically denounced the authorities for minimizing the oil spill's impact.[2] They considered that, contrary to what Pluspetrol had been claiming, the company's emergency action failed to inform the surrounding communities about the incident in a timely manner. They noted that Pluspetrol had acted by spreading a chemical substance (what they called a "white powder") on the river without properly explaining whether it was toxic for the environment and human consumption.

The report by the Ombudsman of Loreto[3] and our fieldwork four months after the oil spill, substantiate that the lack of awareness led to sickness among the population, who continued drinking the contaminated water and experienced stomach upsets, headaches, fevers, and skin problems. Local dwellers as well as community health assistants stressed the increasing cases of sickness in the months following the oil spill and were able to show prevailing physical injuries, such as rashes, scars, and severe skin dryness. In the community of Ollanta, one of the closest to the oil spill, an elder died after serious stomach disorders during the first days.[4] Moreover, local residents added that Pluspetrol's claims of immediate emergency support of water, food, and medicines were false (at least in most communities and during the first weeks). DICAPI's report later corroborated the ineffectiveness of Pluspetrol's contingency plan and indicated that both Pluspetrol and Petroperú (the state institution in charge of promoting investment in exploration and exploitation of hydrocarbons) violated the law by not having properly licensed contingency plans (Dirección General de Capitanías y Guardacostas de Perú [DICAPI], 2010).

Journalist Marisol Choquehuanca from the news program *Reporte Semanal*, who visited some of the affected communities and later released a story on national television, indicated that during those first days after the oil spill, Pluspetrol refused to give her an interview (cf. Choquehuanca, 2010). "Instead," she said, "[Pluspetrol] sent us a communiqué where they assured us that they were covering the needs of the communities." She added that no further explanations were obtained with respect to why the company had thrown a "white powder" that would only hide the crude oil stains (sending it to the riverbed) as part of their contingency plan rather than first warning the communities about the dangerous water conditions.

In the following sections, we focus on the main aspects of the unruly management of the contamination by the state-oil company partnership. We emphasize the struggle for control over the dissemination of information and also over the production of scientific knowledge about contamination. We discuss the modes of "dialogue" and "consultation" administered through specific mechanisms of participation, aiming not just to visualize the strategies of the oil company, but also to discuss indigenous and other responses. Moreover, we attempt to shed light on how these responses reinforce a type of extraction that implies a relative (yet contested) detachment from responsibility.

Modes of Unruly Engagements: Communiqués

Well-formulated and convincing press statements, or what we refer to as communiqués, are one of the modes of "unruly engagements" we identify in the Marañón case. Most communiqués were published relatively frequently in the local newspapers and usually covered entire pages highlighting, for example, that "Pluspetrol confirms its compliance with the agreements with the communities . . . Pluspetrol confirms its openness to dialogue (*voluntad de diálogo*) and the commitment to the well-being of the communities" (La Region, 2010). Despite the vast amount of visual and written evidence on the critical situation that local communities faced due to the lack of clean water and food, the use of communiqués enabled Pluspetrol representatives and central authorities to maintain a public image of things being under control and of their openness to dialogue. Indigenous leaders in Iquitos found it ironic that in some of the communiqués Pluspetrol would mention their "openness to dialogue" Although it seemed to them that after all their way of "dialoguing" was mainly through that one-way form of communication. Many of them were aware that through these expensive full-page statements, Pluspetrol had better chances of getting public support; particularly among the urban population whom they perceived as generally indifferent to undertakings in the rest of the region. Appropriating the discussion through communiqués is an important mechanism to maintain power in contamination management, such as oil spills, and to avoid political disputes about the extractive sector at the national level. In the Marañón case, communiqués enabled Pluspetrol to largely take over decisions about the management of contamination by structuring and limiting direct encounters with affected communities as well as other stakeholders (at least right after the incident). In the words of a *kukama* leader: "[Pluspetrol] closed the dialogue on us . . . confronting face to face is different" (*kukama* leader, interview with author, December 2010, Iquitos). The way this mechanism allows appropriation of power is further linked to problems of participation whereby the company's claims on how contamination management proceeded became legitimized above other versions, in particular above what affected communities asserted. We will discuss more on the issue of participation in the following section by depicting particularities in the meetings and dialogue between the parties during the months after the oil spill.

Modes of Unruly Engagements: Meetings, Dialogue, and Participation

Four months after the oil spill, contamination impacts were still denied by many regional authorities and Pluspetrol. By then, community leaders suspected a deceitful state-company collusion, particularly since negotiations took place through certain selected groups of affected communities and with the exclusion of particular leaders.

Both Pluspetrol and the regional government representatives decided what "affected communities" entailed, and arranged meetings and compensation payments that resulted in some communities receiving emergency support, while others were left unattended. The communities ascribed to the *Asociación Kukama del Bajo Nauta* (Cocama Association of Lower Nauta—AKUBANA) association, for instance, were initially denied emergency support and compensation based on the premise of being too far downriver from where the incident occurred. AKUBANA leaders considered it unreasonable that regional authorities and Pluspetrol could argue that contaminated water and fish would remain restricted to one particular area as the river water flowed, eventually reaching communities downriver like theirs (approximately 250 km from the incident). AKUBANA asserted that their communities had experienced just as many detrimental effects from the oil spill. Pluspetrol invited the AKUBANA leaders to dialogue five months after the oil spill, but after the meeting AKUBANA was still denied any kind of support.

The limited and selected indigenous participation in the management of oil spills was also observed in a meeting organized by the regional government, where Pluspetrol and the two institutes in charge of environmental sampling were invited, but no indigenous leaders were allowed in (at least initially). The exclusion of indigenous leaders was justified on the grounds that the meetings were "technical meetings" where incongruences in the sampling procedures between sampling teams would be discussed, assuming that the indigenous leaders had nothing to contribute. In response to this, indigenous leaders together with local journalists met outside the regional government's building, demanding it to open up all discussions concerning the oil spill given that they were issues of general public concern. Four indigenous leaders were selected to go in. However, their selection was based on the regional authorities' disposition. This explicitly rejected the leaders of the *kukama* association ACODECOSPAT, whom some regional authorities had openly labeled as "intransigent and troublesome"[5] for refusing the company's direct compensation (what the *Kukama* association considered "the company's alms") and for seeking indemnification instead (based on technical measurements of the actual impacts of contamination).

Soon afterward, it became evident that the meeting had not been entirely "technical." The leading scientist of one of the sampling teams in charge of the Marañón case (from DIRESA-Loreto), and seemingly the most capable of technically explaining the sampling procedures and verifying them with the other sampling team, was found outside the building fully unaware that the meeting was taking place.[6] The scientist revealed that the institution's head (apparently its only representative at the meeting) had not notified him that the results of Marañón environmental samples had been already disclosed (after being analyzed in laboratories in Lima) and that they showed no contamination. Moreover, after the so-called technical meeting, one of the community leaders, among the selected four, discreetly mentioned to others that Pluspetrol representatives had barely spoken throughout it. "Instead," he said, "it was mainly the attorney, our own people, who had been talking, defending Pluspetrol, against their own people [us, the affected communities]." Another leader claimed,

> We have been three days here in the regional government and we're not yet being heard ... I think [the regional government] pretty much shows favoritism for the company. For us, the communities' residents

that come to make a just demand for our rights to defend the Marañón and the Amazon, we are practically abandoned by the authorities. (*Kukama* leader, interview with author, October 2010, Iquitos)

In the eyes of the community leaders, the authority and legitimacy of the state in mediating cases of contamination eroded further through the direct exclusion they experienced in addition to the perceived state-company collusion. The case demonstrates that efforts to make technicalities appear the most important issue in the process of contamination management can serve to camouflage exclusion and ostensible collusion.

In response to the selected eligibility criteria for data employed in the oil spill's handling, the *kukama* and other affected community associations themselves organized open meetings at the regional indigenous association's offices, where they invited Pluspetrol and regional authorities to attend for dialogue and clarification. In one of these meetings, where they were to discuss details behind the discrepant results on the level of contamination, neither Pluspetrol nor regional authorities attended. Likewise, representatives from the institution whose results showed no contamination (DIRESA-Loreto/DIGESA) were absent. Only the leader from the institution's sampling team (IIAP), whose report asserted the existence of contamination, attended and explained the findings in his samples to the indigenous leaders. The attitude by some regional state institutions and Pluspetrol in this case confirms the expectations that indigenous peoples will comply with an imposed form of meetings or so-called dialogue tables (*mesas de diálogo*).

In that sense, it is crucial to take a closer look at the interactions between actors in these particular "invited spaces" (Cornwall, 2004) as well as the underlying forms of unruly engagements brought forward through them. The procedural rules that characterize meetings and dialogue tables (cf. Rodriguez Garavito, 2010) encourage the imposition of a particular form of participation by more powerful groups, in this case the regional government and Pluspetrol. For instance, the *kukama* were conscious of the learning process involved in the procedures requested by the company and authorities to enter negotiations, indicating, for example, "[Our association] now has its own legal personality; the company demanded this in order to sit [and negotiate]." However, while procedures to extend *kukama* presence in spaces of participation "are necessary conditions for their formal involvement," they proved not to be "sufficient to enable [them] to participate substantively" (Pozzoni, 2001, cited in Cornwall, 2004, p. 84, see also Knight & Johnson, 1997; Kohn, 2000).

A coercive form of participation was evident in how Pluspetrol dominated the agenda of negotiations. A human rights lawyer, who had been present at several dialogue tables between *kukamas* and Pluspetrol noted, for example, that "the indigenous leaders bring their points, but they are simply inserted into the company's agenda." The same lawyer also commented that, on one occasion, a company representative accused him of "inciting insurgency among the population" because he tried to inform local residents about their rights and simple meeting procedures before the meeting started. The advice he had given included the need to write down minutes, and commitments and signed agreements that the communities could later use to demand their fulfillment by the company. After all, the "existing arrangements" (cf. Ferguson, 2006) of keeping affected communities as ill-informed as possible seemed to satisfy and benefit the company as well as some authorities who continued engaging in business as usual. Moreover, the state failed to act as a mediator of discussions in spaces of negotiation. In a crucial meeting between Pluspetrol and the *kukama* association AKUBANA, for example, no state representatives were present.

Although the indigenous leaders had brought an agenda with three key requests to Pluspetrol, the company declined them and refused to sign the minutes prepared by the indigenous party (attesting to the company's rejection of the indigenous leaders' requests), even after insistent demands. The company alleged that signing minutes was unnecessary because that day's meeting had only been "a dialogue." So, although Pluspetrol representatives tried to show tolerance by listening patiently to all the testimonies, the indigenous leaders felt they had no argument to fight back as they were politely asked to leave the company's installations.

The "invited spaces" where negotiations take place also reveal subtle prejudicial expressions and attitudes that reinforce power asymmetries. For instance, certain comments made by Pluspetrol representatives revealed expectations that indigenous leaders should act in a "civilized" manner: "We have cordially invited you to our house and we want to dialogue like civilized people." In general, there is an underlying paternalistic conceptualization that dialogue in the types of meeting proposed by more powerful actors are a "civilized" form of engagement compared with the "uncivilized" blockades or protests with which indigenous peoples in Peru are increasingly associated. In many ways, the procedural rules in such formalized invited spaces together with the "internalized discourses of discrimination" (Freire, 1972) reinforce even further power asymmetries between the parties, and lead to highly ambiguous forms of dialogue. In the Marañón case, a general feeling of disappointment spread among the affected communities of not being properly heard, suggesting that "having a voice clearly depends on more than getting a seat at the table" (Cornwall, 2004, p. 84). At the same time, these examples also illustrate how indigenous communities, political leaders, and organizations, struggle to enter into and appropriate the rationale of the "invited spaces."

Modes of Unruly Engagements: Politics of Sampling

The shaping of sampling politics by regional authorities and Pluspetrol is another mode of unruly engagement. As noted throughout this chapter, two different institutions handled the environmental samples taken after the oil spill: DIRESA-Loreto (the regional branch of the National Directorate for Health, DIGESA, ascribed to the ministry of health) [7] and IIAP (Research Institute of the Peruvian Amazon, ascribed to the ministry of environment yet considered autonomous). The institutions' findings concerning the level of contamination contradicted each other on major points. DIRESA's reports indicated no presence of hydrocarbons in the Marañón river. They only found a very small concentration of another type of hydrocarbon[8] that "does not disturb the river's sanitary quality" (Ministerio de Salud [MINSA], 2010). DIRESA concluded that "after 60 days from the incident, the water recovered its usual quality" (MINSA, 2010).

In complete contrast, IIAP's reports indicated high levels of contamination. The samples taken three days after the oil spill showed high levels of oil and grease in the river, "exceeding by more than a hundred times National Standards of Environmental Quality for Water" (Instituto de Investigaciones de la Amazonía Peruana [IIAP], 2010a, p. 4). Contrary to what DIRESA-Loreto found, IIAP's first report noted that oil was visible in both water and sediments, and not only in riverbanks and impregnated in river vegetation—as recognized by DIRESA-Loreto. IIAP emphasized the need to undertake a "comprehensive monitoring" of the medium- and long-term impacts of the oil and grease as well as the dispersant (the "white powder" spread by Pluspetrol). IIAP also cautioned about the population's health, well-being, and socioeconomic activities, and the need to account for previous water contamination from the year 2000, when approximately 5,000 barrels of crude oil were spilled in the same area (IIAP, 2010b). According to IIAP's ecological approach, Pluspetrol's cleaning had not only been inefficient but also insufficient and superficial.

Correspondingly, local residents claimed, "It has not been properly cleaned, the white powder only submerged the crude [oil] to the river bottom . . . when the children jump into the water, the oil comes up again, you can see it floating" (Resident of Urarinas district). In addition, IIAP noted that the concentration of lead and cadmium as well as other heavy metals was above the maximum permissible levels in many of the common fish species consumed and traded locally.

Soon after the publication of IIAP's reports revealed high levels of contamination, some public authorities discredited their value. This included the regional government's vice-president, Norman Lewis, who called the reports

> a remarkable act of irresponsibility, because as a result, 59 communities [had] blocked navigation in the Marañón River . . . causing social unrest" (Pro & Contra, 2010). Lewis maintained that IIAP's reports lacked legal value because an attorney had not been present in the sampling procedures. He ratified that DIRESA-Loreto (DIGESA) was "the only organism capable of doing a legal evaluation of contamination in the Marañón River . . . [and they] explicitly show that there is no contamination.

When Lewis was told that the samples of both IIAP and DIGESA were taken during the same field visits, meaning that no attorney was present for either of them, his answer was vague and he appeared to lack knowledge about the actual sampling procedure (Pro & Contra, 2010).

The report of OSINERGMIN (the Supervising Agency for Investment in Energy and Mining) released only a few days after the oil spill also denied contamination, and it served to support Pluspetrol. OSINERGMIN highlighted the effectiveness of the company's contingency plan, indicating that, "the oil spill [had] been controlled and eliminated," and that "there is no presence of hydrocarbon being observed neither in the river water nor on the river banks in the sectors downriver from the incident" (Organismo Supervisor de la Inversión en Energía y Minería [OSINERGMIN], 2010). Since OSINERGMIN is the independent regulatory body overseeing and imposing sanctions on extractive companies that infringe the law in Peru, its position in these cases is significant. According to several local sources, however, OSINERGMIN's observations concerning the Marañón case relied on information provided by Pluspetrol's supervisors (in the Saramuro plant).

During the months following the oil spill, both IIAP and DIRESA-Loreto continued taking samples. Due to the controversy over the level of contamination, regional authorities determined that a team from the capital city, DIGESA-Lima, would assist the regional team DIRESA-Loreto and that an attorney would be present throughout the entire sampling procedure. This meant that the "official" level of contamination, as dictated by DIGESA-Lima, was determined four months after the oil spill. The *kukama* leaders perceived that by the time the DIGESA-Lima team arrived to take new samples, their results would indicate much lower levels of contamination than those indicated by IIAP immediately after the oil spill, given that contaminants would continue dispersing with time. Accordingly, many leaders suspected that the authorities were actively encouraging delay in the sampling procedures, which would eventually help support DIGESA's initial results and would end up minimizing the level of contamination. Additionally, for many, the fact that a DIGESA-Lima team was to take new samples did not guarantee them any more credible results. It seemed very unlikely to them that DIGESA-Lima would contradict previous results from its own institution considering the prevailing pressure. Indigenous leaders also held that DIGESA had previously denied contamination in the Corrientes area (where Pluspetrol is also involved) and only recognized it after an independent foreign monitoring institution revealed that indeed contamination existed.

Furthermore, the ways in which field-sampling procedures are carried out also contribute to understanding how the state-company partnership shaped sampling politics. For instance, some of the field visits for river monitoring included Pluspetrol members and two private environmental analysis providers hired by them (Walsh Peru and CORPLAB). Although the ministry of health's website celebrated the significant improvements in the coordination between Pluspetrol and state institutions at national and regional level (cf. Dirección General de Salud Ambiental [DIGESA], 2010), other actors (at least at the local level) remained skeptical of such collaboration. Some perceived that the company's simple presence during sampling procedures would inflict pressure to comply with what seemed most favorable to the company's interests. For instance, a member of a civil society organization expressed having a sense of uneasiness over his indebtedness to Pluspetrol after using the company's boat and helicopter on previous occasions to reach some communities. The company covers transportation expenses in these cases because of the ostensibly low budget designated by state institutions at the regional level for missions in remote areas.

The restricted way in which the results were disclosed is another point worth highlighting in the handling of sampling procedures. DIGESA's website and regional representatives indicated their full reports would be publicly disclosed. However, the results became known through notifications (in newspaper format) uploaded on the Internet. Moreover, while copies of the notification and the actual report were sent to regional authorities and Pluspetrol immediately after being released, the indigenous party did not receive any (even after several reminders). The indigenous associations became aware of the first report later and through a letter sent by Pluspetrol. This experience illustrates how authorities tend to overlook the role of indigenous and local stakeholders in evolving conflicts. Also, the fact that DIGESA is the only accredited institution with the right to take samples that legally represent the "reality" of contamination effectively prevents the *kukama* and other oil-affected communities from being sources of knowledge about contamination in the areas where they live.

In that sense, the politics of sampling can be further analyzed from a more "cognitive" and "institutional" angle, looking at contamination as part of a "technical discourse" (Karpouzoglou, 2011) in the Amazonian context. As with most other monitoring procedures in the region, the assessment of contamination levels relies entirely on water and (to a lesser extent) fish samples, which are generally examined in laboratories in the capital city of Lima. In other words, contamination levels are determined at some distance from community contexts, whereby residents' testimonies and their own criteria of water quality are included only to a limited extent in the reports.

The Marañón case illustrates how the guidelines for the management of oil spills are based on the adoption of a narrow technical definition of water quality that fails to recognize the multiple meanings and constructions that water users attach to problems of water quality. The reliance on a kind of detached quantitative "science" influences the types of "expert advice" delivered to authorities and the oil company. Thus, the type of advice used to address oil spills and contamination depends largely on how water quality has become "constructed" by DIGESA and its umbrella institution, the ministry of health, through the use of their definition of water quality based on scientific values, the scope of their monitoring program, the production of written texts such as official reports, and the institutional position of DIGESA (which legally has the last word about the status of water contamination) vis-à-vis the exclusion of other sources of information.

Modes of Unruly Engagements: Contingency Plan and Compensation

The lack of a contingency plan or emergency plan is another dimension of the unruly engagements in contamination management in Amazonia.

The Marañón case demonstrates that the lack of a contingency plan allowed Pluspetrol to decide unilaterally when to end the basic emergency support of water and food to the affected communities (two months after the oil spill), despite the fact that contamination levels continued to be contested. In the compensation processes, Pluspetrol and regional authorities also have the power to decide who to engage with, that is, which communities and associations, as well as in which ways. Although indigenous representative bodies exist (AIDESEP and ORPIO)[9] and a concrete indigenous association representing all three affected districts along the Marañón river was created to start formal dialogues after the oil spill (i.e., the umbrella association *Asociacion por la defensa del Río Marañón*), Pluspetrol was able to engage with and favor some communities that willingly entered into temporary alliance to receive compensation while leaving out others that were more difficult to negotiate with.

An example is a group of leaders from the district of Nauta (one of the three affected districts) who took over the umbrella association's name to start its own separate negotiations with Pluspetrol. Leaders of the *kukama* association (ACODECOSPAT) explained that Nauta's association had decided to negotiate on their own because the company had told them that they were willing to negotiate and compensate them only if they did not have to deal with the president of ACODECOSPAT—who was also the leader of the original umbrella association. According to the ACODECOSPAT leaders, the company wanted to divide them from the beginning because the original umbrella association had as its main objective to file a lawsuit against Pluspetrol and obtain appropriate indemnification (rather than negotiating for small unregulated payments of compensation). The ACODECOSPAT leaders commented that Pluspetrol considered it much easier and cheaper to divide the umbrella association and negotiate individually with each association or individual community.

The Nauta association was invited to negotiate directly with Pluspetrol after receiving attention in the media due to a four-day blockade of the Marañón river that they organized. As the Marañón is one of the Amazon river's main tributaries, the blockade meant obstructing an important fluvial connection for trade between Peru's northeastern cities. Much tension emerged during the days when the blockade was in force. Since the breakout of deadly violence in the Amazonian city of Bagua a year earlier, public authorities had in general become much more alert about indigenous protests. Thus, the Marañón blockade received immediate attention and soon afterward a dialogue table was established between the protesting communities, the regional authorities, attorneys, and institutions in charge of environmental sampling. The meetings, which proceeded in the city of Iquitos and together with Pluspetrol representatives, literarily closed the door on leaders from all other affected communities as well as the press. Among the associations that were left outside were the *kukama* association ACODECOSPAT, *Asociación Indígena de Desarollo y Conservación del Samiria* (Association of Development and Conservation of Samiria—AIDECOS) (representing some communities in the Parinari district), *Organización de Juntas Vecinales de Nativos Cocamas de Loreto Nauta* (Organisation of the Cocamas Indigenous Neighbourhood Committees of Nauta—OJUVENACO) (an organized group of neighbors also in the district of Nauta), and groups of leaders from the Urarinas district. On one occasion, when these other leaders and journalists had taken their seats in a conference room where the negotiation with Nauta's association was to take place, a regional authority representative suggested changing rooms, and hence excluding these participants, in order to "facilitate dialogue" with those who were "actually involved." Pluspetrol readily agreed to this suggestion. After days of private negotiations, the Nauta association was able to obtain compensation ranging from USD35 per person to USD1,400 per affected family, as well as 75 tons of food altogether (mainly canned food that ended up being sold in the town of Nauta in exchange for cash).

Another group of communities that decided to initiate separate direct negotiations with Pluspetrol was the Parinari association (representing most communities in the district of Parinari). The Parinari association was the first one to meet Pluspetrol, only four days after the oil spill, in the community of Santa Rita. That day, Pluspetrol and community leaders across Parinari signed an agreement whereby the company committed itself to supply the communities with emergency support of water, food, and medical attention until technical reports indicated that the water was otherwise drinkable again.

Nearly a month after the oil spill, the Parinari association called for a new meeting with Pluspetrol, arguing that the company had not supplied enough water and food in spite of two previous agreements and that sickness continued rising. For this meeting, the communities had prepared a set of requests where, among other things, they demanded long-term sustainable development projects and constant renewal of medical supplies. The regional manager, who had personally attended that day's meeting, indicated that those particular requests did not correspond to the company's mandate. He then added that Pluspetrol allocates, however, a budget called the "economic development fund," which accommodates to the communities' priorities and could support Parinari with 2 million Peruvian soles (approx. USD650,000). After some discussion, Pluspetrol's manager agreed to make it 2.5 million soles instead (approx. USD700,000), which the community members immediately approved and they signed a written agreement.

After the compensation agreement, the Parinari communities stopped supporting the collective demand of the associations of the affected communities. ACODECOSPAT leaders considered that the direct form of negotiation employed by Pluspetrol was part of a strategy to continue dividing affected communities. They became even more convinced of this after realizing that Pluspetrol had acted in a similar manner when handling issues of contamination among *achuar* and *kichwa* indigenous communities in the Corrientes area:

> While we looked for the unity of all the affected [communities], the company managed to convince the leaders of the Parinari district . . . to negotiate with them according to the company's criteria to divide [communities]. (*Kukama* leader of ACODECOSPAT, interview with author, October 2010, Loreto)

A similar process took place with the community leaders of the Urarinas district. Initially, the Urarinas representatives worked closely with ACODECOSPAT under the umbrella association in favor of the lawsuit and appropriate indemnification. However, a few months later, after seeing that communities in Parinari and Nauta had managed to obtain immediate economic benefits from Pluspetrol, they also saw the need to organize themselves separately in order to negotiate. Five months after the oil spill, Pluspetrol called the Urarinas committee in for private negotiations. This was only after the leaders had appeared on the front page of the regional newspaper indicating that if they were not heard their communities would otherwise take "more drastic measures," like occupying the company's oil wells and blocking an important highway in the region. Similar to other cases, the Urarinas association's direct negotiation with Pluspetrol was a complicated process. According to one of the first agreements reached with Pluspetrol, the company had committed itself to supply food and water to all the affected communities. However, the agreed amount never reached the communities and it became a long bureaucratic process trying to prove the company wrong. Moreover, Pluspetrol apparently requested the Urarinas communities to sign an agreement indicating that after receiving economic support ". . . the communities [would] give up any other type of demands for the incident."

This became subject to extended discussion as some leaders refused to sign it despite receiving pressure from their communities to do so, noting that the communities "just wanted the money to come." Furthermore, the Urarinas leaders indicated that Pluspetrol not only requested community representatives to sign the agreement, but entire communities as well. The reason was that in case of future changes of Urarinas' representatives, the document would still be valid and irrevocable and the communities would not be allowed to ask for any other type of support concerning the oil spill.

The lack of a contingency plan gave Pluspetrol power to decide for how long the emergency support was appropriate regardless of the fact that the level of contamination remained contested. It also gave the company power to legitimize a self-made criterion on how far downriver to consider an "affected community." Through the lack of guidelines, Pluspetrol was able to limit participation, decide how negotiations would proceed and based on what terms, and which leaders and associations to include and exclude from negotiations based on their willingness to comply with the company's compensation parameters. Pluspetrol was in charge of distributing basic resources like water, food, and medicines in the emergency and had the last word on how much the support would be adequate.

Moreover, not only did Pluspetrol determine rules for what constituted a contingency plan in correspondence with its own interests, but also the state did not question the improvisation of a contingency plan that was not legally validated. The procedures—as unruly as they are—are taken for granted and even supported by the authorities directly and indirectly. In that sense, oil companies take an active role in "governing" the unruly engagements in Amazonia and local governmental institutions contribute to legitimize the company's role. Nonetheless, Pluspetrol's lack of a legal contingency plan simultaneously provides a potential for affected communities to legitimately demand a replacement of such a form of corporate unruliness for one that reflects the population's real needs and expectations. Indigenous and civil society's responses, although uncertain, are growing in the area and are more fiercely contesting such modes of engagement.

Conclusions

Today, Peru is considered to be undergoing an oil exploration boom. More than 70 percent of Peru's Amazonian territory is currently covered by hydrocarbon concessions, compared with only 7 percent in 2003 (Orta-Martínez & Finer, 2010). The central government of

Alan García (2005–2011) celebrated the expanding extractive frontier, despite increasing levels of socio-environmental conflict across the country. Conflicts have, to various degrees, been linked to an underlying concern about contamination by the extractive industry. According to the Ombudsman's office, socio-environmental conflicts, closely associated with extractive activities, added up to 117 in April 2011, constituting of more than 50 percent of all national conflicts (Defensoría del Pueblo, 2011). The increasing number of confrontations, including violent ones, related to the use and management of water, has caused the national media to refer to Peru's situation as "the war for water" (cf. La Republica, 2010).

Rather than an outright war for water, we see the proliferation of unruly engagements in the many and different interactions, negotiations, alliances, and clashes between the state, the extractive industries, and Amazonian communities and peoples. The "unruly engagements" in the lower Marañón region on which we focus are the specific mechanisms used to control knowledge and information regarding contamination and the spaces for participation in negotiating compensation. These include communiqués released by the oil company concerning the state of contamination and its community assistance; delayed action in the process of sampling, assisting, coordinating meetings and taking decisions; controlling of sampling procedures regarding the level of contamination; restricting the access of the indigenous party to key information before negotiating and bargaining; appropriating power to decide which community gets to be assisted and with how much; partial negotiations where particular groups and leaders are restricted from entering; and dialogue tables that are highly inefficient and reinforce power asymmetries in their modes of participation. Based on the analysis of these types of interactions, we argue that "unruly engagements" are established and maintained through several parallel processes, namely (1) a politics of representation characterized by a control of information dissemination and the production of scientific knowledge, (2) the acceptance and also implementation of participatory mechanisms and discourse, and (3) confrontation as a mode of local claims-making outside of "invited spaces."

A focus on how unruly engagements play out in the Marañón case also arguably sheds light on contamination impacts in the northeastern Amazon region of Peru. Poor information exists on the health status of the region's population and environment despite earlier evidence connecting high levels of hydrocarbons in the water with health consequences for river dwellers whose daily livelihood depends on the river. A lack of in-depth analysis of companies' and government agencies' handling of adverse impacts of oil exploitation prevails (Orta-Martínez & Finer, 2010). In the communities neighboring Pluspetrol's oil block 8E, where the Marañón case occurred, many residents stressed the continuous oil spills and leakages that the authorities do not get to hear about. This continuous contamination is not officially recorded and thus, no attention is given to it unless the episodes are large and visible enough. The fact that river resources are especially important for the *kukama-kukamiria* peoples poses a special concern. The *kukama-kukamiria* are known for their close cosmological relation to water as well as for their sophisticated fishing techniques (Barclay, García, & Payaba, 2010; Rivas Ruiz, 2004).

The diminishing quality of vital resources, due to largely unregistered contamination from the oil industry, and the specific politics of sampling and the instruments of participation employed in order to control and deny contamination, also indicate the limitations and challenges involved in reducing damage and securing well-being for people. Through "unruly engagements" with the affected communities Pluspetrol ultimately achieves effective disentanglement from the social, legal, political, and environmental transformations it generates in the Peruvian Amazon.

Notes

1. ACODECOSPAT stands for Kukama Association for Development and Conservation of San Pablo de Tipishca and represents 54 communities in 5 different districts in the department of Loreto; Nauta, Urarinas, Belen, Maquía, and Sarayacu.
2. Cf. Civil Society Loreto, "Pronunciamiento de la sociedad civil por derrame de petróleo en el Marañón," (Iquitos, June 23, 2010).
3. The Ombudsman's report was based on a three-day field visit to some affected communities four days after the incident, together with representatives of the Kukama association ACODECOSPAT and two journalists from a national television channel.
4. Testimony obtained from the elder's wife who indicated that her husband did not have previous symptoms of sickness. Other community members, including the community health assistant, corroborated this testimony.
5. Published in several newspapers as well as mentioned in several testimonies gathered during fieldwork. An ACODECOSPAT member indicated "even the Superior Attorney [Gallo Zamudio] had taken the liberty of labeling us as intransigent for refusing to negotiate with the company".

6. Percy Cardenas, head of the Loreto Environmental Directorate. Open interview, GOREL-Iquitos, October 28, 2010. Cf. Nosotros no conocemos últimos resultados de Digesa quizá le llegaron al director, *La Region*, October 29, 2010.
7. DIRESA stands for Regional Directorate for Health.
8. Polycyclic Aromatic Hydrocarbons (PAHs).
9. AIDESEP is the national Amazonian indigenous association and ORPIO is one of its regional branches in the Loreto region. According to the ILO 169 Convention, these are the institutions that should be approached for consultation.

References

Appel, H. (2010). Offshore work: Oil and the making of modularity in Equatorial Guinea. Paper presented at the *American Anthropological Association 109th Annual Meeting*, 17–21 November, New Orleans, LA.
Barclay, F., García, P., & Payaba, L. (2010). Demandas Territoriales del Kukama Kukamiria del Río Huallaga y Nucuru. Sustentación jurídico antropológica. Lima, Peru: FEDECOCA.
Choquehuanca, M. (2010, June 27). *Mancha Negra en el Río Marañón* [Television broadcast]. Reporte Semanal. Frecuencia Latina. Retrieved March 8, 2012, from http://elcomercio.pe/planeta/501684/noticiapluspetrol-pudo-prevenir-poblacion-derrame-petroleo-rio-maranon
Cornwall, A. (2004). Spaces for transformation? Reflections on issues of power and difference in participation in development. In S. Hickey & G. Mohan (Eds.), *Participation From Tyranny to Transformation?* (pp. 75–91). London & New York, NY: Zed Books.
Defensoría del Pueblo. (2011). *Reporte de Conflictos Sociales No. 68*. Lima: Defensoría del Pueblo.
Dirección General de Capitanías y Guardacostas de Perú (DICAPI). (2010). *Resolución de Capitanía Guardacostas Fluvial de Yurimaguas N° 004-2010-M*. Yurimaguas, Peru: Marina de Guerra del Peru, Ministerio de Defensa.
Dirección General de Salud Ambiental (DIGESA). (2010). *Digesa Continúa con Evaluación de Contaminación de Río Marañón*. Dirección General de Salud Ambiental, Ministerio de Salud, http://www.digesa.minsa.gob.pe/noticias/noviembre2010/nota154.asp
El Comercio. (2010, June 21). El gobierno aseguró que en 10 días empresa deberá limpiar derrame de petróleo en el Río Marañón. *El Comercio*. Retrieved March 9, 2012, from http://elcomercio.pe
Ferguson, J. (2006). *Global shadows: Africa in the neoliberal world order*. Durham, NC: Duke University Press.
Freire, P. (1972). *Pedagogy of the oppressed*. London, UK: Penguin Books.
García Pérez, A. (2007, October 28). El Síndrome del Perro del Hortelano. *El Comercio*. Retrieved March 9, 2012, from http://elcomercio.pe
Instituto de Investigaciones de la Amazonía Peruana (IIAP). (2010a, October 12). *Informe de Evaluación Sobre la Presencia de Petróleo en los Ríos Amazonas y Marañón*.Iquitos: Instituto de Investigaciones de la Amazonía Peruana.

Instituto de Investigaciones de la Amazonía Peruana (IIAP). (2010b, June 19). *Informe Sobre la Contaminación del Río Marañón Ocasionada por el Derrame de Petróleo*. Iquitos, Peru: Instituto de Investigaciones de la Amazonía Peruana.

Karpouzoglou, T. (2011). Our power rests with numbers. The role of expert-led policy processes to address water quality: The case of peri-urban areas in the national capital region of Delhi, India. Doctoral dissertation, University of Sussex, UK.

Knight, J., & Johnson, J. (1997). What sort of equality does deliberative democracy require? In J. Bohmann & W. Rehg (Eds.), *Deliberative Democracy: Essays on reason and politics* (pp. 279–320). Cambridge, MA: MIT Press.

Kohn, M. (2000). Language, power and persuasion: Toward a critique of deliberative democracy. *Constellations*, 7(3), 408–429.

La Region. (2010, October 29). Nosotros no Conocemos Últimos Resultados de Digesa Quizá le Llegaron al director. *La Region*. Retrieved from http://diariolaregion.com/web/

La Republica. (2010, December 19). La Guerra por el Agua. *La Republica*, Sunday magazine, p. 1.

Ministerio de Salud (MINSA). (2010). *Digesa da a Conocer Resultados de la Calidad Sanitaria de las Aguas del Río Marañón*. Retrieved January 29, 2012, from http://www.minsa.gob.pe/portada/prensa/ notas_auxiliar. asp?nota=9287

Organismo Supervisor de la Inversión en Energía y Minería (OSINERGMIN). (2010). *Informe Tecnico no. 175901–2010-Os/Gfhl-Ueel Derrame de Hidrocarburos en el Río Marañón en Saramuro*. Lima, Peru: Organismo Supervisor de la Inversión en Energía y Minería.

Orta-Martínez, M., & Finer, M. (2010). Oil frontiers and indigenous resistance in the Peruvian Amazon. *Ecological Economics*, 70(2), 207–218.

Pozzoni, B. (2001). Citizen participation and deliberation in Brazil: The case of the municipal health care council of São Paulo. Unpublished doctoral dissertation, University of Sussex, UK.

Pro & Contra (2010, October 29). Informe es irresponsable. Retrieved March 9, 2012, from http://proycontra.com.pe/2010/10/29/informe-es-irresponsable/.

Reed, K. (2009). *Crude existence: Environment and the politics of oil in Northern Angola*. Berkeley, CA: University of California Press.

Rivas Ruiz, R. (2004). *El Gran Pescador. Técnicas de pesca entre los Cocama-Cocamillas de la Amazonía Peruana*. Lima, Peru: Pontificia Universidad Católica del Perú, Fondo Editorial.

Rodríguez Garavito, C. (2010). Ethnicity.gov: Global governance, indigenous peoples, and the right to prior consultation in social minefields. *Indiana Journal of Global Legal Studies*, 18(1), 1–44.

Univisión. (2010, June 22). Sancionarán a Responsables del Derrame de Petróleo en Río de Perú (Ministro).Retrieved March 9, 2012, from http://www.univision.com/contentroot/wirefeeds/world/8239886.shtml.

Chapter 10

Nonextractive Policies as a Path to Environmental Justice? The Case of the Yasuní Park in Ecuador

Chiara Certomà and Lucie Greyl

Introduction

In an era when the race for access to natural resources deeply affects social justice issues, the proposal to leave the oil in the Yasuní Park in Ecuador underground represents an innovative initiative. The Yasuní Park, a UNESCO world biosphere reserve in the Ecuadorian Amazonia, is a hotspot of biological and ethnic diversity whose reproduction capacities have been increasingly jeopardized in recent decades, particularly because of oil extraction activities. The Yasuní-ITT initiative proposes to leave over 846 million barrels of oil in the ground, not only to protect forest biodiversity, but also in order to foster innovative strategies of energy production and consumption, to face climate change, and to advance an alternative model to the carbon emissions market.

This chapter provides a theoretical discussion of the challenges and weaknesses of this proposal from a socio-environmental point of view. It highlights the role of civil society in the development and implementation of the initiative by exploring the philosophical and political ideas in which the arguments of the involved actors are grounded. Finally, it uses the Yasuní case to reflect more broadly on extraction, nonextraction policies, and social justice.

The main philosophical reference point is provided by the environmental justice theory and the way in which it has been mobilized in support of nonextractive claims. The concept of environmental justice calls for the recognition that, through particular mechanisms of spatial displacement and uneven distribution of environmental damages, a disproportionately large part of environmental risk is borne by poor and ethnic minority groups. Although social movements hold non-extractive policies to be a powerful means to promote environmental justice in Ecuador, this chapter suggests that this is not necessarily the case, as some of the arguments manifest a number of theoretical and practical fallacies.

Oil Extraction in Ecuador: Who Gains, Who Loses?

The first oil explorations in the Ecuadorian Amazonia in the 1930s led to little actual extraction, due to the geographical isolation and the strong opposition of local indigenous communities. But by the late 1960s the oil industry had expanded, and by the 1980s the area had been divided into imaginary blocks in order to expedite the granting of concessions for extractive rights to national and multinational oil companies (Centro di Documentazione sui Conflitti Ambientali [CDCA], 2011). The petroleum extraction boom that started in 1972 initially stimulated economic growth and social cohesion. Nonetheless, from 1982 onward, due to the difficulty of efficiently managing the oil income, there was increasing disparity in the allocation of economic resources and very little improvement in social conditions was generated. The two oil booms of 1973 and 1979 facilitated Ecuador's access to international credit, and between 1978 and 1983, whereas the oil industry contribution to national Gross Domestic Product (GDP) grew from 20 percent to 66 percent, the external debt increased 18 times (Fontaine, 2002). Like many other oil-dependent economies, Ecuador quickly decreased investments in all other sources of energy because of the strong reliance on oil-related gains (an effect known as "the Dutch Disease"). The disruptive impacts of oil drilling on environmental, economic, and social conditions made real socioeconomic change almost impossible. As a result, Ecuador has suffered from conditions of political and economic insecurity (Teran, 2007).

Economic diversification in the country is currently low, whereas social, ethnic, and regional disparities are high. Several studies have demonstrated that the increase in natural resources exports is likely to generate little employment creation and unfair income distribution. Summarizing these studies, Larrea and Warnars (2009) state that "dependence on petroleum exports has resulted in low growth and diversification, poor social performance and high environmental impacts" (p. 220). Although the public benefits from the oil industry have been known to fluctuate in past decades, the presence and influence of private oil companies in the Global South has increased. As Ecuadorian economist and politician Alberto Acosta (2009) has argued, like in most countries in the Global South whose economies are based on the exportation of natural resources, in Ecuador extraction has reinforced clientelism, corruption, and rentierism. This echoes economic and energy disparities manifested at the global level. Industrialized countries implement advanced technologies to exploit crude oil reserves more efficiently and often seek alternative energy models in their own backyard. At the same time, they have transferred the losses generated by an inefficient model of industrial development and the huge externalities it produces to poor resource-dependent countries. In turn, countries such as Ecuador are likely to remain trapped in a political space that encourages the reproduction of energy-intensive production coupled with inefficient energy usage (Teran, 2007). The state's economy depends on external financial inputs that subsidize an oil-dependent model in which detrimental social effects (subordination, poverty, and insecurity) are only partially compensated by the gains obtained from oil exploitation. In precarious democracies—whose political weakness is to some extent the effect of international lobbying activity—petroleum extraction has often been a main factor in undermining common goods, deterioration of welfare state provisions, and decrease in people's capabilities and rights (Teran, 2007).

Under the government of President Rafael Correa, from 2006 to the time of writing in 2012, this tendency has been countered. Correa was elected with a mandate for a decisive renationalization of the natural resource sectors and for the empowerment of state-owned companies. In 2007, private companies controlled 50 percent of oil production, but in 2011 they controlled just 30 percent (Banco Central del Ecuador, 2011). The state has increased its control over resource exploitation by privileging state-owned oil companies over foreign oil companies, and in 2010 it approved further reforms of hydrocarbon production. Despite the fact that the petroleum industry is no longer expanding at its earlier rate, it still remains a central sector in the Ecuadorian economy, in which the export of raw materials was estimated at around the 54 percent of total export revenues in 2007. At the same time, decrease in oil production has been accompanied by an increase in oil prices, which has guaranteed high profits for those operating in the sector. In turn, the importance of oil income to overall state revenue makes the shift away from an oil-based national economy particularly difficult, especially because the government looks toward nationalization of the oil industry as the core strategy to finance its reforms and social policies. Indeed, the expansion of the welfare state is another central point in Correa's mandate. In the transition toward renationalization of the oil sector, Correa implemented a tax system for foreign oil companies and imposed new conditions on investments. The income generated by oil taxes has allowed the implementation of a new economic policy, and investment in welfare arrangements that almost doubled between 2006 and 2008 to reach over 7 percent of GDP (Acosta et al., 2009). Thanks to these measures, the economic extractive model has started to generate benefits for Ecuadorians in general, but it has not stopped producing negative social and environmental impacts (Gudynas, 2010).

The Yasuní National Park: A Contested Hotspot

Latin America's oil reserves are relatively minor on a global scale, but many countries are undertaking an increasing expansion of the oil frontier that particularly affects the most remote areas where new reserves are most likely to be found (International Monetary Fund [IMF], 2011). The development of more advanced extraction technologies has supported and opened new frontiers, and coupled with weak conservation legislation, has facilitated the exploration and exploitation of oil in tropical areas, including protected and fragile areas such as the Yasuní National Park (YNP; Oilwatch, 2006). YNP is the most important biological reserve in Ecuador, created in 1979 by interministerial decree, and in 1989 it was declared a "World Biosphere Reserve" by UNESCO (the United Nations Educational, Scientific and Cultural Organization). The park, situated in the Orellana and Pastaza provinces on the border with Peru, contains a unique concentration of flora and fauna species, and it is an area of important biological and ethnic diversity. It is inhabited by several indigenous groups: the Huaorani nation, composed of the *hagaeri, taromenane,* and *onomeñane* peoples, living in voluntary isolation (whose original territory covers most parts of the park area); the *kichwa* and *shuar*; and other rural communities. Notwithstanding its status as a national park and biosphere reserve, as an effect of the expansion of the oil frontier to the most remote areas of the Ecuadorian Amazonia, the Yasuní Park territory has been divided into six exploitation blocks, namely blocks 14, 15, 16, 17, 31, and the ITT block (*Ishpingo Tambococha Tiputini*). The ITT block corresponds to the area covered by the Yasuní-ITT proposal (CDCA, 2011) (see figure 8.1).

Under the Gutiérrez government (2003–2005), the ITT block (estimated as having a rate of production of 107,000 barrels per day) was opened for exploitation by foreign companies. Numerous companies have shown interest, particularly Chevron-Texaco, Total, China National Petroleum Corporation (CNPC), China Petrochemical Corporation (Sinopec), and Petrobras (the Brazilian state-owned oil company); Chevron-Texaco was favored. The blocks' borders and the companies' licenses changed a number of times up to the 2010 renegotiation by the Correa government, when Ecuadorian state-owned companies increased their control of oil resources in the Yasuní area (CDCA, 2011). In March 2007, the Ecuadorian government launched the Yasuní-ITT proposal to leave the crude oil of the ITT block underground, which estimated at a total of about 900 million barrels, corresponding to 10 days of world consumption of oil and to 407 million tons of saved carbon emission (CDCA, 2011)—an amount exceeding the annual emissions of countries such as Brazil or France.

On the basis of the value of the Certified Emission Reduction in the European market of May 2009 (17.66 USD per metric ton), the economic value of the saved emissions is estimated by the Ecuadorian government to be around USD7.2 billion (Iniciativa Yasuní, 2010). Without accounting in monetary terms for the protection of the biological and ethnic diversity concentrated in the YNP, this is approximately the same amount the Ecuadorian state would get for the exploitation of block ITT. Half of USD7.2 billion is expected to be covered in 13 years by a trust fund constituted by international donor contributions and transactions in carbon market (Government of Ecuador, 2010). Initially it was presented as an Energy Transition Fund for which supporting countries would buy bonds to sustain the initiative until the end of 2008. However, because of the difficulties in securing funding, the deadlines have been revised and the government established an agreement with the United Nations Development Program (UNDP), which is now administrating the Yasuní ITT Trust Fund. UNDP is gathering donations received from international and national organizations, international cooperation programs, and individuals. Governments' economic support is also received in exchange for bonds named Yasuní Guarantee Certificates (CGYs). In case the planned minimum amount of USD100 million is not reached by the deadline of December 2011, the CGYs would be exchanged for their market value and the contributors reimbursed by the Ecuadorian state, which would subsequently start the exploitation of the ITT block. On the contrary, in a successful scenario, the money collected through the fund and the capitalization of a 7 percent benefit would be reinvested in renewable energy projects, deforestation prevention and reforestation projects, programs for ecosystem and biodiversity conservation, social development initiatives in degraded areas, and technological innovation (Government of Ecuador, 2010; Larrea & Warnars, 2009). To understand better the complexity and the implications of the proposal it is necessary to review the process that led to its adoption by the government. The Yasuní-ITT proposal originated from the increasing opposition of Ecuadorian indigenous and rural communities to oil extraction activities. In particular, in the YNP, after the first concessions of block 16 to Repsol-YPF and block 31 to Petrobras, local communities mobilized against the oil industry and gathered the support of environmentalist groups, international experts, and intellectuals. At the initiative of the organization *Acción Ecológica* (Ecological Action), an international campaign for the defense of Amazonia against oil extraction activities called *Amazonia por la vida* (Amazonia for life) was launched in 1989 (Fontaine, 2002). For the first time, environmentalist organizations allied with experts, intellectuals, indigenous, and rural communities, giving birth to a united front of mobilizations against oil extraction and its consequences (Bravo, 2005; De Marzo, 2009). On this occasion the traditional opposition between rural communities (usually complaining of a lack of consideration in the environmentalists' campaigns) and indigenous people (concerned about the destruction of the natural resources on which their communities rely), if not totally absent, appeared to be weaker than usual. Organized civil society developed national and international lobbying capacities and their close collaboration with intellectuals and politicians was fundamental in the development of the Yasuní-ITT initiative and its adoption by the national government.

The setting up of the initiative has to be understood in the broader frame of Correa's political agenda. At the beginning of his term, Correa started an ambitious and innovative process to rewrite the Constitution of Ecuador. The new Constitution has been recognized worldwide as the most advanced in terms of environmental and sociocultural rights (De Marzo, 2009). Furthermore, to develop his socialist political project based on wealth redistribution, Correa committed the government to the building up of new relations with indigenous people and ecological movements. He labeled Ecuador a "plurinational" state, resigned from the free trade agreement with the United States, created special indigenous districts, and instituted a social system in which most poor people receive cash transfers to cover basic needs (this last initiative attracted several criticisms; see Harnecker, 2010; Villacreses, 2008). Yet a very critical point relates to the effects of mineral resource extraction, in that while producing environmental degradation, it is also a means to finance social policies and the transition toward clean energy and conservation (Harnecker, 2010). The difficult process of building trust led the government to support and advance some of the proposals coming from the social movements, the Yasuní-ITT initiative being one of them. Notwithstanding that indigenous and environmental movements agree on most parts of the government's political program, their critical gaze has been focused on the difficulties encountered in gathering the initial financial contributions to the trust fund. A major crisis emerged in January 2010 after President Correa decided to step back at the last minute on his decision to sign the agreement with international donors, criticizing the work done by the UNDP Commission in charge for the trust fund, and arguing that it would not guarantee state control over the investments of the fund. In reaction, Roque Sevilla, president of the UNDP Commission, resigned. In August 2011 a new commission headed by Ivonne Baki was established. However, the pertinence and competence of the new commission was contested by Acosta (2009), who claimed that this episode not only brought back the ghost of oil industry interests, but also discredited the seriousness of the proposal. It is also important to consider that Ecuador has been the first country to support such a strong postextractive proposal, and this choice was made over serious economical evaluations. Oil exploitation by national companies respecting high environmental and social standards is economically and politically expensive, and given the potential 847 million barrels underground in the ITT block (the biggest reserves discovered in the last decades in Ecuador), it may turn to be convenient to get income for not exploiting oil. The government, while maintaining an important petroleum reserve for an uncertain energy and economic future, could also set the best price for the payment of the Yasuní initiative. However, faced with the government's statements about the option of turning back toward extractive policy if the trust fund does not amount to USD100 million by the end of 2011 (Fernández, 2010), the Commission is promoting a new international campaign all over the world.

People and Forest: A Postcolonial Narrative

The Yasuní-ITT proposal has been endorsed by different political and social actors, whose arguments invoke a diverse set of socio-environmental theories. A discussion of the narratives these arguments build upon may highlight their affinities as well as their principal contradictions. The government's view of the Yasuní proposal—also subscribed to by the international organizations involved—prioritizes nature preservation; it is justified on the basis of the uniqueness, richness, and inestimable value of the Yasuní biodiversity and the global ecological importance of the tropical forests. This approach builds (principally but not exclusively) upon an idea of nature that very closely recalls the origins of Western environmentalism, when tropical forests were seen as the last remains of the Garden of Eden (Bramwell, 1989; Grove, 1995). At that time, environmental care was interpreted as a luxury for rich countries (and people) with the possibility to invest in nature (Meyer, 1995). This view was implicitly reaffirmed in the first international meetings on environment and development held under the auspices of the United Nations (UN Stockholm Conference on Human Environment in 1972, and the UN Earth Summit held in Rio de Janeiro in 1992). Particularly, parks and natural reserves have long been thought of as dedicated places for preserving authentic wildlife for the well-being and the enjoyment of present and future generations. This often required the exclusion of local inhabitants from such wildlife "paradises" or, in some cases, allowed their presence as merely folkloristic figures (Hinchliffe, 2007).

From the 1980s onward, due in large part to the emergence of postcolonial studies, this view was challenged by a more "people-inclusive" place protection policy, on the basis of the assumption that "conservation is not necessarily about reducing the impact of people, it is about conserving some kinds of impacts, or disturbance" (Hinchliffe, 2007, p. 23). Postcolonial research has focused on the resistance of marginalized populations and on the claim that local communities should be entitled to manage local resources. This view was clearly acknowledged in later UN summits and major reports, like the 1992 Rio de Janeiro UNCED Conference and its *Report of United Nations Conference on Environment and Development*, Mme Ksentini's Report on Human Rights and Environment, and the Johannesburg Earth Summit in 2002. This acknowledgment goes together with the international recognition of indigenous rights whose main pillar is represented by the claim to be the original guardians of nature (especially of the forests). It also constitutes the principal narrative underlying the social movements' understanding of the Yasuní initiative, as clearly shown by the campaign *El Yasuní depende de ti* (Yasuní depends on you), part of *Amazonia por la vida*.

However, on closer examination, it is clear that the postcolonial narrative has produced a shift from the colonial tendency of *denying* the role of local people in conservation, to the postcolonial tendency of *fetishizing* them (Adger, Benjaminsen, Brown, & Svarstad, 2001, see also chapter 3 by McNeish, this volume). This creates a problematic situation. On the one hand, locals' claims adapt to and employ transnational solidarity networks and universal discourses (such as human rights), because the efforts by international environmental organizations, individuals, and political networks to sustain their struggle for the preservation of Mother Earth confirm the legitimacy of their cause (Brosius, 1997). On the other hand, they require boundaries and protective "fences" (legal, ethical, economic, etc.) to be erected around their places; places where they not merely "arrived" first, but to whose soil they claim to belong. Postcolonial narratives produce a view of indigenous identity as endlessly stable, and this reinforces and legitimizes specific political tenets. It is simpler to campaign to save "the noble savage" than to save *people* (as indigenous people actually are), whose heterogeneous identities are the results of different constructions, practices, and policy technicalities in a long history of various hybridizations. Indigenous peoples are not "frozen" at all; they generally demand their identities to be publicly acknowledged in the international arena as part of the center of power, demand a higher standard of living in accordance with their traditions (i.e., the ecological and social order they know and have perpetuated for a long time) and call for the fulfillment of social justice values. Paradoxically, to consider them an intimate part of the natural world, embedded in a completely autonomous system of knowledge, owners of a peculiar heritage of meanings and gatekeepers of paradise's secrets (as conservation projects often suggest) does not allow them to have a history, to have aspirations, or to have individual inclinations—sometimes opposed to those of the wider society within which they are born.

Rural communities (generally poor peasants, shepherds, fishermen, etc.) in the Amazonia experience a slightly different condition. Like indigenous people, rural people also are generally considered to hold an innate sense of place and to be natural experts of environmentally friendly land management (Pimbert & Pretty, 1995). Again, as indigenous people, they are considered to be satisfied with their lifestyle (subsistence or traditional lifestyle), to have limited material and financial aspirations, and not to be "annoyed by the enormous gulf between their level of affluence and that of the foreign conservationists, consultants and tourists whom they interact with on a regular basis" (Foale, 2001, p. 49). In fact, the formula of direct negotiation adopted by oil companies in recent years overturned traditional societal structures, values, and habits by directly bringing local people face to face with the international economic arena. Thus, embracing the romanticized ideal of local people as disinterested natural custodians of the environment disregards the fact that they might jealously guard their land and natural resources and be skeptical of any foreigners having the right to declare them in need of conservation or to limit their economic activities for the sake of global benefit. In turn, local people might both resist the erasure and the appropriation of their land, but also have a more positive attitude toward extractive activity because of the benefits they expect from it. This results in a situation in which "cultures are caught between, on the one hand, the desire for the mobility and material rewards of modernity and, on the other, the nostalgia for a lost purity, stability and traditional coherence which the present no longer provides" (Hall, 1995, p.177).

For quite a long time, petroleum extraction was a profitable business for many and brought some economic benefits, at least for a part of the Ecuadorian population. This is probably the reason why poor people pursuing a means to satisfy their immediate needs (either survival needs or accessories) continue to support oil extraction projects. Evidence that the economic benefits they obtain from oil-related activities are simultaneously undermining their traditional livelihoods does not necessarily turn them to antiextraction causes. Rather, the protection programs aimed at preserving forest and indigenous cultures have frequently been rejected by rural communities of small land-holders and farmers who gain (even if very marginally) economic rewards, because they will be constrained from getting this small (but significant) gain by the environmentalists' fanaticism for forest preservation and protection of native cultures. After all, why should a bunch of indigenous-supported ecofanatics from materially comfortable backgrounds be authorized to put constraints on their development?

The role of indigenous and rural communities in the Yasuní case clearly exemplifies how noninstitutional actors are reshaping political agency in the era of globalization. Together with engaged scientists working on Ecuadorian biodiversity and concerned for the fate of the rain forest, they rallied around a common environmental cause—despite advancing somewhat different claims —and turned it into a terrain for political struggles where new political subjectivities could emerge. Globalization frequently produces undemocratic and disempowering effects, but, at the same time, it fuels local strategies of resistance put forward by social movements and NGOs (Escobar, 2001). Even when geographically immobile and resource-poor, social movements contribute to the formation of the global domain and the virtual public sphere; and, thereby, advance a type of local political subjectivity that needs to be distinguished from what we usually consider "the local" (Castells, 1998; Massey, 1995; Sassen, 2007). Indeed, place-based political agency may interact with global politics in two different ways; it may focus on a local issue and connect it with similar struggles in the world, or it may result in local struggles aimed at engaging global actors (Castells & Cardoso, 2006). In the Yasuní case both these strategies have been mobilized; although social movements worked on the specific issue of petroleum extraction in the protected area, and linked their protest with worldwide nonextractive practices, they also formulated a proposal that requires global attention to succeed. Therefore, in the Yasuní case, a few acres of forest became a globally contested issue entangled in complex economic, political, and social networks.

Environmental Justice Theory and the Yasuní Initiative

The core argument of the new noninstitutional political actors supporting the Yasuní initiative is that nonextractive policies may increase environmental and social justice in a number of ways (Larrea & Warnars, 2009). Indeed, the issue of social justice is closely linked to environmental problems and poverty—both crucial issues in Ecuador. In the traditional conception, the fulfillment of social justice required governments to enact a set of social and political institutions, norms, and provisions that would ensure equality and just distribution of benefits and costs throughout society. By the 1990s the faith in this normative ideal of justice began to wane as activists recognized that the circumstances in which different social groups live have a major role and a one-size-fits-all justice did not necessarily serve everyone equally (Harvey, 1996). Indeed, material wealth, opportunity, health outcomes, educational attainment, job creation, and virtually all of the metrics of quality of life are never equally distributed across space. In the recent decades, the relation between social justice and environmental issues has been highlighted by pointing to a famous remark by Ulrich Beck (1995) who claimed that poverty is hierarchic, whereas smog is democratic. The "democratic" aspect of smog consists in its ubiquitous character; it affects everyone equally and, presumably, it is a matter of concern to everyone.

In the reality of everyday life, however, this is not necessarily the case. Beck's (1995) view fails to recognize that the fact that nobody can avoid environmental risks and damages does not mean that no inequalities in their distribution exist. Environmental problems are not "democratic" at all, because they affect some people more than others. First of all, through particular spatial displacements, environmental problems may overburden lower income countries, marginal peoples, and neglected areas of the planet. Second, the consequences of environmental problems are not randomly distributed; rather they reinforce already existing inequalities (Sachs, 1993). In general, marginalized groups and ethnic minorities are exposed to higher environmental problems because they lack social and economic power, and this, in turn, gives them fewer opportunities to counteract the poverty and social discrimination they suffer from. Beck (1995) acknowledges that some people are more affected than others by the distribution and growth of environment problems, but he tones down this statement by arguing that environmental risks create a *boomerang effect*, meaning that sooner or later even rich and powerful social groups will be influenced by environmental problems.

To counteract this state of affairs, environmental justice theory claims redistributive policies alone are not enough; a mere redistribution of environmental problems would not radically change the structure of global society in which the marginalization of certain groups is pervasive. Real empowerment of marginalized groups and the fulfillment of their claims for healthier environmental conditions thus require a virtuous relationship between participation, recognition, and redistribution (Bromberg, Morrow, & Pfeiffer, 2007). Representation alone does not necessarily guarantee effective empowerment (as the case of the direct negotiation policy by oil companies exemplifies); only when a concerted effort is made to ensure that everyone's point of view is seriously taken into consideration can marginalized groups' claims actually receive equal consideration.

Indigenous and social movements claim that the Yasuní-ITT proposal may improve environmental justice conditions. However, because the Yasuní project's first aim is to protect natural biodiversity and to reduce the environmental impact of oil consumption, social justice is not automatically achieved (Dobson, 1999). Indeed, although it is evident that the petroleum economy in practical terms encourages inequality and injustice, how will leaving oil underground promote social justice, and particularly environmental justice?

How (and *Whether*) Nonextractive Policies Foster Greater Environmental Justice

Different actors have presented a number of arguments in support of the claim that the Yasuní project may advance environmental justice. First of all, they noted that natural resources (especially oil) exploitation and exportation, unsustainable development, poor social conditions, and the perpetuation of poverty are part of the same self-reinforcing cycle. The proposal to leave the oil underground may break this cycle. Second, the Ecuadorian government affirms that in renouncing to exploit petroleum resources it weakens its own financial possibilities for the sake of the planet. This represents a concrete step toward a postcarbon society and a substitution of economic goods values with environmental, social, and moral values. Again, it is known that the lack of financial resources and the dependence on international economic institutions has weakened the agency of poorest countries and made them unable to move toward a sustainable model. The possibility to use the trust fund (without depending on foreign investment) may allow Ecuador to improve its financial and institutional foundation, and to support permanent conservation projects and stronger social justice measures. This may also be effective to avoid the squandering of oil reserves produced by short-term policies; indeed, several countries have adopted a petroleum fund in which oil represents a savings mechanism for the future to be used in specific circumstances (such as prolonged economic recession or a bank crisis) (Teran, 2007).[1]

In the case of Ecuador, characterized by pervasive poverty, any payment saving for future generations could be modified in favor of the majority of people, by stressing infra- (rather than intra-) generational redistribution. At the international level the Yasuní-ITT initiative may rebalance the North-South relations, since Ecuador proposed it in exchange for a greater role within international negotiations (Larrea & Warnars, 2009). This is intended to achieve greater international and internal equality.

However, this proposal is not perhaps without some shadows. From the economic point of view, the use of CGYs on the carbon emission market could also be seen as an acceptance by Ecuador of the international framework of climate change financialization, transferring credit for the right to pollute to rich countries. The Yasuní-ITT initiative broadly relies on the idea that industrialized countries declare themselves willing to improve global sustainability policies; and it offers them an opportunity to move in this direction. Despite government affirmations that the Yasuní-ITT initiative is not a sale of environmental services but a compensation for the lack of gains from oil exploitation, the effective realization of the proposal will still closely resemble a "willingness to pay" policy. Thus, the question is how far will it be possible to replicate such trust funds in exchange for forest conservation and keeping oil underground? It seems unlikely that industrialized countries will be willing (and able) to finance similar proposals in every corner of the world where mineral resources should be left underground and ecosystems preserved.

The Yasuní-ITT proposal is presented as a new mechanism to prevent greenhouse gas emissions, however, considerable doubt exists as to its real innovative character as it may reasonably be regarded as another mechanism to introduce new products into the carbon market (i.e., the CGYs), rather than advancing an alternative commitment to a post-Kyoto regime (particularly the Clean Development Mechanism). If environmentalists and scientists aim to put forward forest preservation they need to find someone who is willing to pay for it. Put this way, the Yasuní proposal does not directly question the pillars of the capitalist model of energy production and consumption, and it does not explicitly question the "geometries of power" (Massey, 1995) in the global economic system. Rather it substitutes dependence on foreign investments in oil exploitation with dependence on foreign subsidies for forest preservation; as a consequence the proposal is ambiguously similar to the classic "willingness to pay" mechanism because someone has to pay for conserving natural treasures. Furthermore, the definition of wild nature areas, which are considered valuable and deserving of conservation efforts, such as the ITT block, often leaves the surroundings for development of business as usual. This is obviously irrational under the perspective of working for a more environmentally sustainable world, particularly because oil extraction will be stopped in the Yasuní ITT area but it will continue in the rest of Ecuador.

Social movements have particularly focused on the relation between nonextractive policies and social justice through the issue of climate change. This is presented as the core reason for shifting toward nonextractive policies, for instance, by Oilwatch. The argumentation develops in the following manner: the expansion of the oil-based economy and deforestation produces impressive social inequalities, ecological imbalances, and geographical injustice (displacement, eradication of people, flows of environmental refugees, and so on). The oil industry is seen as one of the principal sources of social injustice in direct (deforestation, drilling, pollution spills) and indirect ways (greenhouse gas emission and climate change). Climate change is closely related to the oil-based economic model and it particularly affects those directly living on free basic environmental services (such as indigenous people, peasants, and fishermen) (Kolmannskog, 2008; Tsosie, 2007; Westra, 2008). After the failure of Kyoto and the proven inefficacy of emissions trading and environmental services schemes (Martinez-Alier & Temper, 2007), nonextractive policy is regarded as a viable alternative to confront climate change on the bases of precautionary principle and the principle of shared but differentiated responsibility. Ecuadorian experience in this field may be a leading example, as social movements claim. Hence, a straightforward conclusion suggests that ending, or slowing down, the rate of petroleum extraction will enhance social equality and justice. However, from a theoretical point of view, the climate change argument may appear a bit weak, because reducing oil extraction does not automatically reduce climate change. In order to achieve this goal it would be necessary to implement a viable and effective plan for energy production—an aspect in which the Correa plan at the moment is a bit fuzzy. It is unclear which kinds of energy production projects will be funded though the Yasuní Trust Fund: what will be their dimension; what participative processes will be enacted; and whether or not they will lead to centralized production and large scale distribution or small scale, locally distributed, production. Again, climate change reduction will not automatically mean a reduction of environmental injustices unless it is coupled with appropriate social policies and redistributive measures. As a consequence, the realization of the Yasuní initiative will not necessarily improve environmental justice in Ecuadorian society. In turn it is clear that, although nonextractive policies are presented by civil society as a means to foster greater environmental and social justice, this may turn out to be true only under specific conditions. These conditions are relative to the use of the trust fund and the complementary initiatives. The fact that a nonextractive policy in the Yasuní National Park model has been proposed, and that steps have been taken in the direction of its realization, does not guarantee per se that new privileges, elites, and injustices will not emerge as a substitute for the old. The impact on social justice is likely to depend on *how* the proposal will actually be implemented, the fund resources used, the old privileges contrasted, and the marginal voices taken into consideration.

These considerations suggest that to actually produce a change in the collective mentality and a shift toward a postcarbon society where nonextractive politics play a crucial role, the proposal is not sufficient. It would be necessary to question the very theoretical bases on which conservation proposals rely, to consider nature not merely as a physical place, neither a treasure to fence nor a code to be read with scientific formula. Because, as Donna Haraway (1992) reminds us, nature is "neither mother, nurse, nor slave, [...] is not matrix, resource, or tool for reproduction of man [; nature] is, strictly, a common place [...] widely shared, inescapably local, worldly, inspirited [...], is the place to rebuild a public culture" (p. 296). It is necessary to deconstruct the image of the tropical rain forest as "Eden under glass" and configure a politics "not of national parks and walled-off reserves, responding with technical fixes to whatever particular danger to survival seems most inescapable, but of a different organization of land and people, where the practice of justice restructures the concept of nature" (p. 309).

Note

1. This is the case of Norway, Canada, Alaska, Azerbaijan, Sao Tome, and Chad, for instance (Teran 2007).

References

Acosta, A. (2009). *La Maldición de la Abundancia*. Quito: Abya-Yala.
Acosta, A., Jacomé, H., Long, G., Martín-Mayoral, F., Montesdeoca, L., Ramirez, F., . . . Varela, M. (2009). *Análisis de Coyuntura Económica*. Quito, Ecuador: Facultad Latinoamericano de Ciencias Sociales Ecuador.
Adger, W., Benjaminsen, T., Brown, K., & Svarstad, H. (2001). Advancing a political ecology of global environmental discourses. *Development and Change, 32*(4), 681–715.
Banco Central del Ecuador (2011). *Cifras del Sector Petrolero Ecuatoriano.* n° 49–2011. Retrieved March 1, 2012, from http://www.bce.fin.ec/documentos/Estadisticas/Hidrocarburos/cspe201149.pdf
Beck, U. (1995). *Ecological politics in an age of risk*. Cambridge: Polity Press.
Bramwell, A. (1989). *Ecology in the 20th century: A history*. New Haven: Yale University Press.
Bravo, E. (2005). Exploitacion Petrolera en la Reserva de la Biosfera Yasuni—Ecuador. In E. Bravo & Y. Yanez (Eds.), *Asalto al Paraiso: Empresas petroleras en areas protegidas* (pp. 36–77). Quito: Manthra Editores.
Bromberg, A., Morrow, G. D., & Pfeiffer, D. (2007, Summer). Editorial note: why spatial justice? *Critical Planning, 14*, 1–3.
Brosius, J. P. (1997). Endangered forest, endangered people: Environmentalist representation of indigenous knowledge. *Human Ecology, 25*(1), 47–69.
Castells, M. (1998). *The power of identity: The information age—economy, society and culture*. Oxford: Blackwell.
Castells, M., & Cardoso, G. (Eds.). (2006). *The network society: From knowledge to policy*. Washington DC: Center for Transatlantic Relations.
Centro di Documentazione sui Conflitti Ambientali (CDCA). (2011). *Estrazioni petrolifere nel parco nazionale dello Yasuni*. Retrieved July 11, 2011, from http://www.cdca.it/spip.php?article606
Dobson, A. (1999). *Justice and the environment*. Oxford, UK: Oxford University Press.
Escobar, A. (2001). Culture sits in places: Reflections on globalism and subaltern strategies of localization. *Political Geography, 20*(2), 139–174.

Fernández, Á. (2010). Ecuador no Extraerá Petróleo del Parque Nacional del Yasuní. *Energias Renovables, 95*, 72-76. Retrieved January 11, 2011, from www.energias.renovables.com

Foale, S. (2001). Where is our development? Landowner aspirations and environmentalists agendas in Western Solomon Islands. *Asia Pacific Journal of Anthropology, 2*(2), 44-67.

Fontaine, G. (2002, March). Sobre Bonanzas y Dependencias, Petroleo y Enfermedad Holandesa en el Ecuador. *Iconos, 13*,102-110.

Government of Ecuador (2010, July 28). *Ecuador Yasuni ITT Trust Fund: Terms of Reference.* Retrieved March 1, 2012, from http://mdtf.undp.org/document/download/4492

Grove, R. H. (1995). *Green imperialism: Colonial expansion, tropical island Eden and the origin of environmentalism 1600-1860.* Cambridge: Cambridge University Press.

Gudynas, E. (2010). Si Eres tan Progresista ¿Por qué destruyes la naturaleza? Neoextractivismo, izquierda y alternativas. *Ecuador Debate, 79*, 61-81.

Hall, S. (1995). New cultures for old. In D. Massey & P. Jess (Eds.), *A place in the world?* (pp. 175-214). Oxford, UK: Oxford University Press.

Haraway, D. (1992). The promises of monsters: A regenerative politics for inappropriate/d others. In L. Grossberg, C. Nelson, & P. A. Treichler (Eds), *Cultural studies* (pp. 295-337). New York, NY: Routledge.

Harnecker, M. (2010, October 12). *Gobierno de Correa y Movimiento Indigena.* Rebelión. Retrieved September, 2011, from http://www.rebelion.org/docs/114792.pdf

Harvey, D. (1996). *Justice, nature and the geography of difference.* Oxford, UK: Basil Blackwell.

Hinchliffe, S. (2007). *Geography of nature: societies, environments, ecologies.* London, UK: Sage.

Iniciativa Yasuní. (2010). *Valoración Económica de la Iniciativa.* Retrieved July 11, 2011, from http://yasuni-itt.gob.ec/valoracion-economica-de-la-iniciativa-yasuni-itt/

International Monetary Fund (IMF). (2011). *World economic outlook April 2011: Tensions from the two-speed recovery, unemployment, commodities, and capital flows.* Washington DC: International Monetary Fund.

Kolmannskog, V. O. (2008, April). *Future floods of refugees: A comment on climate change, conflict and forced igration.* Oslo, Norway: Norwegian Refugee Council.

Larrea, C., & Warnars, L. (2009). Ecuador's Yasuni-ITT Initiative: Avoiding emissions by keeping petroleum underground. *Energy for Sustainable Development, 13*(3), 219-223.

Martinez-Alier, J., & Temper, L. (2007). Global warming. In Oilwatch, *Leaving crude oil underground.* Bali, Indonesia: IUCN National Committee of the Netherlands.

De Marzo, G. (2009). *Buen Vivir: Per una nuova democrazia della terra.* Rome: Ediesse.

Massey, D. (1995). The conceptualisation of place. In D. Massey & P. Jess (Eds.), *A place in the world?* (pp. 45–86). Oxford, UK: Oxford University Press.
Meyer, E. H. (1995). *I Pionieri dell'Ambiente.* Milan, Italy: Carabà.
Oilwatch. (2006). *Entre el Sueño y la Memoria: 10 años de lucha. 10 años de resistencia.* Quito: Manthra Editores.
Pimbert, M. P., & Pretty, J. N. (1995, February). *Parks, People and Professionals: Putting "participation" into protected area management.* Discussion Paper No. 57. Geneva: United Nations Research Institute for Social Development.
Sachs, W. (Ed.). (1993). *Global ecology: A new arena of political conflict.* Halifax, Nova Scotia, Canada: Fernwood Books.
Sassen, S. (2007). *A sociology of globalization.* New York, NY: W.W. Norton & Company.
Teran, J. F. (2007). The hidden costs of petroleum. In Oilwatch, *Leaving crude oil underground.* Bali, Indonesia: IUCN National Committee of the Netherlands.
Tsosie, R. A. (2007). Indigenous people and environmental justice: The impact of climate change. *University of Colorado Law Review, 78,* 16–25.
Villacreses, R. (2008, January). ¿Los Subsidios en Ecuador Valen la Pena? Un análisis teórico, de sostenibilidad y de los beneficios que generan los subsidios en el Ecuador. *Análisis de Políticas Públicas, 5.*
Westra, L. (2008). *Environmental justice and the rights of indigenous peoples: International and domestic legal perspectives.* Sterling, VA: Earthscan.

Chapter 11

Extraction as a Space of Social Justice? Commodity Production and Labor Rights in Brazil and Chile

Jewellord T. Nem Singh

Introduction

What does post-neoliberal resource governance consist of in Brazil and Chile? Can extractive justice be delivered under this political economy? In this chapter, I attempt to provide a sketch of emerging extraction-based growth strategies by focusing on how states, firms, and labor unions reconstitute their relationship in periods of commodity boom. Instead of binary models of governance between neoliberal and post-neoliberal "moments" that characterize the central Andean region, such historical ruptures and an anti-Washington Consensus agenda seem less apparent in Brazil and Chile. The economic reforms in mining are instead characterized by *political continuities with changes*, in terms of the orientation of state politics and the relationship between business firms and workers. Contemporary strategies of extracting rents for social development in Latin America cannot be simply categorized with reference to the weight of the state in relation to the market, or the degree of globalized integration. Political elites in all countries face public pressures of addressing the poverty and inequality legacies of the past, and the improvement of social justice depends on the ability of these elites to find pragmatic strategies to deliver both growth and social equality that were undermined by the neoliberal policy agenda.

The chapter offers two distinctive cases emphasizing the popular demands for economic and political reforms in the context of commodity booms and the extent to which state elites are responding to calls for a growth strategy beyond resource extraction. I examine

Brazil and Chile, and their petroleum and copper mining sectors respectively, to demonstrate how demands for greater inclusion, voice, and meaningful participation in the management of extractive industries are constrained by the realities of resource dependency and consolidation of exports-led models of growth. In both cases, natural resources are—and will remain—the fulcrum of conflicts between states, foreign and domestic capital, and organized labor unions in recalibrating strategies of growth and inclusion. Although Chile's dependency on natural resources rests on a single commodity that has considerably changed under different models of development, Brazil, in contrast, has a highly diversified export profile through centuries of extractivism ranging from wood, minerals, rubber, agricultural products, and most recently, petroleum. However, petroleum—like copper in Chile—has been a focal point of nationalist mobilization in defense of the right of the (peripheral) state to own and define its development strategy in a world system characterized by unequal terms of trade and inequality in power relations.

Further, the chapter brings in *labor unions* as a political actor contesting state-led projects of inclusion, and this resonates quite strongly with the tradition of political mobilization in twentieth-century Latin America. Left-wing governments of Brazil and Chile have combined the maintenance of exports-led growth model emphasizing the partnership of state and private capital in mineral extraction with the introduction of initiatives to bring in the voices of labor unions and social movements. Therefore, unlike many studies on the new politics of Latin American left (Hogenboom & Fernández Jilberto, 2009; Kennemore & Weeks, 2011), in this chapter I offer a detailed account of extraction reforms to make manifest the fuzzy distinctions between neoliberal and post-neoliberal strategies of extraction. In so doing, I seek to provide a more nuanced view within debates on the differing views about natural resource wealth and development as perceived by state elites and technocrats, on the one hand, and those who pay for development—the workers—on the other hand.

Consolidating Commodity Production in Brazil and Chile

As Haarstad argues in the introductory chapter to this volume, contemporary struggles over natural resources and the social contract between the state, private actors, and civil society illustrate competing claims for redistribution, recognition, and representation. As neoliberal reforms clearly failed to address (sometimes they even reproduced) social inequality and exclusionary decision-making, resource conflicts generated by struggles for social redistribution, recognition and representation have brought about the collapse of political coalitions supporting market reforms in the Andes and beyond. Although Brazil and Chile are part of the broad turn to the left in Latin America, their models of extractive management are far more institutionalized (and proffer greater legitimacy to the private sector) than others and they are indicative of *gradual* institutional change in the governing of natural resources. The distinctions between the discursive and actual policy practices in economic and political reforms need to be made clear to understand the difficulties of institutional transformation aimed at redressing the legacies of neoliberalism (Domingo, 2009; Haarstad & Andersson, 2009; Sawyer, 2004; Silva, 2009).

After some 30 years of neoliberal reforms, mineral extraction in Brazil and Chile has not produced popular mobilization at a scale, intensity, and scope comparable to the Andean countries. Despite the different historical legacies of military dictatorships and state corporatism—Chile being highly marketized and Brazil maintaining a developmentalist statist legacy—both countries have moved toward the gradual institutionalization of reforms legitimized by electoral victories promising a new politics of rebuilding the state without compromising the market. Although elites cautiously accepted the need for the participation of private capital in mining and petroleum, the state in practice never really left its regulatory and productive roles during this period, despite pressures for withdrawal of the state from economic management. One of the main reasons has been the extent of integration of Brazil and Chile in the global political economy. Ideas about the value of private sector participation in enhancing the competitiveness of state enterprises and efficiency in production through outsourcing and technological development have all been widely embraced by state technocrats and state-owned enterprise (SOE) managers. The extractive industries are some of the most internationalized sectors of these countries, with high rates of foreign investor participation, in which outsourcing of services and human resources is an acceptable and legitimate business practice. The state enterprises have been competing with private capital for mineral rights in exploration and exploitation, and follow the same regulations in tax payments, environmental management, and labor standards. In turn, state enterprises act much like private entities, with profitability as the driving force of investment strategy and labor management. How this particular political arrangement between public authority and market actors emerged is discussed in the following section.

Neoliberal Reforms in Extractive Industries

The process of neoliberalization in Latin America was not uniform or straightforward, as the differences between the Chilean and Brazilian cases attest. Chile came first in radically reorienting the role of the state and reintroducing private participation through the Foreign Investment Statute, famously known as DL 600, issued by the military dictatorship in 1974. This was followed by the Mining Code in 1983, still under General Augusto Pinochet, which further depoliticized copper management by limiting executive discretions in mining contracts and transferring this power to the judiciary, privatizing water rights, and recognizing the right of individuals (as opposed to big firms) to acquire mining concessions. Upon the return of civilian democracy in 1990, the governing coalition of Left and Center parties, *La Concertación por la Demócracia* (henceforth *Concertación*), did not alter the institutional framework in managing copper mining.

The standard narrative of Chile depicts the state as hollowed out by deliberate attempts of state elites to strengthen institutional frameworks for facilitating market-driven growth and a thorough expansion of private initiatives across the economy. However, mining reforms were not left uncontested. Instead, they were surrounded by reactions to the excesses of marketized governance, what I will call "moments of politicization." By *politicization*, I mean the contestation of reforms taking place in response to the construction of market societies (Polanyi, 2001), reflected in popular demands for greater inclusions, voices from below, and change in the ways labor and production are valued politically. In the Chilean context, this involved retaining full state ownership of copper mining, through the *Corporacion Nacional del Cobre* (CODELCO). Unlike in many resource-rich developing countries where large-scale mining is dominated by foreign capital, CODELCO maintains its large share in copper production (figure 11.1) and this effectively makes it the biggest producer of copper. Also, its influence over fiscal stability and macroeconomic decisions implies a political role. CODELCO has inexorably served as buffer between the state and private sector since its establishment in 1976 and this remains the historical legacy of Chile's nationalization of copper in July 1971. While the state recognizes the legitimacy of private capital and courts organized business through a probusiness mining framework, CODELCO's strategic importance to Chile necessitates indirect support from the state. For example, CODELCO holds mining concessions to the largest mine deposits in Chile, participates in joint ventures, and its corporate governance proffers extensive powers to

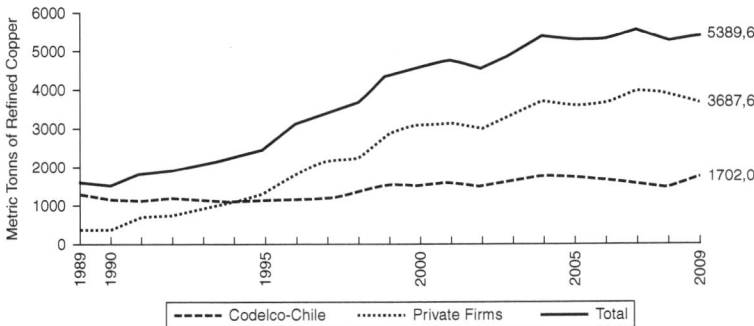

Figure 11.1 Share of public and private copper production in Chile, 1989–2009.

the state despite reforms in its management (Nem Singh, in press). Therefore, political continuities between neoliberalism and what preceded it, as well as continuities between neoliberal governance forms and what some refer to as the reconstitution of the *neostructuralist* state under *Concertación*, reflect the difficulty of identifying the distinctive rupture between neoliberal and post-neoliberal states (Leiva, 2009; Nem Singh, 2010).

In Brazil during the 1990s, attempts to privatize extractive industries (mining, petroleum, and steel) have been manifestly contested as a result of a lack of political consensus around private sector–driven development model and the need for sustained alliances between business and labor unions to successfully deliver economic reforms (Nem Singh & Massi, 2011; Montero, 1998). To begin with, economic nationalism has for long been part of the ideological mainstream in Brazil, so it never left. After a national campaign for state monopoly (1947–1953), the state oil enterprise *Petróleo Brasileiro* (Petrobras) was born and given absolute control over the domestic oil market for nearly 50 years. Both under Getulio Vargas (1937–1948, 1951–1955) and the military dictatorship (1964–1985), the strategy relied substantially on a *developmental state* that incorporated elements of organized interests within the state apparatus as a way of forging consensus around models of growth and political inclusion (Evans, 1979, 1995; Schmitter, 1972; Schneider, 2009; Trebat, 1983). Peter Evans (1979) famously referred to Brazil's strategy as a triple alliance between the state, multinational capital, and domestic industrialists, in which the state took both regulatory and entrepreneurial roles in sectors where private investment was nearly absent and in sectors deemed to be crucial for national security. Indeed, the story of petroleum is one of creation in the face of energy scarcity, a highly insecure

Cold War world order in which self-sufficiency was the only viable solution, and the growing need to address domestic energy consumption (Smith, 1976; Trebat, 1983; Wirth, 1970). Upon the return of civilian democracy in 1985, Brazil embraced the pathway of neoliberal reform. The strategy of Fernando Henrique Cardoso (1995–2002) was to intensify the process of dismantling state control in the sector through privatization, a process that began under Fernando Collor (1990–1992). Amidst intense mobilization of petroleum workers and trade unions, Cardoso successfully ended Petrobras' monopoly in oil exploration and exploitation and opened the oil industry to foreign capital for the first time. However, the privatization of mining—through selling capital stocks of the mining company Vale and ultimately transforming the state enterprise into a private-run firm—was not replicated in the oil industry. The momentum to privatize Petrobras was lost. To this day, state control over the oil sector is reflected in the ownership structure of Petrobras, and the large extent to which it participates in oil exploration, development, and production in the country.[1] While petroleum remained a state monopoly for more than 50 years, Petrobras was also driven to expand internationally to become competitive in the world market. The credence of a private sector–driven model of growth did not materialize completely in Brazil, with the oil sector largely open for private firms for investments in oil exploration and development but not necessarily ownership of the biggest player in the market—Petrobras. With such competitive advantage, foreign and domestic oil companies have opted for a cost-effective investment strategy, which is to work together with Petrobras rather than compete with the firm directly. Table 11.1 shows the degree of Petrobras' control of the domestic oil market, and that the refining and processing of crude oil remains completely a Petrobras affair. What is evident is that Brazil's legacy of state intervention has not been fundamentally altered; if anything, neoliberal reforms in extractive industries are domestic adjustment strategies in relation to an increasingly globalized international economy (Doring & Santos, 2011; Nem Singh & Massi, 2011).

In Brazil and Chile, then, neoliberalism has influenced the balance between states and markets significantly in the sense of proffering greater legitimacy and authority to private capital. However, the consequences are far more varied and complex than most academic literature suggests. The evidence presented here indicates that no consensus has emerged around marketization of resources, and this is reflected in a significant contestation of market reforms.

Table 11.1 Petrobras' oil production, explorations, and development share ownership

	Petrobras as 100% concession owner	Petrobras as 50% joint partner	Petrobras as minority partner (1%–49%)	Petrobras as majority partner (51%–99%)	Private capital as 100% concession owner
Blocks in Exploration Phase	113	31	29	56	175
Percentage of the Total (404)	28.0%	7.7%	7.2%	13.9%	43.3%
Fields Under Development	36	3	8	4	10
Percentage of the Total (61)	59.0%	4.9%	13.1%	6.6%	16.4%
Producing Fields	254	2	11	3	41
Percentage of the Total (311)	81.7%	0.6%	3.5%	1.0%	13.2%

Note: Numbers in parenthesis represent total number of oil blocks in exploration, fields under development, and producing fields as of December 31, 2009.
Source: Data from ANP Annual Report 2010.

Changes in the Margins: New Extractivism in Brazil and Chile

There are gradations of support for leftist governments across Latin America, but what arguably cements the democratic legitimacy of the left is the failure of neoliberalism to deliver economic growth, lessen poverty and social inequality, and deepen democratic practices. This is particularly the case for highly contentious reforms of labor and extraction (Grugel & Riggirozzi, 2009; Panizza, 2009). Post-neoliberalism, if one marks its temporal boundaries, begins with the erosion of social pacts between elites and organized social groups that were forged under the pressure to liberalize national political economies in the two countries. In some countries, periodic moments of resistance took place, most emblematically mobilizations around the rejection of privatization of water in 2000 and gas in 2003 in Bolivia, *El Argentinazo* in 2001, and *El Caracazo* in Venezuela in 1989. Elsewhere, the rise of left governments was primarily mediated by institutional channels—electoral victories—with a clearer social democratic agenda in economic reforms. Brazil and Chile fit into the latter category, in which leftist parties were engaged in forging a political consensus around economic governance by accepting the role of private capital in managing the challenges of globalization. Left-wing governments in Brazil and Chile have promised a political project of rebuilding the state, expanding citizenship rights, and placing social justice at the core of reforms.[2]

It can be argued that what facilitated the new political project in Latin America is a global context marked by sustained growth rates and high commodity prices. According to Economic Commission for Latin America and the Caribbean ([ECLAC] 2010b), the combination of a favorable external environment and better macroeconomic management has resulted in economic growth, building up of reserves, controlling inflation, reducing public debt, and achieving fiscal and current account surpluses. In South America in 2010, the largest proportion of foreign direct investment (FDI) went to the natural resources sector (43 percent), followed by the service (30 percent) and manufacturing (27 percent) sectors. Natural resources are an important FDI destination and the weight of the primary commodities sector in investments has actually increased compared to the period between 2005 and 2009 (ECLAC, 2010a, p. 9). China is the third largest investor in Latin America (after the United States and the Netherlands) with a share of 9 percent, with its transnational firms investing over USD15 billion in 2010. China's investment to Brazil grew from USD255 million in 1990 to USD9.564 billion in 2010, and its regional strategy was to invest in the extraction of natural resources mainly in the hydrocarbons sector, and to a lesser degree, mining (ECLAC, 2010a). There seems to be a "fit" between Chile's export profile and China's demand in these sectors, which is not the case for other industries like textiles and footwear (Barton, 2009a). China's presence is now widely felt across the region and its engagement with Latin America creates simultaneous competitive and complementary effects (Hogenboom & Fernández Jilberto, 2010; Jenkins & Dussel Peters, 2009; Phillips, 2011).

At the same time, left-wing governments were apprehensive in rejecting free market policies that have been embedded for two decades. The Chilean experience is exemplary of the difficulties in challenging the neoliberal ideology. In the 20 years of the *Concertación* government being in power, the first decade (1990–2000) was about maintaining the credibility of Center parties (mainly Christian Democrats) in forging a political consensus by embracing Pinochet's free enterprise approach in the economy. In the second decade (2001–2009), the renovated socialist and communist parties took the driving seat of the governing coalition and it was only under Ricardo Lagos and Michelle Bachelet that key changes in mining policy were gradually introduced. For example, labor reforms were tackled immediately by Lagos, the royalty tax was passed in Congress in 2006, and subcontracting law followed suit in 2007. In October 2009, Michelle Bachelet ushered in the debate in Congress to abolish the law that directly transfers 10 percent of CODELCO's profits to the military for arms modernization, which is currently discussed in National Congress under the right government. While these are important moves to introduce the "social" question into *Concertación*'s platform, on the whole, this does not go far enough to shift the weight of mining governance away from big business. The Chilean state remains wary of any opposition in conferring mining contracts to foreign capital. Despite the externalities of mining—environmental degradation and tensions in firm-community relations—popular support has failed to mount greater state protection for mining communities.

Similarly, the Brazilian Workers' Party (PT) has been transformed by the shift in its role from opposition to governing party. As the main opposition in the 1990s, PT forced the Cardoso government to justify its neoliberal program (1995–2002) but they hardly succeeded in offering an alternative political project of change. Upon assuming power in 2003, Lula da Silva expanded social policy and antipoverty alleviation programs, though its expenditure was constrained by fiscal and monetary discipline. In the petroleum sector, Lula began to understand the difficulty of challenging the discourse of global market integration and this was manifested by his more reconciliatory position with the regulatory agency in charge of overseeing the market opening and breaking of state monopoly, the *Agencia Nacional do Petróleo* (ANP). As a senior official in ANP argues in an interview:

> When Lula was elected, backed up by the trade union movement, he saw he could not appoint the directors because [they] have already been appointed. There was a feeling . . . that he had won the power but he has not had the power over the agencies . . . But over time, President Lula and the PT were recognizing the importance and relevance of regulatory agencies . . . There was, in his second term, a reverse process of what occurred in the first term: strengthening the environmental, regulatory, and controlling agencies. PT tackled Cardoso's neoliberal policy by strengthening these agencies despite PT being ideologically against it. (ANP Senior Official, interview with the author, August 2010, Rio de Janerio)

Until his last year in office, Lula followed *political continuity with minimal changes* with respect to the role of the state in the oil industry. Trebat (1983) distinguished the roles of the state in the economy as a *regulator* and as a *direct participant*. As a *regulator*, the Brazilian state has maintained its classic allocative, stabilizing, and distributive functions through a variety of policy tools, such as monetary, credit, and fiscal policies, trade and exchange rate policies, and price controls. As a *direct participant* in the economy, the state has reduced its role as owner of banks and enterprises in response to the negotiated privatization of key public firms and financial institutions. However, one must not forget that neoliberalism, rather than a critical juncture restructuring state-market-labor relations, is in fact an interlude between the old and new development state in Brazil (for extensive discussion of this point, see Arbix & Martin, 2010; Nem Singh & Massi, 2011).

Above other evidence on Petrobras' competitive position vis-à-vis foreign oil companies, the move of Lula da Silva during his second term (2007–2010) toward establishing a new institutional framework to be applied specifically for strategic areas with proven oil reserves (the so-called *pre-salt* blocks) affirms the view of the pivotal role of the state in governing natural resources. Put differently, the politicization of oil—which is, today, at the heart of policy debates in Brazil's aspirations of becoming an energy superpower—is in fact a historical outcome brought about by the confluences of decisions made by different actors, namely the military government (which had continuities from Vargas' oil policy since 1930), Petrobras, the small number of private actors, and organized labor in the petrochemical and refining sectors. In a nutshell, the historical legacy of oil governance is to create an exceedingly politicized debate on energy security, and therefore, a generally negative public sentiment toward the privatization of oil and mining.

To sum up, the debates on post-neoliberalism and resource governance reflect the political and policy efforts of refocusing the role of the state in the economy, through for example the use of royalty payments and export taxes as tools for social redistribution, without necessarily compromising the alliance between states and private actors. Support for left governments is rooted in the broad appeal to expand beyond economic growth and to include social development as the goal of state intervention in the context where historically embedded inequalities have remained unaddressed by statist and neoliberal policies. As Grugel and Riggirozzi (2011, p. 7) point out, post-neoliberalism aspires to a radical distribution of political power away from traditional elites while working with the grain of the global economy. Within the extractive sector, post-neoliberalism is about whether reforms can bring in participation, voice, and agency for the affected communities, marginalized groups, and mining workers.

This implies, above all, going beyond constructing export growth models that overlook class inequality, disproportionate distribution of "environmental bads," and histories of marginalization in the name of capitalist modernization.

Labor Unions and Social Justice

The victory of left leaders and parties across Latin America at the turn of the millennium was essentially about a promise to reconstitute state-society bargains and a renegotiation of citizenship particularly with traditional actors like labor, and new ones like social movements, local communities, and neighborhood associations. In the heyday of neoliberalism market reforms have also been associated with the dramatic collapse of historic alliances between Left parties and labour unions, either as a result of the weakening appeal of the Left or the renovation process that widened the distance between these actors (Burdick, Oxhorn, & Roberts, 2009; Levitsky, 2003; Nem Singh, 2012). For some, the decline of labor parties and trade unionism is indicative of the "end of politics" and the triumph of liberal democracy (Colburn, 2002; Fukuyama, 1992). Nevertheless, the apparent fading of union activism does not necessarily lead to the demobilization of civil society and of politics as such. Instead, what is recurring together with the demise of traditional interest representation (i.e., labor politics) is the reorganization of citizenship claim-making from one space to another—a shift from the politics of redistribution associated with trade unionism to a new politics of representation and recognition. Other case studies in this volume attest to this. The radicalization of indigenous politics and the rise of popular movements contending the political alliances supporting neoliberal projects quite vividly illustrate the transformation of contentious politics as a result of the limits of traditional modes of representation.

In contrast, popular demands to contest neoliberalism in Brazil and Chile did not come from a strong social movement, although periodic resistance from communities did take place. Instead, social mobilization has rested on the historically militant trade unions in mining and petrochemical sectors. Because labor unions in extractive industries remain the most organized, with highly compensated workers facing increasing job insecurity, worsening employment conditions, and growing informality in the economy, labor politics serves as the main arena for contestation of rights and citizenship claims.

Post-neoliberalism, with regard to extractive justice, is intrinsically about the capacity of unions to exert pressure on both state and private firms to adhere to labor rights and to open institutional channels to mediate conflicts on social compensation and environmental regulations. The degree to which unions are able to expand political spaces to negotiate labor rights vis-à-vis the growth-oriented goals of state technocrats and enterprise managers is crucial to achieving social justice. However, this is no simple task. Tensions between developing institutional arrangements for greater participation and actual practices of consultation and participation are complex and contradictory. State enterprises are required to perform both the roles of a profit-maximizing company *and* of a public firm with social goals such as offering employment. Often the need to increase the value of extracted minerals does not always coincide with other public goals. In the context of public enterprises, SOEs make difficult choices in managing labor conflicts. For example, while collective bargaining agreements offering bonuses and social benefits to avoid work stoppage tend to benefit permanent workers, the broader firm strategy of subcontracting and outsourcing services distributes losses across temporary workers. What is evident is the continuing fragmentation of workers' collective organization in exchange for individualized benefits held by some sections of the working classes. In other words, the economic imperatives of extracting rents undermine opportunities of representation and recognition for some groups, such as the unorganized workers, local communities, and social movements. At best, local communities have been compensated through voluntary codes of conduct as exemplified by corporate social responsibility projects. While unions have had the mobilizing capacity to command national strikes, this organizational power does not translate into substantive claim-making that incorporates demands for social justice.

In Chile, the state enterprise is faced with dual pressures of responding to workplace demands from mining unions and demands for cultural rights from indigenous communities living within the mining areas. In the case of state-controlled mineral extraction, CODELCO and the *Federacion de los Trabajadores del Cobre* (FTC) have, for almost 20 years, negotiated wages and social benefits, contract compliance, and job security through collective bargaining agreements. The *Alianza Estrategica* (Strategic Alliance) between workers and the state enterprise was founded in 1994 within the context of the perceived loss of competitiveness of CODELCO, loss of credibility, and skepticism as regards the state's capacity to manage the transition toward becoming the "best" copper firm in the world (Villarzu, 2005). The Strategic Alliance consists of two phases, during which different compromises between the state enterprise and the workers were made. Phase I (1994–1999) aimed at regaining competitiveness, profitability, and credibility through the "modernization of CODELCO." Its goal was to reduce the costs of extraction to less than 10 centavos per pound, increase production by 500,000 tons, and productivity by 50 percent. Phase II (1999–2006) sought to maximize the economic value of the company's workers and the transfer of profits (dividends) to the state through the so-called common project of the firm. In practice, this would mean doubling the economic value and increasing the surplus production of CODELCO.

In the process, the modernization of CODELCO required exceedingly stable relations between management and workers. According to Villarzu (2005, pp. 10–12), the index of conflictivity as a measure of success of the program waned from 3.3 percent, between 1990 and 1993, to 1.4 percent, between 1994 and 2005. Since 1993 there has also been a decline, in absolute terms, in the frequency rate of accidents, which signify the improving standards of health and safety measures in mining operations. Equally, those with permanent contracts (called *trabajadores de planta*) have successfully won generous benefits and received bonuses to reduce conflicts and avoid work stoppage. However, because subcontracting has become the dominant practice both for CODELCO and private mining firms, to respond to global demands for cost effectiveness and production efficiency, new categories of workers have been formed (called *trabajadores contratistas*) whose salaries, benefits, and general working conditions are worse than those of plant workers. As is evident from the absence of any major strike in the past 20 years in CODELCO, this state strategy of managing labor has succeeded in co-opting the once militant mining unions by addressing the bread-and-butter issues of workers at the expense of collective labor rights. However, in the private sector, this paternalistic relationship between the state managers and plant workers was never consolidated. Instead, firm-worker relations in private mining are characterized by ephemeral tranquility and permanent friction as exemplified by the number and frequency of workers' strikes.

Despite the absence of the state in mediating labor conflicts, mining workers have remained quite powerful in organizational and political terms. The mining industry stands out from other sectors for its high levels of unionization (around 90 percent), thereby justifying the term *labor aristocrats* frequently applied to the mining workers, in comparison to the representative confederation of poor workers, *Central Unitaria de Trabajadores de Chile* (CUT). In terms of their clout in commanding strikes, mining workers clearly have the ability to halt production and make a credible threat to both state and private firms. The lessons of the mining strike of plant workers in Escondida Mine in 2006 compelled *Minera Escondida*, the second biggest mining company after CODELCO, to offer a generous package of wages, bonuses, and social benefits to avoid labor conflicts in October 2009. Yet this is not an achievement for all the workers. As expressed by a leader of *Federación Minera del Chile* (FMC),[3] the division between the permanent and subcontracted workers has consequences for the disproportionate allocation of labor rights among workers:

> Collective negotiations in private mining are very hard . . . CODELCO has a good paternalistic administration and in the private sector things are different . . . the only form of advancing . . . [causes] with the lack of social benefits [as a result of subcontracting] is through collective negotiations. The contract we have achieved is the best in both public and private mining but not for all, Escondida has 2,253 unionized workers, it cannot advance in the same manner . . . it depends on organizational capacity of unions . . . it has only been possible to advance our interests through tough protests . . . We were on a twenty-five-day strike and I led them and we won through force (Leader, Federación Minera de Chile, interview with the author, November 2009, Antofagasta).

In response to the series of workers' strikes in Chile that began in 2006, the political classes debated in Congress, and in 2007 eventually passed, the Subcontracting Law to regulate business practices in hiring third parties and overseeing contract compliance of subcontracted firms across all sectors of the economy. There are now more stringent rules on outsourcing and large-scale mining firms are now aware of those companies that follow labor regulations. What remains clear, however, is that the institutional framework has failed to respond to the demands for social equity among the workers and that the world of labor is plagued with divisiveness and fragmentation. Most crucially, the extent to which the law has actually benefited ordinary workers remains to be seen.

In Brazil, state corporatism created extensive controls over the labor movement. This was done through single-union representation per category of worker and dependency on financing of union activities through the *imposto sindical* (union tax). Under difficult circumstances, a trade union movement autonomous from the state developed in the metallurgical sector in São Paulo in the 1970s and formed the *Central Única dos Trabalhadores* (CUT) in 1983, which also constituted the founding members of the PT. In the 1990s, Cardoso attempted to weaken trade union resistance through labor reforms institutionalizing labor flexibility and competitiveness. While Lula and

PT were against labor reforms as opposition, it was more difficult to reverse Cardoso's policy when they came to power. Still, a few gains were won by the workers under PT, such as having a trade union leader in the position as minister of labor and achieving a steady increase in wages. Nevertheless, labor flexibility was in line with Brazil's response to competitive pressures, in which the most organized sectors—metallurgical, banking, steel, public sector, and petroleum—were all exposed to global competition (Sandoval, 2001). The combination of privatization of steel, banks, and petroleum, technological changes, and overall restructuring of sectors in response to competitiveness (such as changing banking practices of foreign private banks and closing subsidiaries of state enterprises) made it difficult for CUT to offer alternatives to the privatization program. Although CUT still commands representation of workers, new forms of collective action emerged in response to the weakening power of labor and the need for novel ways of contesting neoliberalism, for example through the rural workers' movement (MST) and the movement of the unemployed (*neo-camelos* and *perueiros*).

In the oil sector, Cardoso had to face opposition from the confederation of petroleum workers (affiliated with CUT), the *Federação Única dos Petroleiros* (FUP), to pursue the privatization agenda, from the famous workers' strike in 1995 until the end of his second term in 2002. Throughout the Cardoso presidency, FUP and CUT jointly mobilized to counter the passage and implementation of the law liberalizing the petroleum sector. In June 1999, *petroleiros* (petroleum workers) across the country participated in the call of FUP to pressure Cardoso to suspend the auction that would transfer the possession of 27 oil-producing areas to multinational firms. The workers organized a national campaign in defense of state monopoly and Petrobras' strong role across the hydrocarbons chain. Specifically, their campaign *Privatizar Faz Mal ao Brasil* (Privatizing is Bad for Brazil) was the slogan of workers' demands in 2001 and became the center of debate at the national assembly of workers (VII CONFUP).

In light of the discovery of the pre-salt oil reserves in the coastal areas of Brazil in 2007, the statist solution of unions to "the oil question" was publicly expressed when they sought for the renationalization of Petrobras and eventually supported Lula's proposal to create a new state enterprise (Petrosal) to represent state interests in the negotiation of oil contracts. In the big debate around the redistribution of royalty taxes, that is giving other states and the federal government more share of the potential oil revenues, the petroleum workers in Rio de Janeiro—the main oil-producing state—mobilized in defense of the right of the oil-producing state to keep its bigger share of the revenues. The political strategy of this movement has been to link their campaign to the highly nationalistic *O Petróleo é Nosso* (The oil is ours) campaign, thereby, asserting the state as both entrepreneur and regulator of the oil industry.

While the labor movement generally has indeed weakened, the strategic importance of oil meant that *petroleiros* have maintained their organizational and political capacity to resist privatization and influence national debates on oil management. However, as the passage of the Petroleum Law suggests, the capacity of unions to mobilize is a necessary but insufficient condition to alter the dynamics of power relations in policy-making. The workers have failed to challenge the discourse of competitiveness inherent in the logic of privatization. Equally, subcontracting and labor flexibility remain as the basis of labor management in the oil industry. Nevertheless, subcontracting is not as extensive in the oil sector as in other parts of the economy (e.g., in steel and banking) because Petrobras retains substantial control in the petroleum chain. Above all, Petrobras still follows the rules on hiring and firing of workers applicable in the public sector. Petroleum workers continue to hold the reputation of labor aristocrats, although they are more politicized and have a more direct relationship with the broader national confederation movement than do the Chilean copper miners.

The world of labor is complex. One reality is that labor rights are disproportionately distributed across groups of workers. The differences in their working conditions generate friction among the working classes, which in turn make the tasks for unions to craft cogent proposals formidable. While union capacity to strike indicates the authority of labor leaders over ordinary workers, this does not reflect in any way their influence to command resistance beyond the workplace. On the one hand, post-neoliberal resource governance accepts the necessity of private capital-driven development to take part in the increasingly competitive global economy. On the other hand, unlike their counterparts in the central Andes, labor management in Brazil and Chile has been very politicized. Labor reforms and agreements in the workplace are negotiated between states and organized labor as a result of the dual functions of state enterprises. It is clear that labor politics continues to be the fulcrum of resource conflict in Brazil and Chile.

Conclusions

The new politics of left governments in Latin America is complex and contradictory. We do not find neat ruptures between neoliberal and post-neoliberal policies, and the cases of Brazil and Chile illustrate the point quite lucidly. Whereas growth strategies aim to strengthen the role of the state in economic management, political elites are also pragmatically trying to make democratic politics more meaningful by making explicit references to social equality, class politics, and voices from below as constitutive of governance. As I show in this chapter, labor unions have made clear gains during the past 20 years of economic restructuring in Brazil and Chile. States are more inclusive, legitimate, and far more open to societal pressures. But the political challenges pose constraints to the attempts of Brazil and Chile to find alternative pathways of growth.

Clearly, renewed state activism sits alongside a strategy for growth that is based on increasing dependency on natural resources. In Chile, there has been a move from a more diversified export base—consisting of salmon, wine, fruit, and other nontraditional exports in the 1990s—toward a return to copper dependency at the turn of the millennium (Barton, 2009a; 2009b). Chile conforms to the "new extractivism" in Latin America, characterized by the growth strategy of intensive and extensive exploitation of natural resources principally conducted with the strong presence of the state through greater regulation, taxation, and royalties (Gudynas, 2010). For example, royalty payments are now financing projects toward research and development to promote innovation. This approach involves linking the productive bases of the economy to the extractive industry through public-private partnership, which will pay for investments in infrastructure, human resource development, and technological development in mineral extraction. Nevertheless, Chile is still a state dependent on commodities and thus vulnerable to external shocks and international price fluctuations, and the necessity for innovation and economic diversification incessantly lingers as a policy challenge.

In Brazil, although we find an emerging consensus for a stronger state in managing natural resources (and the economy more generally), a major policy debate rests on the capacity of PT to sustain growth by moving from resource extraction toward industrialization. This involves complex coordination between state agencies, most notably in the natural resources and economic planning sectors, but also the state must acquire public acquiescence in its overall policy direction. National policy plans suggest awareness of the issues they face, including the need to enhance bureaucratic competency and guarantee private sector participation in key strategic industries.[4] But there are also challenges beyond growth strategies; questions about the domestic legitimacy and democratic credentials of a strong state have now emerged.

Brazil cannot replicate the corporatist authoritarianism of the twentieth century. Lula's antipoverty strategy is one way of gaining public confidence to address historically rooted social inequalities. The PT experiment of democratizing the centralized state is another remarkable experiment to introduce direct democracy alongside representative institutions. In governing natural resources, the redistribution of mineral rents has become the focal point in national debates. Under a new law (12.351/2010), a national social fund will be created whose budget will be apportioned from the royalty taxes. The fund is directly linked to the Office of the President, and will be mobilized by the federal government to address poverty, inequality, and regional development. The law specifies the sources of financing, such as participation fees and royalties, to finance prospective projects ranging from education, culture, sports, public health, science, and technology, to the environment, and the mitigation and adaptation to climate change. Lula's new political discourse has managed to move public support away from the highly technocratic approach to managing oil of Cardoso toward a new developmentalist state agenda where renewed activism involves embracing social development as an equally important goal of state intervention. Lula's successor, Dilma Rousseff, understands the challenges of extractivism, and being a technocrat herself in the ministry of mines and energy under Lula, she knows the limits of expanding social policies, financing state enterprises, and using mineral rents for social development. Arguably, we are witnessing the construction of a post-neoliberal state in Brazil, one that is characterized by economic pragmatism and political commitment to social justice.

To sum up, Brazil and Chile challenge the sweeping claims of some scholars around notions of success in managing natural resources. Although they are not explicitly post-neoliberal states, their commitment to strike a social contract that is minimally acceptable for states, firms, and organized labor shows incremental changes toward such a platform. Yet there is a lack of alternative constructions of models for managing labor and negotiating conflicts in the workplace, exemplified by the difficulties of unions to promote labor rights for all categories of workers and the absence of an effective labor reform project. Ultimately, the challenge for resource politics is finding an appropriate balance between the demands of the global international economy on one hand, and addressing popular dissatisfaction in delivering growth and equity in societies known for their centuries of social inequality and exclusion on the other.

Notes

1. As of February 2011, the combined share of the Federal Government, BNDES, and BNDESPAR constitute 45 percent of capital stocks to the Brazilian state, giving the state control over management decisions. For further details, see Nem Singh & Massi, 2011.
2. We should note that Chile has been ruled by an alliance of Right parties since 2010, with two major parties at the core of this political grouping; *Union Democrática Independiente* (Independent Democratic Union—UDI) and *Renovación Nacional* (National Renovation—RN).
3. Mining Federation of Chile (FMC), the confederation of 21 mining unions in the private sector.
4. See *Plano Nacional de Mineração 2030*. Ministério de Minas e Energia. Secretaria de Geologia, Mineração e Transformação Mineral, 2011.

References

Arbix, G., & Martin, S. B. (2010). *Beyond developmentalism and market fundamentalism: Inclusionary state activism without statism.* Paper presented at the Workshop on States, Development and Global Governance, University of Wisconsin Madison, US, March 12–13, 2010.

Barton, J. (2009a). The impact of China's global expansion on Chile. *World Economy and Finance Research Programme Working Paper Series*, No. 6, February. University of East Anglia, UK.

Barton, J. (2009b). The impact of China's global expansion on the copper export value chain and the textiles import value chain in Chile. *World Economy and Finance Research Programme Working Paper Series*, No. 7, February. University of East Anglia, UK.

Burdick, J., Oxhorn, P., & Roberts, K. (Eds.). (2009). *Beyond neoliberalism in Latin America? Societies and politics at the crossroads.* Basingstoke UK: Palgrave Macmillan.

Colburn, F. (2002). *Latin America at the end of politics.* Princeton, NJ: Princeton University Press.

Domingo, P. (2009). Evo Morales, the MAS, and a revolution in the making. In J. Grugel & P. Riggirozzi (Eds.), *Governance after neoliberalism in Latin America* (pp. 113–145). Basingstoke, UK: Palgrave Macmillan.

Doring, H., & Santos, R. (2011). Post-developmentalist state and steel sector: Is it possible to talk about a new brazilian development path? Paper presented at the workshop on post-neoliberalism: Towards a new political economy of development for Latin America?, University of Sheffield, UK, October 7, 2011.

Economic Commission for Latin America and the Caribbean (ECLAC). (2010a). *Foreign direct investment in Latin America and the Caribbean.* Santiago de Chile: United Nations Publications.

Economic Commission for Latin America and the Caribbean (ECLAC). (2010b). *Time for equality: Closing gaps, opening trails. Thirty-third session of ECLAC.* Santiago de Chile: United Nations Publications.

Evans, P. (1979). *Dependent development: The alliance of multinational, state, and local capital in Brazil.* Princeton, NJ: Princeton University Press.

Evans, P. (1995). *Embedded autonomy: States and industrial transformation.* Princeton, NJ: Princeton University Press.

Fukuyama, F. (1992). *The end of history and the last man.* New York, NY: Free Press.

Grugel, J., & Riggirozzi, P. (Eds). (2009). *Governance after neoliberalism in Latin America.* Basingstoke, UK: Palgrave Macmillan.

Grugel, J., & Riggirozzi, P. (2011). Post-neoliberalism: Rebuilding and reclaiming the state in Latin America. Paper presented at the Society for Latin American Studies (SLAS) Annual Conference, University of St. Andrews, UK, April 8–10, 2011.

Gudynas, E. (2010). Agropecuaria y Nuevo Extractivismo Bajo los Gobiernos Progesistas de America del Sur. *Territorios, 5,* 37–54. Retrieved March 8, 2012, from http://www.gudynas.com/publicaciones/articulos/GudynasAgroNuevoExtractivismoTerritorios10.pdf.

Haarstad, H., & Andersson, V. (2009). Backlash reconsidered: Neoliberalism and popular mobilisation in Bolivia. *Latin American Politics and Society, 51*(4), 1–28.

Hogenboom, B., & Fernández Jilberto, A. (2009). The new left and mineral politics: What's new? *European Review of Latin American and Caribbean Studies, 87,* 93–102.

Hogenboom, B., & Fernández Jilberto, A. (Eds.). (2010). *Latin America facing China: South-South relations beyond the Washington Consensus.* New York & Oxford: Berghahn Books.

Jenkins, R., & Dussel Peters, E. (Eds.). (2009). *China and Latin America: Economic relations in the twenty-first century.* Bonn, Germany: Deustches Institut für Entwicklungspolitik.

Kennemore, A., & Weeks, G. (2011). Twenty-first century socialism? The elusive search for a post-neoliberal development model in Bolivia and Ecuador. *Bulletin of Latin American Research, 30*(3), 267–281.

Leiva, F. I. (2009). *Latin American neostructuralism: The contradictions of post-neoliberal development.* Minneapolis, MN: University of Minnesota Press.

Levistky, S. (2003). *Transforming labour based parties in Latin America: Argentine Peronism in comparative perspective.* Cambridge, UK: Cambridge University Press.

Montero, A. P. (1998). State interests and the new industrial policy in brazil: The privatisation of steel, 1990–1994. *Journal of Inter-American Studies and World Affairs, 40*(3), 27–62.

Nem Singh, J. T. (2012). Chile's mining unions and the "new left," 1990–2010. In B. Cannon & P. Kirby (Eds.), *Civil society and the state in left-*

led *Latin America: Challenges and limitations to democratization* (2012). London, UK: Zed Books.
Nem Singh, J. T. (2012). Who owns the minerals? Re-politicising natural resource governance in Brazil and Chile. *Journal of Developing Societies, 28*(2), 229–256.
Nem Singh, J. T. (2010). Reconstituting the neostructuralist state: The political economy of continuity and change in Chilean mining policy. *Third World Quarterly, 31*(8), 1413–1433.
Nem Singh, J., & Massi, E. (2011). The politics of natural resources: A critical appraisal on the "return of the state" in Brazil. Paper presented at the Workshop on Post-Neoliberalism: Towards a New Political Economy of Development for Latin America?, University of Sheffield, UK, October 7, 2011.
Panizza, F. (2009). *Contemporary Latin America: Development and democracy beyond the Washington consensus.* London & New York, NY: Zed Publications.
Phillips, N. (2011). Re-ordering the region? China, Latin America and the Western Hemisphere. *European Review of Latin American and Caribbean Studies, 90*, 89–99.
Polanyi, K. (2001). *The great transformation: the political and economic origins of our time.* Boston, MA: Beacon Press.
Sandoval, S. (2001). Working-class contention. In M. A. Font & A. P. Spanakos (Eds.), *Reforming Brazil* (pp. 195–216). Oxford & New York, NY: Lexington Books.
Sawyer, S. (2004). *Crude chronicles: indigenous politics, multinational oil, and neoliberalism in Ecuador.* Durham, NC: Duke University Press.
Schmitter, P. (1972). *Interest conflict and political change in Brazil.* Stanford, CA: Stanford University Press.
Schneider, B. R. (2009). A comparative political economy of diversified business groups, or how states organize big business. *Review of International Political Economy, 16*(2), 178–201.
Silva, E. (2009). *Challenging neoliberalism in Latin America.* Cambridge, UK: Cambridge University Press.
Smith, P. S. (1976). *Oil and politics in modern Brazil.* Toronto, Canada: Macmillan.
Trebat, T. J. (1983). *Brazil's state-owned enterprises. A case study of the state as entrepreneur.* Cambridge, UK: Cambridge University Press.
Villarzu, J. R. (2005, October 21). *CODELCO y El Modelo de Alianza Estrategica* [PowerPoint presentation].
Wirth, J. D. (1970). *The politics of Brazilian development, 1930–1954.* Stanford, CA: Stanford University Press.

Chapter 12
Conclusions

Håvard Haarstad

This book began by noting the optimistic prospects for a resource-based development in Latin America. Democratic consolidation, governments elected on socially responsive platforms, and stable economic growth were pointed to as indications that the region's natural resources can be used and stewarded for the benefit of broad sectors of the population. At the same time we noted some enduring challenges, and some emerging ones as well, that should remain in sight and subject to critical assessment. It is primarily these challenges that occupy the pages of this book. This is not, I believe, because we as authors do not recognize the positive impacts that resource extraction (if done well) can bring to society. It rather is because we are wary of the legacy of resource extraction in the region, and because our professional and normative orientations draw our attention toward power differentials and injustice. Political practices and governance models should continuously be subject to critical analysis and assessment in the hope that such analysis may contribute better practices.

The introductory chapter framed the analyses in this book in two ways: one aimed to understand the political spaces for civil society actors pressing claims toward natural resource governance and the other to assess how emerging models are contributing to social justice. In this chapter I will draw up some conclusions on the basis of the discussions in the chapters.

The Political Spaces for States and Civil Society

The first question posed in the introduction was as to how can we understand the political spaces for civil society actors to press claims toward the ways in which natural resources are governed? The authors seem to agree that economic dependence on natural resource extraction, particularly hydrocarbons, *narrows* political spaces for governments (and thereby often for civil society as well) and restricts policy options. Despite political rhetoric that has been associated with the new left, of making extraction subservient to social and environmental needs, it is evident that this does not involve significant steps toward anything resembling a postextraction society. Instead, government leaders of all ideological shades are pressing for an expansion of extractive activity in ways that often contradict earlier promises. Several of the cases illustrate that at the local level, indigenous and community groups do not experience significant differences between current regimes of extraction and those of the neoliberal era. Tensions between local claims and national extractive strategies has been a recurring theme, pointing to the difficulty of reconciling new local rights to participation and territory with national revenue generation and the attraction of investment. This contradiction between local political spaces and national development policy discourses appears as a central characteristic of the current natural resource governance problematic. Governments are in different ways "playing the national development card" (to use a phrase from chapter 6 by Barton, Román, and Fløysand, this volume) to legitimize priorities for the types of outcomes that show up in the national accounts. Some of these priorities would be hard to argue against; social programs such as cash transfer schemes have been expanded in many countries, notably in Brazil and Bolivia, and financial flexibility has enabled countries to break out of the debt cycle. High commodity prices and significant investor interest in Latin America make extractive expansion an attractive option. Also, many governments are now in a position to increase taxation and impose restrictions on companies with "sunk" investments (what economists refer to as dynamic inconsistency). This suggests the national development card can be played with some justification. At the same time, many of us had expected, or at least hoped, that "post-neoliberalism" would involve political and institutional innovations that could overcome contradictions between local and national development discourses and aspirations. The evidence presented in these chapters does not suggest that such innovations are particularly widespread.

While other authors have seen regional integration and ideological alliances as means to increase national energy sovereignty, there is little to suggest that this is translated into a break with the path dependence of resource extraction or new political spaces for local actors. Instead, a regional initiative such as Initiative for the Integration of Regional Infrastructure in South America (IIRSA) has exacerbated tensions between local territorial claims and national development agendas, and illustrated that modernization comes with a cost for certain actors. Haarstad and Campero stress the economic imperatives that tie the hands of governments in terms of renewing extractive strategies, regardless of ideological alliances, regional initiatives, and post-neoliberalism. Regional alliances condition possibilities for local development in much the same ways that international market forces, and trade and investment agreements do—they facilitate interstate cooperation and foreign investments in ways that bind governments to particular economic policy actions. In practice, few of these policy actions seek to open local political spaces for participation. They focus primarily on economic development concerns and often impose sanctions on governments that prioritize differently. This is not to suggest that regional or international alliances and treaties are illegitimate or antithetical to the interests of Latin American countries. But they do seem to make issues of local development and local participation more complex and problematic.

Why is the path dependence of natural resource extraction so hard to break out of? The different chapters provide parts of what is likely the answer. There are some obvious economic factors. In comparison to the large informal sectors in Latin American economies, the extractive sector provides a source of revenue that is much easier to tax and manage. Extractive activity comes with long-term investments in infrastructure that can not easily be used for other economic purposes. Government leaders may bet on a service and supply industry developing in connection with the operations of large companies, providing jobs, and more taxable revenue. International trade in certain resources, notably gas, requires long-term contracts that stipulate penalties for failure to deliver (and for failure to buy). Finally, international market integration through resource export can offer access to markets, capital, and technology that would otherwise not be available. Economic factors such as these seem to play an important role in structuring the policy spaces for governments, making it difficult to diversify priorities.

There are also some political factors. The scalar logic of national democracy seems to favor extraction. Opposition to extractive activity is often composed of smaller, localized groups, which constitute a fragmented political force. While halting, delaying, or changing a particular extractive project in an immediate sense only benefits a group in one locality (and possibly only a nonrepresentative faction within that locality), expanding extraction creates revenues to support priorities benefiting a much broader constituency. At least, national-level politicians will tend to see it that way. When government leaders play the national development card they cater to the electorate as a whole, rather than discrete communities, particular movements, or "militant particularisms." (The cash transfer programs in Bolivia are accompanied by an advertising campaign stressing that the programs are paid for by nationalization, or in other words, by gas extraction.) And the extractivist lobbies may be a considerable political force in its own right. Further, contemporary leftist leaders in Latin America might be confident that, despite temporary conflicts around particular projects, civil society movements will still back them in an election. If the leaders in power have no serious contenders from the left flank, the traditional elites and the rightist parties may provide the only alternative for the electorate. Hence, leftist leaders are not significantly challenged to heed the demands of extraction critics. It may also be the case that researchers have overestimated the influence of national and international advocacy networks critical to extraction. While the chapters in this book elaborate on the rich mobilizing tactics of local groups, indigenous movement organizations, and their international networks, it is not clear that they are significantly backed by sufficiently influential political forces at the national scale. National political leaders across the continent seem to have realized that expanding extraction to fund national developmentalist projects is the smart thing to do politically, as well as economically.

The Governability of the "Local"

The question of whether there still are spaces for civil society to shape the ways natural resources are governed remains. While the chapters in this book are often pessimistic about the possibilities for substantive influence, they also reveal how extraction of resources is deeply entangled in the local and regional contexts in which it takes place and how this creates opportunities and channels for influence. The chapters by Anthias and Guzman-Gallegos, in particular, show us that oil companies are forced to negotiate with local cultures and organizations to secure the conditions for extraction. As Anthias puts it, transnational oil companies cannot "merely swoop down from above to extract gas; they must navigate existing geographies."

This means that long-term trajectories of extraction will shape current relations between local actors and oil companies, because past experiences with extraction can generate hostile attitudes toward new extraction or provide local actors with significant competence in dealing with companies. Local organizations have gained this competence through decades of struggles for land rights and cultural recognition, and these rights are now mobilized knowledgably toward changing the ways natural resources are governed. Indigenous and other actors are skillfully using rights to participation, litigation, round-tables, and international activist networks to press their claims. According to McNeish in chapter 3, processes of prior consultation and legal action have perhaps become the most common way of expressing indigenous concerns and interests. This has been backed by international conventions and related national legal reforms, and has spurred formal agreements between companies and communities and given rise to local socio-environmental monitoring of extractive projects. Indigenous actors are also promoting their interests by negotiating directly with companies, initiating their own businesses, and purchasing land privately to advance control of resources and sovereignty over land. Other examples from the chapters illustrating the diversity of strategies include securing support from a transnational oil company for a credit cooperative and for a local development fund. As Hall mentions, indigenous populations and farmers have looked into possibilities of accessing Reduced Emissions from Deforestation and Forest Degradation (REDD) financing for protecting their forests. Anthias describes how Bolivian *guaraní* organizations tried to stop a *Tierras Comunitarias de Origen* (TCO) titling process because they thought they would get faster results if they began purchasing private properties within the TCO, in turn becoming private property holders. It remains to be seen how widespread such initiatives will become, but they already suggest that indigenous actors are meeting the pressures of modernity and extraction in much less predictable ways than we tend to assume.

This diversity of strategies and entry points into the national economy brings home the important point, stressed most forcefully in chapter 3 by McNeish, that we have to maintain a complex understanding of the goals that indigenous and local groups have in dealing with the extractive sector. They have few possibilities of stopping an extractive project if the government is determined to push it through—but more often their aim is actually to shape project designs, mediate environmental impacts, and negotiate for increased monetary benefits. Attempts to veto projects are most likely results of perceived closure of opportunities to guide the process or receive relevant benefits, and not necessarily an expression of a desire to live undisturbed and untouched by modernity. If this is a correct observation, then the existence of local political spaces and the opening of new ones will not necessarily halt the expansion of extractive activity or shrink government revenue, but also improve the governability of the extractive sector, lower conflict levels, and help create more predictable outcomes for all involved. A broader understanding of the aims and interests of local actors is important both for their actual concerns to come to the fore, and for our analysis of why environmental conflicts emerge.

The chapters make clear that new legislation to strengthen local participation and rights have to some extent created new political spaces for actors in civil society. Rights granted through constitutions or laws are not implemented perfectly, and the chapter by Humphreys Bebbington and Bebbington suggests that in many cases rights to prior consultation are circumvented outright as governments deem them too important for "national interest." Other authors in this book, such as Okamoto and Leifsen, and Guzman-Gallegos, illustrate that participation can be undermined and circumvented through informal power arrangements at the local level. But at the same time, it appears that new rights provide discursive rallying points and organizational resources that sharpen claims and mobilize campaigns. Even when not implemented to full effect, rights give people a sense of entitlement and strengthen their feeling of disenfranchisement when their rights are not respected. Gone are the days (if there ever were such days) when extraction was just a matter for states and companies. Several chapters argue that companies attempt to make onshore extraction as detached from local contexts as possible (chapter 9 by Okamoto and Leifsen), to create "extractive spaces" that commodify local places (chapter 6 by Barton, Román, and Fløysand). Yet the degree of conflict and friction that this generates suggests that these attempts are not completely successful, and most likely they will never be. Extractive companies are dependent on some degree of collaboration with communities, perhaps more than ever before. The companies seem to be realizing this, so they are engaging local communities directly through supplying welfare services, backing particular candidates for local office, or information campaigns. (Many have pointed out that indigenous and local actors are upscaling their political activity; perhaps the response from transnational companies is a downscaling of theirs?) For better or for worse, the focus on local rights brings local actors and impacts into the equation, creating a new terrain for interest negotiation and conflict. The increased levels of conflictivity that several of the chapters point to should not just be interpreted as a direct result of increased extraction, but also as a renewed sense of entitlement among local actors.

The fact that the local scale is a central terrain for conflicts over extraction does not imply that they can be understood without an acute attention to the broader picture. As Certomà and Greyl write of the Yasuní case in chapter 10, this volume, "A few acres of forest became a globally contested issue entangled in complex economic, political, and social networks." As political geographers are prone to emphasize, "local" conflicts are rarely merely local when one takes a closer look, they are always embedded in national and international processes and discourses. That said, it is telling that international advocacy networks play a minor role to substantive outcomes of environmental conflicts in the accounts of this book. Anthias in chapter 7 points to the importance of transnational alliances for the organizing strength of the *Asamblea del Pueblo Guaraní Itika Guasu* (Guaraní People's Assembly Itika Guasu—APG IG), and Guzman-Gallegos argues that transnational advocacy was part in pressuring Repsol to agree to a settlement. In this sense international networks are to some extent widening political spaces for local actors by providing some finance and threats of negative publicity for the companies. But in general we do not know enough about these networks, their interests, or the ways in which they operate to assert that they have a broader effect on how resource conflicts transpire and are resolved. Their influence is often assumed rather than documented. Moreover, the accounts in this book suggest that the political spaces created by international advocacy networks are potentially dangerous. McNeish in chapter 3 argues that advocacy networks tend to distort the claims of local actors to conform to unnuanced "ecological noble savage" prejudices, and Guzmán-Gallegos in chapter 8 stresses how they structure flows of resources in exclusionary ways with the likely effect of supporting those political actors who reinforce their own preexisting positions. In analyses of resource conflicts, transnational advocacy networks certainly have to be taken into account, but we should not overestimate their impact and or ignore the political effect of their particular interests and discourses.

There are also other political actors who are possibly misjudged in analyses of conflicts of extractive resources. Chapter 11 by Nem Singh brings our attention to organized labor and its importance for the politics of new extractivism in Brazil and Chile. In contrast to most of the other chapters, he stresses the role of trade unions in mining and petrochemical sectors as the main arena for contesting the neoliberal model of resource governance. One lesson that can be drawn from this is that we often tend to overlook organized labor as a transformative actor in resource politics. He argues for example that, due to their organizational capacity and the strategic importance of oil, the *petroleiros* (petroleum workers) in Brazil have forcefully resisted privatization and influenced national debates on oil management. But some of the conclusions are remarkably similar to the general trend asserted in the other chapters looking at countries where indigenous organization are more central to civil society; even if representatives from social movements (trade union or indigenous) gain powerful positions in governments, substantive changes in the extractive model is unlikely. The embeddedness of the extractive sector in the global economy limits the opportunities for such changes.

That brings us back to the more general conclusion already alluded to above. The contributions here concur in viewing economic dependence on extractive industries and the political incentives that this creates as a significant deterrent to the development of substantive changes to extractive models. Improvements are seen in legislation and political discourses stressing local rights to participation and territory, but constraints such as national development priorities and power differentials within local communities and between local communities, the state, and companies hinder the legal and discursive improvements from being translated into significantly wider political spaces for local and civil society actors. Increasing levels of conflict seem to be in large part a result of an increasing sense of entitlement among civil society actors without a corresponding experience of being heard.

The Challenge of Social Justice

A point was made in the introduction that natural research extraction and governance have such deep impact on society that they can not just be considered technical or administrative matters. Issues of social justice have to be taken into account and considered at different scales. I asserted that Nancy Fraser's conceptual work, seeing it as a combination of redistribution, recognition, and representation, is a useful tool with which to disentangle the abstract and normative notion of social justice and create a framework for reviewing the case studies.

The chapters in this book have all been concerned with different social justice aspects of the cases they have considered, in particular power differentials between different actors, the misdistribution of environmental harm and the weaknesses in participatory procedures. Above all, they have illustrated the clash between a technical-administrative logic of natural research governance on one hand, and the diverse social justice dilemmas this governance brings about. Chapter 4 by Hall on the implementation of REDD in Latin America illustrates well the potential mismatch between a highly technical governance regime and the complex realities on the ground. The economic incentives and formal property ownership models on which the REDD scheme is based correspond poorly with the legal and customary entitlements, communal ownership, and sociocultural traditions of resource use of the indigenous and community groups occupying much of the Amazon forests. Humphreys Bebbington and Bebbington, in chapter 2, and Barton, Román, and Fløysand, in chapter 6, show how those protesting extraction projects often do so on the basis of very different conceptions of justice than those promoting them, and these conceptions are at times incompatible. This suggests that the process of developing "just" models of natural resource governance is highly complex and will never be fully accomplished. National-scale redistribution of extractive revenue is necessarily in tension with the participatory representation and the recognition of the territorial integrity of groups living in vicinity of extractive projects. A "just" model of governance is not one that erases these tensions, but one that accommodates these different conceptions of justice reasonably well.

On the question of how emerging models and practices around natural resource governance contribute to improving social justice, these studies dispel a set of common myths about contemporary resource politics in Latin America. First, they reject that the region has now entered a "post-neoliberal" era of resource governance wherein the injustices of the neoliberal era has been overcome. Given the continuities and enduring justice problematics they have pointed to, the notion of "post-neoliberalism" is not particularly useful for understanding current resource extractive practices (though it works better as a term for a particular political discourse). Second, they reject the common view that the justice claims of indigenous peoples and local communities against the state are primarily asserting cultural recognition against economic development and modernization. These political claims are as much claims for representation in governance processes at different scales and for a redistribution of opportunities associated with extractive activity and economic development. Finally, they dispel the myth that macroeconomic progress generates opportunities across other scales and economic spaces. There is a significant disconnect, or as some of the authors here say, a "clash of logics," between benefits generated at the macroeconomic scale and the opportunities generated locally.

Ultimately, what can be drawn from the chapters is that the initiatives and processes tending toward improved social justice outcomes from extraction often work against one another. In other words, improvements in one type of justice often generate problems for the promotion of other types of justice. The most illustrative example is perhaps how the extraction-funded, redistributive social policy of Bolivia undermines representative justice for local communities. In turn, the enduring challenge for the states in question is finding the appropriate balance between different conceptions of justice and integrating these in coherent models for resource governance. The states in question have yet to find an appropriate balance between the demands of the international market and national redistribution, on the one hand, and local sovereignty and agency, on the other. It is not for me to say precisely how this balance should be struck in particular contexts. But this volume suggests that much remains in incorporating local agency, local opportunity, and local sovereignty in the emerging governance models. Improved design and administration of consultation processes is an important element in this, as some authors here have suggested. Bureaucratic and political decentralization has been offered as a solution, so has a check on oil company power and privilege and increased attention to local communities' actual (as opposed to preconceived) claims. In a more abstract sense, extractive activity has to be configured within the different development needs of communities, regions, and countries, rather than being imagined as quick and simple way to generate state revenue (which these cases show that it is definitely not).

I want to end by stressing that finding this balance between different concerns is not simply a question of conforming to some detached normative academic ideal. Current events in Latin America illustrate forcefully that the extractive industry will not have the long-term political stability and policy predictability it needs unless its associated social and environmental disruption are broadly perceived to be compensated for by development prospects for broader sectors of the population. If there is one mark that the post-neoliberal discourse has left on the region, it is the sense that natural resources belong to society and that political action to claim them will not be completely in vain.

Contributors

Penelope Anthias is a PhD student in the Department of Geography, University of Cambridge, UK. She began research on indigenous land titling and resource conflicts in TCO Itika Guasu in 2008–2009, while based at the Centro de Estudios Regionales de Tarija (CERDET), and recently completed a one year of PhD fieldwork in the same territory.

Jonathan Barton is a geographer, and associate professor at Pontificia Universidad Católica de Chile. His publications include books on democracy, globalization, environmental regulations, and political geography in Latin America, as well as papers in *Revista de la CEPAL, EURE, Comercio Exterior, Estudios Públicos, Geoforum, Area, Journal of Latin American Studies*, and *Bulletin of Latin American Research*, among others.

Anthony Bebbington is Higgins professor of environment and society and director of the Graduate School of Geography at Clark University, professorial research fellow in the School of Environment and Development, University of Manchester, and research associate of the Centro Peruano de Estudios Sociales. He is a member of the US National Academy of Sciences and has been fellow at the Center for Advanced Studies in the Behavioral Sciences, Stanford.

Cecilia Campero is a PhD candidate in Architecture and Urban Studies at Pontificia Universidad Católica de Chile. Her research reflects her broad interests in extractive industries, development and governance in countries such as Bolivia and Chile.

Chiara Certomà is a post-doctoral research fellow in environmental politics at the Sant'Anna School of Advanced Studies in Pisa, Italy, and teaches political ecology for postgraduate and PhD courses. She does research on environmental politics, postmodern philosophy, and cultural geography.

Arnt Fløysand is professor at the Department of Geography, University of Bergen. His studies and publications have dealt with processes of globalization, in particular how discourses, narratives and rules of conduct are informing practice of resource extraction of multiscaled socioeconomic actors and other driving forces explaining industrial restructuring and development. His work has been based on case studies from Chile, Peru, Norway, Spain, and Estonia.

Lucie Greyl is an anthropologist, and a coordinator and research projects manager of the Documentation Centre on Environmental Conflicts (CDCA) in Rome, Italy. She coordinates CDCA participation in the FP7 funded project Environmental Justice Organisations, Liabilities and Trade (EJOLT). During the past four years she has developed her research qualification on ecological economics and environmental politics related to environmental conflicts and social justice.

María Antonieta Guzmán-Gallegos obtained her doctorate in 2010 from the Department of Social Anthropology at the University of Oslo. She has done extensive fieldwork with the Amazonian *Kichwa* of Ecuador, focusing on *Kichwa* notions of personhood, of kinship relations, and of indigenous leadership. She has also worked with extractive industries, development, and state formation.

Håvard Haarstad is a postdoctoral research fellow at the Department of Geography, University of Bergen, Norway. His current research concerns the political economy of natural resources, in Latin America and elsewhere. His work has been accepted in journals such as *Political Geography*, *Geoforum*, *Antipode*, *Globalizations*, *Latin American Politics and Society*, and *Contemporary Politics*.

Anthony Hall is a professor of social policy at the London School of Economics. He has written extensively on deforestation and sustainable development issues, with a focus on Brazilian Amazonia. His latest book is *Forests and Climate Change: The Social Dimensions of REDD in Latin America* (Cheltenham: Edward Elgar, 2012).

Denise Humphreys Bebbington is research assistant professor at the Institute for Development, Community and Environment at Clark University. Previously she has been Latin America Coordinator for Global Greengrants Fund, Inter-American Foundation Representative to Peru, and Catholic Relief Services Sub-Director in the South America region. Her publications have appeared in *Latin American Perspectives*, *World Development*, *Development and Change*, *New Political Economy*, *Area*, among others.

CONTRIBUTORS

Esben Leifsen is a social anthropologist and senior lecturer in international environment and development studies at Noragric, the Norwegian University of Life Science. He has extensive research experience from Latin America, and is currently working on issues related to oil extraction in the Peruvian Amazon.

John-Andrew McNeish is a senior researcher at Christian Michelsens Institute (CMI) and associate professor at the Department of International Development, Norwegian University of Life Sciences (UMB). McNeish recently coedited the book *Flammable Societies: Studies in the Socio-Economics of Oil and Gas* (London: Pluto Press, 2012). He is also leader of the Norwegian Research Council funded project *Contested Powers: Towards a Political Anthropology of Energy in Latin America*.

Jewellord T. Nem Singh is a PhD candidate in the department of politics, University of Sheffield, UK. His research examines the politics of natural resources in Latin America. His most recent publications focus on the politics of institutional change in Brazil and Chile, and appear in *Third World Quarterly*, *Journal of Developing Societies*, and *Journal of Critical Globalisation Studies*.

Tami Okamoto holds interdisciplinary degrees from the University of British Columbia (BSc) and the Norwegian University of Life Sciences (MSc) focused on natural resource management and development. She is currently working on research projects on environmental governance in Latin America at the Centre for Development and the Environment (SUM), University of Oslo.

Álvaro Román is a sociologist, and PhD candidate in architecture and urban studies at Pontificia Universidad Católica de Chile. His work is focused on governance and spatial transformations related to transnational economic flows in southern Chile. His publications concern transformations in traditional communities, power relations in governance systems, and spatial restructuring.

Index

ACODECOSPAT (Kukama Association for Development and Conservation of San Pablo de Tipishca) 183, 190, 191, 192, 195n1
Acosta, Alberto 28, 29, 201, 205
Acuerdo de Amistad 148
Acuerdo Energético del ALBA 95–6
additionality 74
Agencia Nacional do Petróleo (ANP) 225
AGIP. *See* Arco Oriente-AGIP
AIDESEP (Inter-Ethnic Association of Indigenous Lowland Peoples) 24
AKUBANA *(Asociación Kukama del Bajo Nauta)* 182–3
ALADI *(Asociación Latinoamericana de Integración* - Latin American Integration Association) 95, 98
ALBA 91–2, 95–6, 98
ALBA-TCP agreement 95
Alianza Estrategica (Strategic Alliance) 228–9
Amazon Fund 64, 67
Amazon Gas 53
Amazonia
 colonization of 159
 contestation in 178
 indigenous organizations in 196n9
 land titles in 72
 oil explorations in 200–2

Amazonian strike (Peru, 2008) 24
Andolina, R. 8
ANP *(Agencia Nacional do Petróleo)* 225
Anthias, Penelope 13, 242, 243, 245
APG *(Asamblea Pueblo Guaraní)* 46, 47, 48–9
APG IG *(Asamblea del Pueblo Guaraní Itika Guasu)*
 establishment of 131
 on gas interests 142
 international advocacy and 245
 Morales government and 140–1, 145–7
 Repsol and 137–8, 147–9
 aquaculture industry 118–20
 arbitration, international 88, 90, 91, 92–3
Arco Oriente-AGIP 155, 160–1, 162, 166–9
Argentina
 Bolivia's trade with 97–9
 Chile's gas trade with 121
 Chile's treaty with 114–15
 international arbitration and 93
 REDD and 67
 state-owned companies in 92
Asamblea del Pueblo Guaraní Itika Guasu (APG IG). *See* APG IG
Asamblea Pueblo Guaraní (APG). *See* APG
aschuar people 50–1, 192

INDEX

Asociación Kukama del Bajo Nauta (AKUBANA) 182–3
Asociación Latinoamericana de Integración (ALADI – Latin American Integration Association) 95, **98**
ASODIRA (Association for Indigenous Development in the Amazonian Region) 169, 170
authoritarianism/use of force 23–5, 25–6, 32, 117

Bachelet, Michelle 224–5
Bagua conflict (Peru, 2009) 24, 84
Barrick Gold 115–16
Barton, Jonathan 13, 247
Bebbington, Anthony 11, 12, 42, 244, 247
Beck, Ulrich 209, 210
bilateral donors 66
bilateral investment treaties (BITs) 87–8, 93–4
bilateral treaties 87–95
Binational Mining Treaty 114–15
BITs (bilateral investment treaties) 87–8, 93–4
Bloque del ALBA 95
Bolivia
 arbitrations against 91
 constitutional reforms in 5
 constitution of 93, 95, 142
 extractive strategies in 13–14
 government policy in 25–8, 42
 hydrocarbons development in 21, 45–9, 99–100, 131
 indigenous groups in 45–9
 interstate relations of 85, 95–6, 97–100
 local-national conflicts in 83–4
 neoliberalism in 132–3
 REDD and 64–5, 67
 regional countermovement and 101
 social policy of 41, 248
 See also Morales administration

Bolsa Floresta program 70
Brazil
 Bolivia's trade with 97–9
 CCT programs and 69
 labor unions in 230–2, 245–6
 land titles in 72
 national policy in 233–4
 neoliberalization in 221–2
 PES in 70, 76
 post-neoliberalism in 223–4, 225–6, 234
 REDD and 64–5, 66–7
 resource dependency of 218
 social policy of 41
Brazilian Development Bank (BNDES) 22
Brazilian Workers' Party (PT) 225, 230–1, 233
Brunet, A. 93
Brysk, Alison 56
buen vivir (living well) 11

de la Cadena, M. 42–3
Caipipendi Block. *See* Campo Margarita
Calvo Doctrine 86–7, 93
CAM *(Coordinadora Arauco-Malleco)* 117
Campero, Cecilia 13, 241
Campo Margarita (Margarita Gas Field), Tarija, Bolivia 46, **134, 135**
CAN *(Comunidad Andina)* 8, 95, **98**
carbon emissions, saved 203
carbon markets 64–5
carbon sequestration. *See* REDD
Cardoso administration (Brazil) 222, 225, 230–1
cash transfer programs 11, 27, 41, 69–70, 240, 242
Central Única dos Trabalhadores (CUT) 230–1
CERDET (Tarijeño Regional Research Centre) 46
Certomá, Chiara 14, 245

INDEX 255

CGG *(Compagnie Generale de Geophysique)* 166
CGYs (Yasuní Guarantee Certificates) 203, 211
Chase-Smith, R. 23
Chevron 50
Chicago Boys economists 111
Chile 13, 107–25
 centralization in 123–5
 claims for just development in 109–10
 constitution of 110–11
 development model of 107, 110–13
 hydropower in 120–3
 indigenous conflicts in 116–18
 labor unions in 228–30
 mining in 111–12, 114–16, 224–5
 neoliberalization in 220–1
 plantation forestry in 116–18
 post-neoliberalism in 223–5
 resource dependency of 218, 233
 salmon aquaculture in 118–20
 socioenvironmental conflicts in 107–8
China 2, 224
Choquehuanca, Marisol 181
CIDOB (Indigenous Confederation of the Bolivian Orient) 48
citizenship reforms 5
Clean Development Mechanism (CDM) 63
climate change 212–13
climate change financialization 211
climate mitigation mechanisms. *See* REDD
Coalition for Rainforest Nations 63
Coasean economics 68–9, 70, 72
CODELCO *(Corporacion Nacional del Cobre)* 111, 220–1, 228–9
collective autonomy 51
Colombia 5, 21, 30–1
colonialism 43–4, 131, 136, 159, 163–5. *See also* postcolonialism
communiqués 181–2

Compagnie Generale de Geophysique (CGG) 166
compensation
 for land use 137–8, 167–8
 for oil spill contamination 182, 189–93
Comunidad Andina (CAN) 8, 95, 98
CONADI (National Corporation for Indigenous Development) 117, 118
Concertación government (Chile) 220, 224–5
concessions 21, 158, 193–4
conditional cash transfer (CCT) programs 69
conflicts. *See* socioenvironmental conflicts
conservation 206–7. *See also* environmentalism
constitutional reforms 5
contamination
 effects of 180, 194–5
 levels of 186–8
 from oil exploration 50
 spread of 182–3
 technical discourse and 189
contingency plans 180, 189–93
Convention on Indigenous and Tribal Peoples by the International Labour Organization (ILO 169) 5–6, 11, 118, 137, 159, 179
Convention on the Settlement of Investment Disputes between States and Nationals of Other States (ICSID Convention) 88, 90
Cooperacción (NGO) 21
Coordinadora Arauco-Malleco (CAM) 117
copper industry 114, 218, 220–1
Corbera, E. 69
Corporacion Nacional del Cobre (CODELCO) 111, 220–1, 228–9

INDEX

Correa, Rafael 28–30, 100, 201–2, 204–5
corruption 75
Costa Rica 66, 74
Cremades, B. 93
CUT *(Central Única dos Trabalhadores)* 230–1

Dagnino, E. 18
decision-making
 centralization of 111, 123–5
 exclusion of local actors from 11
 indigenous conflicts and 117–18
 regional countermovement and 101–2
Decree Law 701 (1974, Chile) 116
deep entanglements 156, 242–6.
 See also unruly engagements
deforestation 61, 62, 63, 65, 74–5, 77
democracy 5, 110, 123, 209–10.
 See also neoliberalism; social justice
detachment 14, 155, 177–8, 244.
 See also unruly engagements
DICAPI (General Directorate for Harbor and Coast Guards) 179, 180
DIGESA-Lima 188–9
DIRESA-Loreto 183, 184, 186–8
discrimination 179, 185–6.
 See also stereotypes
disentanglement 172–3, 178–9.
 See also detachment; unruly engagements
distribution of resources
 AGIP and 167–9
 carbon sequestration and 61–2
 enclave formation and 173
 as exclusionary/unjust 157
 OPIP and 171–2
 resource curse and 8–9
 theoretical approaches to 156
DL 600 (Foreign Investment Statute) (1974, Chile) 220

"The Dog-in-the-Manger Syndrome" (García) 23

Earth Summit (1992) 62
ecological nobility 44–5
Economic Commission for Latin America and the Caribbean (ECLAC) 224
Ecuador
 Arco-AGIP and 161–2
 concessions in 21
 constitution of 5, 159, 204
 economic development in 200–2
 government policy in 28–30
 oil industry in 50, 200–2
 state-company partnerships in 155–7
 withdrawal from BITs 93–4
 See also oil extraction in Ecuador; Oil field 10
Ecuadorian Institute for Agrarian Reform and Colonization *(Instituto Ecuatoriano de Reforma Agraria y Colonización – IERAC)* 167
EIA (environmental impact assessment) 115, 117, 122–3, 169–70
EITI (Extractive Industries Transparency Initiative) 7, 96–7
emergency support 180, 182, 191
enclave formation 14, 156–7, 159–63, 166–9, 172–3
Endesa 121, 122
Engle, K. 52
entrepreneurship 53–4
environmental impact assessment (EIA) 115, 117, 122–3, 169–70
environmentalism
 dam conflict and 122–3
 as inspired by indigenous peoples 43–4
 as luxury 206
 as obstructing economic growth 23
Yasuní-ITT initiative and 204

environmental justice 210–14.
 See also social justice
environmental justice theory
 199–200, 209–10
Environmental Law (1994, Chile)
 117
Environmental Regulations for
 Hydrocarbon Activities (1995,
 Ecuador) 161–2
equal treatment clauses 90
Escobar, A. 55
Evans, Peter 221
export-oriented economies 108,
 111–12, 119, 123–5, 218
extractive businesses
 Amazon Gas 53
 Barrick Gold 115–16
 Chevron 50
 CODELCO 111, 220–1,
  228–9
 Endesa 121, 122
 Maxus 137–8
 Occidental 51
 Petrobras 99, 221, 222, **223**,
  231–2
 Repsol 46, 47, 135–6, 137–8,
  147–9
 Talisman 50–1
 Texaco 50
 YPFB 46, 99, 135, 143
 See also oil companies;
  Pluspetrol
Extractive Industries Transparency
 Initiative (EITI) 7, 96–7

FCPF (Forest Carbon Partnership
 Facility) 64, 66, 67, 73
Federação Única dos Petroleiros
 (FUP) 231
*Federacion de los Trabajadores del
 Cobre* (FTC) 228
Federación Minera del Chile 230
Ferguson, J. 178
Fløysand, Arnt 13, 247
foreign direct investment
 (FDI) 1–2, 88–9, 224

Foreign Investment Statute (DL
 600) (1974, Chile) 220
foreign investors 87–8, 89, 119–20
Forest Carbon Partnership Facility
 (FCPF) 64, 66, 67, 73
forestry conflict 116–18
forests 61–2, 63, 71–2, 77n2.
 See also deforestation
Fraser, Nancy 4, 10, 246
free trade agreements 96
Free Trade Area of the Americas
 (FTAA) 87, 88, 95, 96
FTC *(Federacion de los Trabajadores
 del Cobre)* 228
Fundación Unir Bolivia 27
FUP *(Federação Única dos
 Petroleiros)* 231
Futemma, C. 72

García, Alan 22–3, 84, 100
García administration
 (Peru) 22–4, 96, 193–4
García Linera, Álvaro 28
Girvan, N. 91
globalization 8, 208–9, 219
gold mining 114–16
Gonzales Espinosa, A. C. 97
governance of extractive
 industry 17–34, 83–102
 in Bolivia 25–8, 42, 95–6,
  97–100
 in Chile 224–5
 in Colombia 30–1
 continuity of 17–20
 in Ecuador 28–30
 expanded investment and 20–1
 international regime of 86–91
 interstate relations in 85–6
 local-national relations and
  100–2
 Morales administration and 83–4
 in Peru 22–5, 95, 96–7
 regional countermovement and
  91–5
 regional narrative of 22–32
Gow, D. D. 56

Gowdy, J. M. 70
Greyl, Lucie 14, 245
Grugel, J. 226
guaraní people
  compensation for land use and 137–8
  land use conflicts of 14, 45–6, 130–2
  in negotiations with Repsol 47, 147–9
  in negotiations with state 47–8, 145–7
  private property ownership by 147, 243
  See also APG IG *(Asamblea del Pueblo Guaraní Itika Guasu)*
Gudynas, Eduardo 6, 18, 42
Guzmán, Jaime 111
Guzmán-Gallegos, María Antonieta 14, 242, 244, 245

Haarstad, Håvard 13, 15, 218, 241
Hale, C. R. 133, 139
Hall, Anthony 13, 243, 246
Hall, Stuart 42
Haraway, Donna 213
HidroAysén dam conflict 108, 113, 120–3
Hörmann, M. 95
Humala, Ollanta 24–5, 84, 96
Humphreys Bebbington, Denise 11, 12, 244, 247
hydrocarbons concessions 21, 193–4
hydrocarbons development 99–100, 131
Hydrocarbons Law (2005, Bolivia) 142
hydroelectricity 120–3

ICSID 90, 91, 93
ICSID Convention (Convention on the Settlement of Investment Disputes between States and Nationals of Other States) 88, 90

IERAC *(Instituto Ecuatoriano de Reforma Agraria y Colonización* - Ecuadorian Institute for Agrarian Reform and Colonization) 167
IIAP (Research Institute of the Peruvian Amazon) 179, 184, 186–8
IIRSA (Initiative for Integration of Regional Infrastructure in South America) 8, 22, 40–1, 85, 92, 240–1
ILO 169 (Convention on Indigenous and Tribal Peoples by the International Labour Organization) 5–6, 11, 118, 137, 159, 179
indigeneity 43
Indigenous Confederation of the Bolivian Orient (CIDOB) 48
Indigenous Fund of Bolivia 141
indigenous groups 39–57
  aschuar 50–1, 192
  discrimination against 179
  displacement of 159
  economic marginalization of 11
  goals of 243–4
  kichwa 162, 163–9, 171, 174n2, 174n3, 192
  Kukama 182–6, 190–1
  leadership structures of 51–2
  mapuche 116–18
  modernity and 54–6
  participation of 242–3
  Pluspetrol and 182–6, 190–1
  stereotypes of 13, 39–40, 42–5, 206–7
  strategies of engagement used by 56–7
  struggle for rights by 20
  surui 74–5
  in Tarija, Bolivia 45–9
  u'wa 51–2
  weenayek 45, 46–7
  working with extractive businesses 52–3

INDEX

in Yasuní National Park 202
See also guaraní people;
  indigenous organizations;
  indigenous resistance;
  indigenous rights
Indigenous Law (1993, Chile) 117
indigenous organizations
  AKUBANA 182–3
  compensation for Marañon case
    and 190–3
  in Ecuador 174n6
  mobilizations of in Peru 24
  oil spill management and 183
  OPIP 161, 165, 166–7, 169–72
  in Peruvian Amazon 196n9
  See also APG IG *(Asamblea del*
    Pueblo Guaraní Itika Guasu)
indigenous resistance
  as direct action 117
  exclusionary character of oil
    extraction and 157
  Marañon case and 190
  to oil extraction in
    Ecuador 165, 166–7, 169–72
  OPIP and 169–72
  See also social movements
indigenous rights
  in Ecuador 159
  land rights and 137–8
  under Morales administration
    140–7
  neoliberalism and 139
  recognition of 206–7
indirect expropriation clauses
  89–90
Initiative for Integration of
  Regional Infrastructure in
  South America (IIRSA) 8,
  22, 40–1, 85, 92, 240–1
INRA 131, 133, 135, 136, 138,
  146, 147
Instituto Ecuatoriano de Reforma
  Agraria y Colonización
  (Ecuadorian Institute
  for Agrarian Reform and
  Colonization - IERAC) 167

Inter-American Commission 11
Inter-Ethnic Association of
  Indigenous Lowland Peoples
  (AIDESEP) 24
international conventions 243
international governance regime
  countermovement to 91–4
  rise of 86–91
Interpol 75
interstate relations
  of Bolivia 95–6, 97–100
  importance of 85–6
  of Peru 85, 95, 96–7
  regional countermovement and
    101
investment 1–2, 21, 87–9, 93–4,
  119–20, 220, 224. *See also*
  REDD
invited spaces 184–6
Itika Guasu
  establishment of as TCO 131–2
  location of **134**
  Morales government and 140–4
  obstacles to TCO titling in
    133–4
  Repsol's land-use agreements in
    135–8
  See also APG IG *(Asamblea del*
    Pueblo Guaraní Itika Guasu)
ITT block *(Ishpingo Tambococha*
  Tiputini). See Yasuní-ITT
  initiative

just development 109–10
justice 124–5, 247–8
  environmental 199–200,
    209–10, 210–14
  See also social justice

Kellogg, P. 92
Keyano-Pimee Exploration 53
kichwa people 162, 163–9, 171,
  174n2, 174n3, 192
kinship relations 163–4, 165–6,
  173
Klein, A. 97

Kosoy, N. 69
Kukama Association for Development and Conservation of San Pablo de Tipishca (ACODECOSPAT) 183, 190, 191, 192, 195n1
Kukama people 182–6, 190–1. *See also* Marañon oil spill
Kyoto Protocol 63

labor unions 15
 importance of 245–6
 as political actor 218, 233–4
 social justice and 227–32
Lagos, Ricardo 224–5
land, commodification of 112, 124
land titling. *See* property rights; TCO titling
Larrea, C. 200
Laurie, N. 8
Law 3477 (2006, Bolivia) 26
Law of Consultation *(Ley de Consulta)* (2011, Peru) 12, 84, 179
leakage 74
legal actions 47–8, 49–53, 243
legislation
 concerning copper mining 220
 concerning plantation forestry 116–17
 concerning subcontracting 230
 for indigenous rights 159, 165
 oil enclave formation and 172
 for PES 76
 regulating prior consultation 12, 45, 84, 142–3, 179
 strengthening local participation 11–12, 244
 strengthening state's role 23–4
Leifsen, Esben 14, 244
Lentini, J. A. 93
Lewis, Norman 187
Ley de Comunas (1937) 165
Ley de Consulta (Law of Consultation) (2011, Peru) 12, 84, 179
Ley Reservada del Cobre (1958, Chile) 111

local dynamics 163–6
local governments 117–18, 119–20, 242–6
local-national conflicts, Chilean 107–8
 over gold mining 114–16
 over hydropower 120–3
 over plantation forestry 116–18
 over salmon aquaculture 118–20
local-national relations 83–5, 100–2, 240–1
Lula da Silva, Luiz Inácio 225–6, 230–1, 234

McNeish, John 11, 12, 18, 243, 245
mapuche people 116–18
Marañon oil spill 14, 177–95
 communiques about 181–2
 compensation for 182, 189–93
 disentanglement and 178–9
 effects of 180
 environmental sampling and 186–9
 lack of contingency plan for 189–90, 193
 meetings about 182–6
 Pluspetrol's detachment from 180–1
 proliferation of unruly engagements and 194–5
Margarita Gas Field (Campo Margarita), Tarija, Bolivia 46, **134**, 135
Maxus 137–8
May, P. H. 69
Melo, M. 161
MERCOSUR 7, 95, **98**
Mexico 66, 69, 70
Minas Conga conflict 25
Minera Escondida 230
mining
 in Chile 111–12, 114–16, 224–5
 in Colombia 21, 30
 in Ecuador 29

management of 220–1
Minas Conga conflict 25
unionization and 228–30
Mining Code (1983, Chile) 220
mining concessions 21
modernity 54–6
Morales, Evo 11, 25, 27, 65, 100.
 See also Morales administration
Morales administration (Bolivia) 13–14
 agreements with APG 47–8
 contradictions of 83–4, 144
 indigenous rights and 140–7
 interstate relations and 95–6
 plurinationalism and 139–40
 policy decisions of 99
 TIPNIS conflict and 25–7
Muradian, R. 69

National Corporation for Indigenous Development (CONADI) 117, 118
National Development Plan of Colombia 30
national development policy 240–2
nationalism 218, 221
nationalization
 arbitration claims and 91
 in Bolivia 83, 99, 143
 in Brazil 221–2, 231
 in Chile 220–1
 in Ecuador 158, 201–2
 impact of on indigenous groups 46
national social fund 234
nature 206–7, 213–14. *See also* environmentalism
Nauta association 190–1
negotiations with oil companies
 by APG 47
 discrimination in 185–6
 indigenous concerns and 242–3
 by *kichwa* 167–9
 land titling struggle and 145–7
 in Marañon case 190–3

Nem Singh, Jewellord T. 14, 18, 245
neoliberalism
 in Bolivia 132–3
 in Brazil 221–2
 in Chile 110–11, 220–1
 indigenous movements and 5–6, 132
 indigenous rights and 139
 post-neoliberalism and 14–15
 reforms and 86–7
 social inequality and 218–19
 See also post-neoliberalism
NGOs (nongovernmental organizations)
 APG IG and 147–8
 dam conflict and 122–3
 enclave formation and 173
 globalization and 8
 impact of 245
 indigenous campaigns and 50–1
 kichwa and 171
 Pascua Lama conflict and 115
 resource circulation and 157
noble savages 44, 207
Noel Kempff Mercado Climate Action Project (NK-CAP) 67
noneconomic rights 97–8
nonextractive policies. *See* Yasuní-ITT initiative
nongovernmental organizations (NGOs). *See* NGOs
nontraditional agricultural exports (NTAX) 112, 116–17, 119
North-South Institute 31
Norwegian government 64

Occidental 51
oil companies 14
 legal actions against 50
 nationalization of 91, 221–2
 negotiations with 46–7, 145–7, 167–9, 190–3, 242–3
 social programs/services and 157, 162, 168–9
 See also extractive businesses; Pluspetrol

oil extraction in Ecuador 155–74
  dependency on 200–2
  establishment of Oil field 10
    and 159–63
  history of 158–9
  indigenous demands and 166–9
  indigenous resistance to 165,
    166–7, 169–72
  local dynamics and 163–6
  management of 28–9
  unruly engagements and 155–7,
    172–4
Oil field 10 (Pastaza, Ecuador)
  establishment of 159–63
  indigenous response to 165,
    166–72
  local dynamics and 163–6
  unruly engagements and 172–4
oil spills. *See* Marañon oil spill
Okamoto, Tami 14, 244
OPIP (Organization of Indigenous
  Peoples of Pastaza) 161, 165,
  166–7, 169–72
OSINERGMIN (*Organismo
  Supervisor de la Inversión en
  Energía y Minería* - Supervising
  Agency for Investment in
  Energy and Mining) 187
Our Common Future (Brundtland
  report) 109

Parinari association 191–2
participation
  circumvention of 244
  environmental justice theory on
    210
  in extractive development 53–5
  of *guaraní* 145–50
  limitations of 52
  in oil spill management 182–6
  OPIP's demand for 170
  resource dependence and 239–42
  unruly engagements and 182–6
Pascual, U. 69
Pascua Lama conflict (Atacama,
  Chile) 108, 114–16

payments for ecosystem services
  (PES) 54, 62, 66, 68–70, 76
Peru
  arbitrations against 91
  concessions in 21, 193–4
  government policy in 22–5
  interstate relations of 85, 95,
    96–7
  local-national conflicts in 84
  prior consultations in 50–1
  resource governance in 7, 178–9
  See also Marañon oil spill
PES (payments for ecosystem
  services) 54, 62, 66, 68–70, 76
Petrobras *(Petróleo Brasileiro)* 99,
  221, 222, **223**, 231–2
petroleum funds 211
Pinochet, Augusto 113, 220
Pizango, Alberto 24
plantation forestry conflict
  (Auraucanía, Chile) 108,
  116–18
plurinationalism 139–40, 144–5,
  150, 204
Pluspetrol 177
  communiqués by 181–2
  compensation by 190–3
  dialogues with 182–6
  environmental sampling and
    186–9
  lack of action by 180–1
political spaces 4, 5–8, 239–42
postcolonialism 131–2, 206–7.
  See also colonialism
post-neoliberalism
  ambiguity of 6
  in Brazil 223–4, 225–6, 234
  in Chile 223–5
  extractive justice and 217–18
  labor unions and 227–8
  neoliberalism and 12, 14–15
  as problematic concept 247
  regional countermovement
    and 101
  withdrawal from international
    governance and 91–4

See also governance of extractive industry; neoliberalism
poverty 209–11. *See also* social justice; social policy
prior consultation
 circumvention of 244
 in Ecuador 159
 guaraní and 137–8
 high-profile cases of 49–53
 indigenous concerns and 243
 legislation around 12, 45, 94, 142
 limiting national economic development 100
 process of 143
privatization
 in Bolivia 132
 in Brazil 221–2, 231–2, 245–6
 FDI and 88
 See also nationalization
Proambiente (PES initiative) 66, 70
property rights
 in Chilean indigenous conflicts 116–18
 collective 23, 66, 129, 139, 165, 166–7
 guaraní and 131
 other indigenous rights and 137–8
 REDD+ and 72–3
 in TCOs 135
 See also TCO titling
PT (Brazilian Workers' Party) 225, 230–1, 233
PTPA (US-Peru Trade Promotion Agreement) 96

Radcliffe, S. 8
Ralco dam project 113, 117, 121
recognition
 defined 10
 environmental justice theory on 210
 of *guaraní* 148–9
 of indigenous rights 206–7

redistributive politics and 227, 247
REDD (Reduced Emissions from Deforestation and Forest Degradation) 61–77
 economic incentives and 68–70
 effectiveness of 73–6
 funding for 62–7
 indigenous groups and 243, 246–7
 resistance to 64–5
 as resource curse 13
 as resource extraction 61–2
 social complexity and 71–3
Redford, K. 44
redistribution
 of benefits from extraction 11
 Correa administration and 204
 defined 10
 environmental justice theory on 210
 extractive growth and 19–20
 recognition/representation and 227, 247
Reduced Emissions from Deforestation and Forest Degradation (REDD). *See* REDD
regional integration 13, 83–102
 effects of 95–102
 international governance regime and 86–91
 interstate relations and 85–6
 local-national conflicts and 83–5, 240–1
 processes of 22
 trend toward 7–8, 91–5
representation 10, 227, 247
Repsol 46, 47, 135–6, 137–8, 147–9
resource curse 8–9, 19
resource dependence 19, 200–2, 218, 233, 239–42
Riggirozzi, P. 226
Rodríguez-Gavarito, C. 52
Román, Álvaro 13, 247
Rousseff, Dilma 234

salmon aquaculture industry 108, 118–20
sampling 183, 186–9
SAN-TCO. *See* TCO titling
Santos administration (Colombia) 30
Sawyer, S. 167
Sevilla, Roque 205
"Social-environmental development in Caipipendi Block" (Repsol) 138
socialism 204
social justice
 dilemmas of 246–8
 dimensions of 4, 10
 enhancements in 33–4
 forestry conflicts and 118
 labor unions and 227–32
 Yasuní-ITT initiative and 209–10
social license 115–16
social movements 5–6, 8, 24, 113, 132, 204, 208–9. *See also* indigenous resistance
social policy 68–70, 225–6, 248
social programs/services
 funding of by extraction 19, 41, 201–2
 national development policy and 240
 oil companies and 157, 162, 168–9, 244
socioenvironmental conflicts
 Bagua conflict 24, 84
 complexity of 6, 10–11
 defined 110
 of *guaraní* 14, 45–6, 130–2
 HidroAysén dam conflict 108, 113, 120–3
 hydrocarbons conflicts 45–9
 involvement of national/international processes in 244–5
 local-national conflicts 83–5, 107–8, 113–23, 240–1
 Minas Conga conflict 25
 motivations for 32–3
 number of in Colombia 30
 number of in Peru 194
 over land-use agreements 137–8
 proliferation of 41–2
 stereotypes of 12–13, 39
 TIPNIS conflict 25–7, 48–9, 83
 SOEs (state-owned enterprises) 92, 219, 228–9
Starn, O. 42–3
state-company partnerships
 in Ecuador 155–7
 in Marañon case 179–80
 meetings/dialogues and 182–6
 sampling politics and 186–9
state-owned enterprises (SOEs) 92, 219, 228–9
stereotypes 13, 39–40, 42–5, 206–7. *See also* discrimination
Stern, N. 65
subcontracting 167–8, 228–9, 232
Subcontracting Law (2007, Chile) 230
surui people 74–5

Talisman 50–1
Tarijeño Regional Research Centre (CERDET) 46
TCO Itika Guasu. *See* Itika Guasu
TCOs (*Tierras Comunitarias de Origen* - Original Communal Lands) 46, 129, 131–2
TCO titling 129–50, 243
 early years of (1996-2006) 133–40
 establishment of Itika Guasu as 131–2
 under Morales administration (2006-2011) 140–7
 opposition to 133–4
 third-party claimants and 135–6
 technical discourse 189, 246–7
Texaco 50
third-party claimants 135–6, 146–7
Tierras Comunitarias de Origen (TCOs) 46, 129, 131–2
Tierras Comunitarias de Origen (TCO) titling process (SAN-TCO). *See* TCO titling

TIPNIS *(Territorio Indígena y Parque Nacional Isiboró Securé)*
   conflict   25–7, 48–9, 83
Tompkins, Douglas   122
transnationalization   7–8
treaties/agreements
   bilateral   87–95
   Binational Mining Treaty   114–15
   BITs   87–8, 93–4
   of Bolivia   95–6
   international   7
   interstate   97–100
Trebat, T. J.   225–6
Tuan, Yi Fu   109, 110

UNASUR   91–2, 95
UNCITRAL (United Nations Commission on International Trade Law)   88, 91
UNDP (United Nations Development Program)   203, 205
UNDRIP (United Nations Declaration of the Rights of Indigenous Peoples)   45, 142, 179
UN Framework Convention on Climate Change (UNFCCC)   63
unions. *See* labor unions
United Nations Commission on International Trade Law (UNCITRAL)   88, 91
United Nations Conference on Environment and Development (UNCED) (Earth Summit) (1992)   62
United Nations Declaration of the Rights of Indigenous Peoples (UNDRIP)   45, 142, 179
United Nations Development Program (UNDP)   203, 205
UN-REDD program. *See* REDD
unruly engagements   14, 177–95
   by AGIP   167–9
   contestation and   178

defined   156, 177
effects of oil spill and   180–1
modes of   181–93
oil extraction in Ecuador and   155–7, 172–4
proliferation of in Peru   194–5
state heterogeneity and   178–9
Urarinas association   191, 192–3
Uribe administration (Colombia)   30
US-Peru Trade Promotion Agreement (PTPA)   96
u'wa people   51–2

Vare, Pedro   48
Vatn, A.   70
Venezuela   5, 41, 92, 95–6
Villarzu, J. R.   229
violence. *See* authoritarianism/use of force

Warnars, L.   200
water quality. *See* contamination
weenayek people   45, 46–7
welfare services. *See* social programs/services
willingness to pay policy   211–12
World Bank   64, 66, 67, 88

Yacimientos Petrolíferos Fiscales Bolivianos (YPFB)   46, 99, 135, 143
Yasuní Guarantee Certificates (CGYs)   203, 211
Yasuní-ITT initiative   199–214
   complexity of   14, 245
   Correa administration and   28–30
   environmental justice and   209–14
   launch of   203–5
   locals' view of   206–8
   negative aspects of   211–13
   postcolonialism and   206–7
Yasuní ITT Trust Fund   203
YPFB *(Yacimientos Petrolíferos Fiscales Bolivianos)*   46, 99, 135, 143